WASHINGTON:
MAGNIFICENT CAPITAL

WASHINGTON:
MAGNIFICENT CAPITAL

Photography by FRED J. MAROON

Text by A. ROBERT SMITH *and* ERIC SEVAREID

1965
DOUBLEDAY & COMPANY, INC., GARDEN CITY, NEW YORK

PREVIOUS BOOKS BY THE AUTHORS

by A. Robert Smith
The Tiger in the Senate: the Biography of Wayne Morse

by Eric Sevareid
In One Ear
Not So Wild a Dream
This Is Eric Sevareid

FIRST EDITION

Library of Congress Catalog Card Number 65-24912
Copyright © 1965 by Doubleday & Company, Inc.
All rights reserved
Printed in the United States of America

All photographs in this book were taken by Fred J. Maroon
The *Look* Magazine Photos © Cowles Magazines and Broadcasting, Inc.

CONTENTS

CHAPTER ONE   The City of Our Age   9

CHAPTER TWO   On the River Potomac   19

CHAPTER THREE   Mr. President   31

CHAPTER FOUR   The Lawgivers   55

CHAPTER FIVE   Oyez! Oyez! Oyez!   79

CHAPTER SIX   The Diplomats   87

CHAPTER SEVEN   The New Warriors   105

CHAPTER EIGHT   The Bureaucracy   115

CHAPTER NINE   The Washington Correspondents   119

CHAPTER TEN   The Persuaders   127

CHAPTER ELEVEN   Washington after Five   131

CHAPTER TWELVE   The Inner City   149

CHAPTER THIRTEEN   The Outer City   195

CHAPTER FOURTEEN   Treasure Troves   211

CHAPTER FIFTEEN   Rites and Pageants   227

Index   245

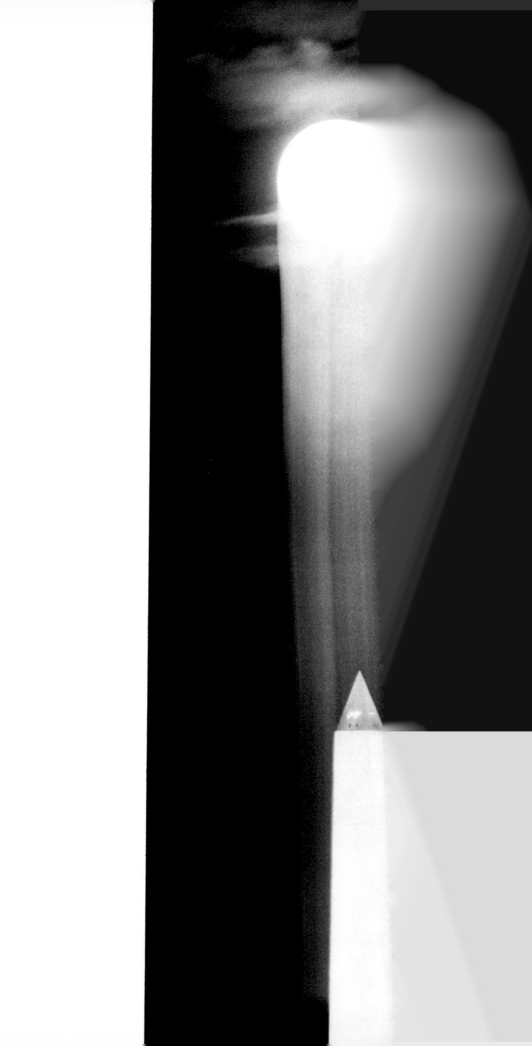

To EVELYN PETERSEN METZGER,
whose inspiration, enthusiasm, wit,
encouragement, and editorial artistry
were indispensable to this creation
and its grateful creators.

CHAPTER ONE

The City of Our Age

Washington, the capital of hope, is the city of our age. Though our age is still young, and only the hazy outlines of the Washington imprint are perceptible, we know it will be different from that of philosophical Athens, or mercantile London, or conquering Rome.

Younger than any of the great capitals, almost provincial by their standards, Washington is the most disarming of all. To the visitor it presents itself as a collection of quiet stone museums, a crisscross of boulevards lined with heroic statuary and arching trees. Yet beneath this serene façade Washington commands more power than all of the old capitals combined. Its power, though measurable in military and fiscal might, is fortunately not limited to that. In this age of collapsing colonialism and rising independence of the less advanced realms, and the related Negro revolution in the United States, Washington's power is generated as much by the spirit as by the sword.

The magnificence of Washington is the embodiment, if an imperfect one, of a glorious ideal. It is the working out in human terms of the precepts of Locke and Paine and Jefferson that government is the creature, the servant, of man and not the reverse. Monarchs have fallen in profusion since the American Declaration of Independence proclaimed this truth to be self-evident; but tyrants remain to challenge and suppress this truth, at times with terrifying cruelty.

Symbolic gateway to the city of our age, Dulles International Airport links Washington by jet with all the continents. Its soaring tower and terminal, one of the last works of architect Eero Saarinen, were dedicated by President Kennedy in 1962 to the memory of President Eisenhower's Secretary of State, John Foster Dulles, a principal architect of American involvement in the worldwide quest for freedom.

The master does not become the servant without a struggle.

How widely the idea and habits of freedom will spread remains to be seen. In one way, without much conscious effort, the West has greatly influenced the world. This is seen in the universal desire for American clothing, amusements, techniques, and gadgets. However some people may deplore this conformity to American standards, it represents variety and freedom for millions of people liberated from the more rigid conformities of village and tribe. A terrible discontent has gripped these people, stimulated more by what the West is than by what the Communists claim to be. Through modern communications, a far different and better kind of life has been revealed to them. It is a life founded not merely on economic and material wants but on a deep yearning to be part of a life of consequence associated with the West.

What America has set into motion is a revolt against anonymity. It begins quite often and quite spontaneously in some areas with the arrival of a group of Americans dispatched by Washington, principally American GIs. One Nigerian, analyzing the influence of GIs in Africa, said it stemmed from the Africans having seen the GIs behave as ordinary mortals, occasionally breaking up property, full of good feeling toward them one moment or fighting them the next. The Africans suddenly realized that the white men were very much like them. The spell of the white master, cast across that continent by centuries of colonial mores, was broken. The Declaration of Independence phrase, "that all men are created equal," had reached them at last.

It is one thing unintentionally to set off a revolution of discontent with the old, quite another to help shape and channel its energy into a new pattern of freedom by which men may realize the fruits of equality. This

Spring in Washington is heralded by the arrival of the cherry blossoms and the first busloads of out-of-town school children, the eager vanguard of an army of eight to ten million sight-seers that overrun the capital each year. This group has just visited the nation's highest tribunal, the Supreme Court, and is headed toward the Library of Congress; these are two of the attractions on Capitol Hill.

is the fundamental struggle of our age. Nowhere is this struggle for freedom against authoritarianism more keenly observed, more encouraged, more suffered over than in Washington. Virtually all decision-making, at the White House, in the Cabinet, at the State Department, in Congress, is performed against an inescapable awareness of this struggle. More than half the national budget is consumed by programs and facilities designed to foster the prospects of freedom around the world.

While this struggle across the globe takes on a thousand forms, much of it beyond any direct control or immediate influence from Washington or anywhere else, Washington is banking on the long-term effect: that the basic yearning of all men to be free as God intended, and the whole movement of man out of darkness into the sun will progressively break the bonds of oppression that remain. To the extent that Washington fosters this movement toward individual life, liberty, and the pursuit of happiness, it exerts more power in the world than all of the conquering legions of the past. And to that extent Washington makes its lasting imprint on our age.

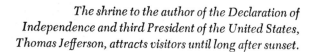

The shrine to the author of the Declaration of Independence and third President of the United States, Thomas Jefferson, attracts visitors until long after sunset.

This granite gingerbread structure (left) on Pennsylvania Avenue next to the White House is an ornamental expression of the beaux-arts style that influenced Washington architecture in the nineteenth century. When completed in 1888, it was the capital's most elaborate government building, containing the State, War, and Navy departments. The twentieth-century rise of the United States as a great power dictated larger quarters for its growing diplomatic-military bureaucracy. Today the Executive Office Building contains offices of the Vice-President, National Security Council, Budget Bureau, and part of the President's staff that spilled out of the White House offices.

Washington's core is laid out with the Mall at the east-west axis, bounded by the Capitol and the Lincoln Memorial, and a north-south axis running from the White House (below) through the Washington Monument to the Jefferson Memorial. Scenes like this make it America's most handsome city.

By day or night, the Capitol is Washington's most magnificent structure. On a knoll described by L'Enfant as "a pedestal waiting for a monument," it dominates the city. Construction of the Capitol has gone on for nearly a century and three quarters; the great iron dome was not set in place until the Civil War, during which time work continued at Lincoln's command as "a sign the Union shall go on." Here it is reflected in the glass front of a new federal office building (opposite) on Constitution Avenue. Inside the Capitol, Congress at work reflects the views and moods of the people of the United States.

In Washington, the crossroads of our age, the standard conversational gambit is "Where are you from?" People come by train (below, at Union Station), by airplane, auto, and bus from every part of the country and the world. Arrivals and departures spark a good deal of the social machinery of the city. It's a rare visitor who doesn't find an excuse for returning. The semipermanent residents, such as U.S. senators, usually stay on indefinitely, for, as the saying goes, "They never go back to Pocatello."

CHAPTER TWO

On the River Potomac

Neither as frantic and sophisticated as New York, nor as muscular as Chicago and Pittsburgh, nor as charming as San Francisco and New Orleans, Washington is the most handsome of American cities.

Washington is also virtuous and bland; it has never submitted to a tyrant, or succumbed to a king. It is innocent of the blood of the Paris mobs, the London Tower, the Roman amphitheater. It knows only democracy, with its mixture of ideals and bloodless cunning, its rhythm of talk and action within the law.

It has always been and will always be, in one sense, "a city of magnificent intentions," as Dickens put it. Dickens meant no compliment, for he was measuring the shabby Washington of 1842 against the standards of European capitals. Indeed, until recently, Washington and the mores of its inhabitants have always been on the safe side of small-town America, the legendary source of strength and self-reliance in the American fiber. No big-city ways for this Washington. Roll up the sidewalks after dark, observe the blue laws, own your own home, keep the streets clean, hold a steady job, respect the merchants and bankers, take the kids to the park on Sunday.

It owes this trait to the decision that brought the capital to the rural Potomac Valley in 1800 as much as to the mood of America for the century and more that followed.

The capital city was conceived, of course, in that famous compromise between President Washington's Secretary of State, Thomas Jefferson, and the Secretary of the Treasury, Alexander Hamilton. Hamilton agreed to align northern support for a southern site in the Potomac Valley in return for Jefferson's promise to deliver Virginia support for Hamilton's plan to

Boating and fishing along the Potomac go on almost the year round, from sunup until past sundown.

have the federal government assume all state debts incurred during the Revolutionary War. The Congress, meeting temporarily at New York, passed a bill that President Washington signed into law on July 16, 1790, authorizing him to select a site "on the River Potomac" for creation of a federal district as the permanent seat of the United States Government. The capital was then temporarily removed to Philadelphia for a decade until the new capital city was ready to receive its makers. In this early departure from the European custom of denoting a great established city as the capital, the United States subjected its capital to the ridicule of such visitors from the Continent as Dickens. Today, however, Washington has achieved what even its fondest founders never expected: it has drawn to itself the vital center of power and decision-making from New York, transferring it from the titans of commerce and industry to the political power elite at Washington.

What sort of place was the Potomac Valley and how did it shape the life of this foundling city? The river itself, rising in the Allegheny Mountains, meanders southeasterly to the lower Chesapeake Bay. Potomac is an Algonquin Indian term meaning "where something is brought" or, more freely translated, a "trading place." The earliest English traders and settlers, notably Captain John Smith from the first colony at Jamestown, fifty miles below the mouth of the Potomac, explored the Potomac up to Little Falls, a rocky gorge just above the present Chain Bridge on the northern outskirts of the city. They traded with the friendly Piscataway Indians, who grew corn, tobacco, and potatoes in the area. The colonists' settlements were raided after friendly Chief Powhatan was succeeded by Opachankano, and the colonists retaliated by burning a large Indian village at the juncture of the Anacostia and Potomac just below the city where Fort McNair stands today.

The traders and trappers who paddled their canoes up the Potomac into the West were followed in the mid-seventeenth century by the planters, who were to leave an indelible mark upon the valley and the capital city. The combination of cheap, accessible land along the river, the importation of African slaves, and the English market for tobacco gave rise to huge plantations. George Washington's eight thousand acres and George Mason's fifteen thousand acres were modest holdings compared with the three hundred thirty thousand acres of Robert Carter. The affluent but genteel plantation culture fathered an American aristocracy that supplied the new nation with its outstanding political leaders, Washington, Jefferson, Madison, Monroe, Mason, and the Lees. They dominated the government until the age of Jackson.

The aristocracy secured and held its power, it should be noted, not by its wealth but by the strength of its personalities and minds. By the end of the eighteenth century, when Washington city was being founded on worn-out tobacco land, the plantation economy was ruined. Washington, Mason, Madison, Jefferson, and Monroe were all in financial distress, some forced to sell their property to meet their debts. Washington held Mount Vernon but it was in poor condition at his death in 1799. This depression was a factor in bringing the new capital to the Potomac Valley, for Washington was hopeful that the city would become a great commercial center, accessible to Europe by ocean vessels, to the heartland of the continent via canals that would be built to the West.

Congress had given him a range of forty miles along the Potomac in which to select a site, between the Anacostia River and the Conococheague Creek upstream. The President never considered the stretch above the fall line just upriver from Georgetown because of his conviction that the capital should be a deep-water port. The choice of a ten-miles-square district, carved out of the Maryland and Virginia shoreland between Georgetown, Maryland, and Alexandria, Virginia, delighted the residents and commercial interests of these adjacent port towns, which had survived tobacco's decline by switching to the wheat trade that dominated the valley's agriculture until the Civil War.

Washington's vision of a great commercial city soon went aglimmering. Although the Chesapeake and Ohio Canal was built from Washington across the Cumberland Gap to the West, it proved no match for the Baltimore and Ohio Railroad, sponsored by rival Baltimore merchants, and the new turnpikes that made that Chesapeake Bay port the commercial gateway to the West.

It was perhaps the capital's good fortune that it was left to find its destiny solely as a government encampment, undominated by resident commercial interests. In any event, its location on the River Potomac was wiser than the compromisers knew; for the Potomac, more than the Mason-Dixon line, became the border between the industrial North and the agricultural South. In the nation's greatest internal strife, the War Between the States, the capital and its decision-makers sat on the geographic divide.

But by what good fortune did this capital become the handsomest of American cities? First there was the President's wise selection of Pierre Charles L'Enfant, a French engineer who fought with the Americans in the War for Independence, to lay out the city on the Maryland side within the new District. (The portion of the District staked out on the Virginia side was later returned to that state as unneeded land, and today forms Arlington County, which has become a vast suburban bedroom.) L'Enfant's plan, preserved in a relief map atop his tomb in front of the Lee Mansion in Arlington Cemetery, reflects the influence of a childhood spent in the garden and park at Versailles, where his father was an artist in the royal court. It called for sweeping vistas, broad avenues, fountains and cascades, squares, public gardens, statuary, a grand promenade lined with embassies, a dignified house for the President and another for the Congress on a hill commanding the city. It was a noble plan from which to commence.

The President persuaded the chief landowners to convey to the government all the land within the District. Part would be allocated for sites of federal buildings, part would be sold as residential lots to raise funds to underwrite the government's construction program, and part would revert to the original owners, appropriately increased in value by the pace of development. The first auction of lots went badly and alarmed the commissioners in whom Washington had invested authority for building the capital. L'Enfant complained that this approach was open to speculators; and when he refused to co-operate by providing a plat for the bidders, the idealistic Frenchman was regretfully dismissed, an early casualty of pragmatism in the American capital.

Washington's low skyline accents its public buildings.
Visible from the hills of Arlington, Virginia, across the
Potomac, are the dome of the National Gallery of Art,
the Capitol, Library of Congress, Washington Monument,
and Lincoln Memorial.

The commissioners accepted a proposition from a syndicate that included Philadelphia's Robert Morris, richest man in the country; the proposition allowed the syndicate to buy three thousand lots at cut rates in return for a promise to build seventy houses and to lend the government twenty-two hundred dollars per month until the public buildings were completed. The syndicate subsequently went bankrupt, stigmatizing Washington as a poor-risk town for investors, and retarding preparations of the capital. It was a tremulous beginning.

When the government was moved from Philadelphia in 1800, the population of Washington was three thousand, and the public buildings were but an earnest of the Washington that was to be. President and Mrs. Adams moved into the White House to find "not a single apartment finished" and "not the least fence, yard, or other convenience, without." "The great unfinished audience-room [today the East Room]," the First Lady wrote her daughter, "I make a drying-room of, to hang up the clothes in. The principal stairs are not up, and will not be this winter." The Capitol on Jenkins Hill two miles to the east consisted of one small flat-roofed unit into which the House and Senate, Supreme Court, Circuit Court, and Library of Congress were temporarily crowded. The Treasury Department's sixty-nine employees moved into the first completed public building just east of the White House. The forty employees of the State, War, and Navy departments moved into their partly finished headquarters on the west side of the White House. And the nine Post Office Department workers took up rented quarters at Ninth and E streets. To this day, despite a public building boom of recent years, the government has never caught up with bureaucracy's expanding space requirements; it rents offices in commercial buildings throughout the city.

In its early years, the capital city fulfilled few of L'Enfant's dreams. Neither the Congress nor the local citizenry was prepared to pay the price of a beautiful city. L'Enfant's prescription for avenues no less than 160 feet wide and streets at least 80 feet broad was intended to give the city an airy spaciousness, but the dust and mud from these unpaved thoroughfares destroyed the esthetic intent. Pennsylvania Avenue, intended as the grand boulevard linking the Capitol and the White House, was a swampy morass tangled with elder bushes. Here again the values of the plantation culture of the Potomac Valley infused the capital city. Instead of becoming a cosmopolitan center on the order of Old World capitals, Washington for years retained a country village atmosphere. It had racetracks (one in Lafayette Square) and gaming houses. It revealed the tastes of the planters in its mansions surrounded by stables and kitchens, such as the White House, Octagon House at New York Avenue and Eighteenth Street, and in Tudor Place, Georgetown's most impressive residence. The city's fine gardens, blazing with blooms from March to October, originated in this period.

By the end of the Civil War era the city's facilities were deplorable. Jefferson had improved Pennsylvania Avenue by lining it with Lombardy poplars but they lasted only thirty years. It was the first and only street equipped with oil lamps – but Congress stipulated that they be lit only when it was in session, which was but a portion of the year. The streets often flooded during storms and became badly rutted. Drinking water was contaminated. At least three presidents – Van Buren, Pierce, and Buchanan – had moved from the White House to the cooler heights above Georgetown during the summer to escape fevers occasioned by the Potomac's swampy shore. Lincoln preferred the Soldiers' Home, well beyond the northern city limits then.

This neglect of public facilities was corrected during Grant's administration when the District of Columbia became a territory, administered by a governor, Alexander Shepherd, an energetic thirty-seven-year-old politician-contractor who plunged into a public improvement program. Shepherd's expenditures evoked congressional howls but his program of paving streets, planting seventy thousand trees, building sidewalks, and adding underground water and sewer lines brought Washington respect as a city. It attracted a well-to-do class of winter residents who put up many of the fine mansions along Massachusetts Avenue and created a heady social season.

The Algonquin Indians who traded with the English settlers from Jamestown named the river Potomac, meaning "trading place," long before Washington became the center of national and international political trading. These Indian artifacts, part of the collection in the Smithsonian Institution, were photographed on the site of an ancient quarry in Rock Creek Park that once yielded quartzite for Indian weapons and tools.

Even the Washington Monument was at last finished. For two decades it had stuck out like a sore thumb from a fist of land at the end of the Mall, incomplete at the 152-foot level because of the weird shenanigans of the Know-Nothings. The Know-Nothings, an extremist political party of the period, who were antiforeign and anti-Catholic, one night in 1854 stole the block of marble from the monument grounds that had been presented for inclusion in the shaft by the Pope, a memento from the Temple of Concord in Rome. After defacing the Pope's stone and chucking it into the Potomac, the Know-Nothings later seized control of the Washington Monument Society, the private organization that solicited funds for the project. This development discouraged contributors and forced a halt of construction in 1855. There it stood until 1876, when Congress decided to finance completion by the Army Engineers. In 1884, the monument received its capstone, thirty-six years after it was started, a delay unavoidably memorialized by a difference of shading in the stones. The finished obelisk of colossal proportions is generally regarded as an improvement over L'Enfant's idea for a less imposing equestrian statue of General Washington.

The turn of the century brought the beginning of the era of the city beautiful. Senator James McMillan of Michigan in 1901 got Congress to create a special park commission, which he headed. Congress in 1890, at President Harrison's request, had already given the city the magnificent Rock Creek Park, which today offers woodsy refuge (and a natural setting for the zoo) for four miles through the heart of the city, one of the largest central urban parks in America. Senator McMillan's commission followed by recommending a far-sighted plan of additional parks, fountains, and water recreation facilities along the Potomac. Since then the park system for the national capital area has been expanded to 33,712 acres, notably by reclaiming the Potomac's tidal flats and acquiring shorelands along much of the Potomac and Anacostia rivers. Ironically, the Potomac itself has for years been one of the country's most polluted rivers, unfit for swimming. When the plantation mansions faced the river, it served as a beautiful, clean avenue; but when the towns embraced the railroad a century later, they turned their backs to the river and spewed both human and industrial waste directly into its channel. Reclaiming the Potomac as a clean waterway will take years but the work is progressing.

In addition to park development, the McMillan Commission inspired the removal of an ugly wart from the face of the Mall. This was an old railroad depot which the immensely powerful Pennsylvania Railroad had got permission to build where the National Gallery of Art now stands. The campaign for its removal led to construction of the handsome Union Station a few blocks north of the Capitol. This is one of the city's most attractive gateways, offering the arriving visitor a panorama of fountains, shaded parks, grassy slopes surmounted by the gleaming dome of the Capitol. As for the Mall itself, the Commission altered L'Enfant's idea for a grand promenade, lined with embassies, along which would pass parading legions and Sunday strollers, an American Champs-Elysées. Instead, the Mall is a swath of green, lined with museums, lively with busloads of school children and tourists by day, lifeless by night.

The Commission picked the site at the far end of the Mall for the Lincoln Memorial, Washington's most awesome marble tribute, and for its reflecting pool. It also proposed construction of the city's most beautiful Potomac crossing, Memorial Bridge, whose graceful stone arches offer an appealing gateway from Virginia, in contrast to the purely utilitarian steel spans thrown across the river at Roosevelt Island, Fourteenth Street, and Jones Point in recent years. The Francis Scott Key Bridge, a striking structure of high arches, crosses the river at the foot of Georgetown.

Like the East and West Potomac parks, the Washington National Airport just across the river was created by filling in low-lying shoreland. It gives the capital an aerial gateway only a short drive from downtown. The jet age impelled the addition of Friendship International Airport near Baltimore and Dulles International Airport to the southwest on a verdant Virginia plateau. From all three fields, the visitor reaches Washington via federal parkways, uncluttered by commercial signboards. The end of the trip from Friendship brings the visitor through the slums of Northeast Washington, but the drives from Dulles and National offer an unimpeded view of the city's majestic skyline.

Georgetown, originally a thriving commercial port, now uses the river mainly for recreation. Here a crew man practices at dawn beneath the spires of Georgetown University.

The face of the city is rapidly changing. From atop the Washington Monument, looking west beyond the White House (in foreground) and up Sixteenth Street, one sees a complex of new office buildings, hotels, and apartments.

That skyline, dominated by the Washington Monument, the Capitol dome, the Washington Cathedral, and the spires of Georgetown University, is protected by a law banning skyscrapers.

During Taft's administration the mayor of Tokyo presented two thousand flowering cherry trees to the First Lady, who planted the first one along the Tidal Basin. A plant disease forced replacement of this lot but ever since 1915 the springtime arrival of the pink cherry blossoms has been a public event, subsequently hailed in colorful pageantry and promoted as a tourist magnet.

In the past half century, as the town has grown up and pushed outward, it has also been at pains to decorate its interior. Since 1910 it has had an esthetic guardian, the Commission of Fine Arts, to advise and stimulate public support in the cause of the city beautiful. Although it has limited authority to veto bad taste, the Commission has enhanced Washington architecture, statuary, and natural beauty in parks and gardens. Indeed, the movement in behalf of urban beautification in other American cities, faced with the more severe problems of industrial grime and blight, was inspired by the effort that brightened Washington.

But the movement is never-ending. The two and a quarter million population of greater Washington is growing faster than that of any American city but Los Angeles. The pressure for more modern office and apartment buildings, for parking space, for freeways threatens the city's historic landmarks and attractive old buildings at every hand. And behind and beyond its marble temples Washington reveals the same social symptoms that deface much of urban America. Since World War II Washington has become the tail of the Atlantic megalopolis, a writhing dragon of congestion that sprawls from Boston Bay to the Potomac Valley. As such it has suffered festering slums, traffic jams, rising crime rates, overcrowded schools, restless and destructive youth. Having these conditions at the back step of the national capital has induced federal officials and Congress, however cautiously, to enlist the minds and money of the federal government in an effort to do something about them.

City on the Potomac: Split Personality

The two faces of Washington, federal and local, see remarkably little of one another. There are workers and merchants and professional men and women who are born, live, and die within the city. They know the conditions of trade and pleasure and crime, they know the schools and bus routes and the intricacies of local taxes. But for many of them the federal government is an alien and mysterious thing, about as strange and distant to them as it is to most Texans. To many of them the Capitol, the White House, or the Department of Commerce are merely landmarks, locations for bus stops, or parking places. Many have never been inside these places in their lives; these structures form the landscape for their eyes but not their minds, and the creatures who inhabit the interiors they know only through the artificial intimacy provided by broadcasts and newspaper columns.

The political community, on the other hand, pays scant heed to the city. Its member congressmen, journalists, federal officials, diplomats, military officers, and others who feed upon the government are more likely to have their origins elsewhere. Since the political community thinks of itself as a collection of the most influential persons from the several states, a native of the District of Columbia must become adept at explaining this embarrassing circumstance by pointing out that Father came here with the Wilson administration and the family is really from Virginia or Massachusetts or Illinois or anywhere but Washington, D.C. The local tax collector bows to this Washington syndrome by requesting each resident to report taxes paid to "State of domicile," no questions asked, making Washington the only place in the country with a subordinate claim on its taxpayers.

Members of the political community can call to mind the names of the senators on the Foreign Relations Committee but not the names of the District commissioners. The second sections of Washington's *Star* and *Post*, which cover local affairs, are unintelligible to them. They vaguely know there are nests of wickedness lurking in the shadows of the city, but just where they are is left unexplored.

And so the two communities of mind and purpose and acquaintance dwell here, together yet very far apart, a little uneasy in that special loneliness of the forced alliance. The residential community keeps Washington functioning as a place of habitation. The political community keeps Washington in the headlines, the focal point of the world.

If we were to penetrate the political community with X-ray vision, observe its values and its behavior cycles, identify for a moment with its activators, we might be tempted to doubt the maxim that America is governed by laws rather than by men.

The rhythm of boisterous human events here is so much more compelling than the solemn accretion of a body of law. The eyes of Washington, as well as the country and the world, focus on the human ferment in which new laws are enacted and old laws revised or repealed, not so much for the law as for the drama in which it is born or dies. Occasionally a law becomes a noticeable part of a citizen's life, as when the postman brings "Greetings" from the President via the local draft board, a reminder that youth is subject to a national consensus; or when the postman brings a Social Security check, a monthly assurance that age is not forgotten in the youthful turmoil on the Potomac. But once a law is enacted, the drama of its rough passage over, more often than not it slips beyond the threshold of public awareness into the household of bureaucracy, there to be administered by the anonymous multitudes of the civil service.

Because Washington dotes on the dynamic, the political community is fascinated with every scrap of news about what the President will next propose, about every minor disagreement that has leaked from last week's Cabinet meeting, about who is "in" and who is "out" with the President, about new names on the White House dinner guest list, about gamy disclosures from the latest congressional investigation.

In this purely human trait, Washington has a common bond with every other seat of power across the ages and around the globe, the courts of czars and Caesars and queens, the harems of sheiks, the cronies of dictators, the favorites of tribal chieftains. Whether supported by a tree of liberty or authoritarianism, the political status climbers forgather and chatter in the upper branches, convinced at the very least that those below gaze enviously aloft.

If gossip is the private currency of this community, law and the established procedures of a free society are its stable foundation. Consequently Washington is only superficially like a royal court but substantially and lastingly like a New England town meeting.

Once the President and the Congress have opened the annual meeting in January, the floor is open to all who wish to speak, to influence their brethren as they might, to contribute insight or confusion to the collective national judgment. In the last analysis, to observe this drama of American statecraft, whether its momentary results are wise or foolish, is to perceive the *raison d'être* of Washington. And it is to understand why Washington will never be a capital within a city but always a city within a capital.

Reflections of the capital's most impressive monuments to the nation's two greatest leaders, Washington and Lincoln, shimmer across the waters of the Potomac.

CHAPTER THREE

Mr. President

The chief activator of this political community, the leading actor in the drama of statecraft, is the President of the United States. He, along with his Vice-President, is the only officer who goes before all the voters to seek his mandate. He, alone, has an over-riding responsibility to serve not one section of the country or one segment of the population, but the nation, the people as a whole. In a country so broad and varied, this is an enormous obligation. It is also a magnificent opportunity for a man of vision and creative purpose.

Consequently the eyes of the nation which turn toward Washington more often than not focus on the man in the White House. This graceful mansion has been the home and office of the President since President John Adams moved in on November 1, 1800. The next day Adams, writing to his wife, said: "I pray Heaven to bestow the best of Blessings on this House and all that shall hereafter inhabit it. May none but honest and wise Men ever rule under this roof." Franklin Roosevelt had Adams' prayer carved on the mantel of the State Dining Room.

The design of the President's House, as it was first called, was submitted in 1792 by an Irish architect, James Hoban. It drew upon the Palladian architecture of mid-eighteenth-century Europe. A rival design based on Renaissance architecture, submitted anonymously by Thomas Jefferson, was among those rejected. But the White House of today is the blending of many afterthoughts, most of which were incorporated after the British burned the town in the War of 1812. That fire gutted the President's House and only a quenching thunderstorm saved the exterior

Washington's self-absorbed political community dotes on social-political gossip, such as who rates one of these White House dinner invitations.

walls. When it was rebuilt, its smoke-blackened walls made of Maryland sandstone were painted white.

The interior was gutted once again, purposely, 135 years later during the Truman administration, this time to strengthen the sagging floors with structural steel. During the War of 1812 fire, the only article of interior decoration saved was Gilbert Stuart's portrait of Washington, which Dolley Madison stripped from its frame before fleeing. The portrait hangs in the East Room. During the Truman reconstruction, all the interior paneling and decorative details were faithfully removed, stored, and then reinstalled. Truman also added a balcony on the south portico, but a more significant change was made by Theodore Roosevelt when he added the west wing of executive offices connected to the house by a colonnade. This wing contains the President's office, the Cabinet room, each looking out upon the garden, the offices of his staff, a reception room for waiting visitors, and a work room for newsmen assigned to the White House beat. For all the burdens of the job, the President at least has the ultimate in fringe benefits: he can walk to work and avoid the jarring rush-hour traffic.

More than a historic shrine, the White House is a center of laughter and tears, of worries and hopes as the home of the nation's First Family. Two presidents, Harrison and Taylor, and Lincoln's son Willy, and Wilson's first wife died in the house. Wilson subsequently proposed to a comely widow while standing on the south portico. Cleveland at forty-nine took a twenty-one-year-old bride in the mansion, and then chafed as newsmen followed to their honeymoon retreat at Deer Park, Maryland. Teddy Roosevelt's youngsters slid down the front hallway stairs on tin trays. Truman bawled out the Washington *Post's* music critic for not raving over daughter Margaret's singing. Eisenhower sharpened his golf game on the back lawn and became piqued at squirrels burying nuts in his putting green. Caroline Kennedy rode her pony, Macaroni, in the back yard and romped with John, Jr., into the President's office. The Johnson daughters have gone twisting, as Secret Service men have chaperoned them on their dates.

The house, consisting of more than a hundred rooms, from the movie theater in the basement to the solarium on top, offers comfortable living quarters for the First Family on the second floor while preserving the flavor of the past in the first-floor public rooms. The first floor is tastefully furnished with period antiques and hung with paintings of the presidents and several First Ladies. Of all the First Lady portraits, the most discussed for some years was the full-length likeness of Grace Coolidge. The red flapper dress was criticized as indecently, if stylishly, short for the dignified First Lady. At length the artist was summoned to lower the hem to her ankles. Coolidge, uneasy about the crimson color, suggested changing it to white. When the artist defended red as a good contrast with the white collie by her side, the President suggested painting the dress white and the dog red.

Tuesday through Saturday mornings these rooms are opened to the public. The line forms early at the East Gate, often stretching several blocks along the iron fence. In 1964, 1,840,146 visitors entered the vaulted archways of the ground-floor hallway, climbed one flight to the first floor and entered the East Room, scene of many balls and receptions, then passed through the Green, Blue, and Red Rooms to the State Dining Room, where the President is host to visiting royalty and other dignitaries, then through the main hallway and out through the columns of the north portico and down the driveway to Pennsylvania Avenue.

Though his privacy is assured within the White House, the President today finds it increasingly awkward to move outside his eighteen-acre estate in the heart of Washington. Gone are the days when John Quincy Adams managed a solitary swim in the Potomac or Teddy Roosevelt hiked with a companion through Rock Creek Park, fording the stream as necessary. Truman, the last President to walk regularly through the streets, rose at dawn in order to do it. When Lyndon Johnson has strolled beyond the gate in midday he has been mobbed.

Franklin Roosevelt loved a story that illustrated the carefree days of a century ago that contemporary

presidents yearn for. Secretary of State Seward, walking home from his office one evening, heard a man calling to him from behind an iron fence which then enclosed Lafayette Square across Pennsylvania Avenue from the White House. Seward discovered that the British minister and the wife of the Spanish minister, preoccupied with their rendezvous on a park bench, had not noticed the watchman locking the gate for the night – and now they were stranded in this embarrassing circumstance. A discreet diplomat, Seward agreed to fetch the man with the key. While searching for him among the White House outbuildings, Seward encountered President Lincoln, who asked what he was up to. Seward explained the international crisis in the shadows across the street, and the President volunteered to help. Failing to find the key man, the President and the Secretary of State each shouldered a ladder and hastened to the rescue. Placing one ladder against the inside of the fence and the other outside, they helped the flustered lady and her escort over the barrier and watched them hurry off into the twilight.

Today the fence is gone from Lafayette. It's around the White House grounds, and the President can't get past it without Secret Service men, a benevolent imposition on every Chief Executive since McKinley's assassination. Wilson once ducked out the front door and got as far as the Treasury building before he was overtaken by his guards. He had just wanted to go to the bank and do a little shopping, alone.

Wilson was the last President to travel about Washington in a horse-drawn carriage, which is now exhibited in the Smithsonian's new Museum of History and Technology. Presidents took to the motorcar in the twenties and to the air in the thirties. Eisenhower began the practice of using a helicopter, taking off directly from the south lawn of the White House to fly to a weekend retreat in the Maryland hills or to his farm at Gettysburg. Today a Marine Corps helicopter ferries the President on short trips or to nearby Andrews Air Force Base, where he boards one of the several jet airliners ever ready for lengthy presidential journeys.

When the President travels within the city, police are alerted in advance to clear traffic from his intended route. Since the assassination of President Kennedy, the President's limousine has become a veritable armored car, complete with bulletproof glass. It is always trailed by an open touring car filled with armed Secret Service men, whose twenty-four-hour-a-day duty is to protect the President and his family against physical threats. Theirs is an impossible task; for presidents, unlike monarchs and tyrants, are also politicians who never escape the compulsion to mix with crowds, to shake hands, to wave to people along parade routes, to stand before vast audiences. This they cannot do behind armor plate or bulletproof glass. Thus, four presidents have been shot to death: Lincoln while attending Ford's Theatre in downtown Washington; Garfield while entering the old railroad station located where the National Gallery now stands; McKinley while shaking hands at an exposition in Buffalo; Kennedy while driving in an open car through the streets of Dallas.

The President's office is an oval-shaped, comfortably furnished room with glass doors giving out on the lawns and magnolias. In that oval room, the focus of all the turbulent forces of a jostling humanity, there is quiet, not the quiet of the scholar's cluttered study but that humming quiet of an orderly engine room where all the parts are oiled and working smoothly. Here the President receives visitors of all stations: Future Farmers of America and past commanders of lodges and legions, Girl Scouts and boy wonders of the arts and sciences, new ambassadors assigned to Washington, and, with growing frequency, the heads of most of the world's nations; members of his Cabinet, of Congress, corporation presidents and union leaders, governors, educators, clergymen, and, inevitably, the owners of the Washington baseball club with a season's pass and an invitation to toss out the first ball of the season.

If the President contemplated each morning those intrusions upon his domestic tranquillity that disturb him most, he would not likely think of the tourists who pass quietly through the White House, or of these daily visitors to his office, who give him a window on the world at all levels. He would think, rather, of the problems which refuse to pass quietly, of foreign crises on which he is briefed by his aides, often before he has greeted the First Lady good morning; of domestic conflicts which, in the democratic scheme, he can never wholly avoid during most of his waking hours. For wherever he goes, in or out of the White House, the President can never escape the hurricane of pressures and influences that swirl about him.

Most presidents have offered acid comments on this unavoidable circumstance. Jefferson regarded the presidency as a "splendid misery," and Jackson called it "dignified slavery." Said Lincoln: "It is a white elephant on my hands, and hard to manage." Although Teddy Roosevelt said, "I enjoy being President, and I like to do the work and have my hand on the lever," he described the anguish of the office as "one long strain on the temper, one long acceptance of the second best, one long experiment of checking one's impulses with an iron hand and learning to subordinate one's own desires to what some hundreds of associates can be forced or cajoled or led into desiring." Wilson said the office "requires the constitution of an athlete, the patience of a mother, the endurance of an early Christian."

Most presidents have emphasized their loneliness in the White House. Eisenhower described it poignantly: "The nakedness of the battlefield when the soldier is all alone in the smoke and the clamor and the terror of war is comparable to the loneliness – at times – of the presidency. These are the times when one man must conscientiously, deliberately, prayerfully scrutinize every argument, every proposal, every prediction, every alternative, every probable outcome of his action and then – all alone – make his decision." Moreover, as Kennedy once observed, "Unfortunately your advisors are divided. If you take the wrong course, and on occasion I have, the president bears the burden, responsibility, quite rightly. The advisors may move on to new advice."

Not even those early waking moments before he descends from his private quarters are free from the agony of lonely decision-making. By pressing a bedside button he can lower the windows to keep the winds of nature from chilling his bedroom; but for all the political buttons he presses each day from his executive office, there is no shutting out the winds of conflict that howl through the capital. The headlines of the Washington *Post* and the New York and Chicago newspapers laid on his bed table tell him so each morning. Though his vast powers and manifold decisions shaped much of the news, though his press secretary skillfully put the President's best foot forward, the Chief Executive comes to this moment with the morning papers with all his humanness as a man exposed to the cutting edge of a free society. Besides the professional opinionators who chide him in editorials and columns, he must face the political elements of conflict that have surfaced in print: the Senator from Georgia demanded...the Governor of California objected...the Congressman from New York criticized...the investigating committee charged...the grand jury indicted...the Supreme Court overruled...the Gallup poll reported a decline...

Instead of seeking restrictions on the right of free speech and free press that foster criticism, the President must rely upon his own powers to persuade, to cajole, to intimidate, to defend, to counterattack, to appeal for public support, which ultimately matters most. Strong presidents thrive on this challenge, weak ones seek to avoid it. Successful leadership of this sort is an imperative of a successful free society.

The President is surrounded by a small staff of loyalists who identify with him, who take office and leave when he does, who supply his personal needs for accurate information, for drafts of speeches, for fresh ideas, for the latest quips to lighten his day.

President Washington had but one secretary. Teddy Roosevelt's staff numbered twenty-five, Hoover's seventy-five, and F.D.R.'s two hundred and fifty. Today's Chief Executive has a news secretary, an appointments secretary, and a personal secretary, several special assistants and administrative assistants, and an Army, an Air Force, and a Naval aide. And the secretaries, assistants, and aides all have secretaries, assistants, and aides. Most of them meet the qualifications prescribed by F.D.R. when he created the post of administrative assistant—"high competence, great physical vigor and a passion for anonymity." The ear of the President has become so difficult for any but the most powerful figures in Washington to reach that most callers are gratified to have a few moments of the time of one of his secretariat. Today no one is admitted to the White House offices without an appointment or credentials, which are checked by guards at the gate.

Since 1921 the President has had an auxiliary staff to supervise the federal budget. Housed in the old State, War, and Navy building next to the White House, the Budget Bureau screens all spending requests from the various government departments and assists the President in preparing his annual budget request before it goes to Congress in January.

One long step beyond his staff stands the Cabinet, a collection of men and an occasional woman chosen by the President to head the great departments of the government that form the substance of the executive branch. The Cabinet stood taller, and closer to the center of power, before the White House staff assumed its current role of importance to counsel the President. When the Cabinet meets it is like a board of advisors, possessing only such influence and authority as the President grants. Lincoln, once opposed unanimously by his Cabinet, announced a Cabinet vote as follows: "Seven nays, one aye; the ayes have it."

The President, his secretariat, and the Cabinet comprise the power elite of the executive branch. Directing the work of 2,500,000 civil servants and expenditure of a hundred billion dollars a year, they command a managerial evolution that has been transforming the American way of life. From Washington, year by year, under yet another new law, another segment of the national life is planned, circumscribed, stimulated, protected, subsidized, or regulated. Washington's managers supervise a few production lines, such as those for postage stamps and dollar bills, but their primary energy is devoted to turning out decisions. The country asks, "Am I eligible for...?" and the civil servant in the Farmers Home Administration or the Social Security Administration decides, on the basis of existing law and precedents, "yes" or "no." He didn't write the law or set the precedents, but he makes the decisions. In triplicate. When the answer is "no" the country may retort, "There ought to be a law." If this message comes through loud and clear to Congress, then the decision passes to Capitol Hill. What will Congress decide? —this is the perennial question in Washington.

When Washington gets down to work each year, it begins on precisely this note. It's the President, speaking for the country as he senses its needs, who tells Congress, "There ought to be a law." He delivers his message in person early in January before a joint session of Congress in the form of the annual State of the Union address.

There is a quadrennial rhythm to these State of the Union addresses that goes far toward creating the working mood of Washington, if not the country. If the President is new to office, he generally finds the country worse off than if he is in the twilight of his tenure, content with real or fancied achievements past. If he is facing re-election, he finds positive gains have been made but more to be done. Whether the President seeks to create or reflect a national mood, his State of the Union message is the score by which

No. 1600 Pennsylvania Avenue at Christmas time.

The First Family's Christmas tree in the entrance hall (left). The crèche displayed in the East Room (opposite). Jacqueline Kennedy was the first to display the Nativity scene in the White House.

The Diplomatic Reception Room on the ground floor, a boiler-furnace room in the nineteenth century, and the place from which Franklin Roosevelt broadcast his "Fireside Chats" has been furnished as an early-nineteenth-century parlor to receive guests arriving at the South Portico for state functions. The presidential seal is above the doorway (left). The walls were decorated during the Kennedy Administration with "Scenic America" wallpaper printed in France from wooden blocks over a century ago and peeled from an about-to-be-demolished house in nearby Maryland. The paper in the close-up (opposite) behind a gleaming wall sconce shows visitors at Niagara Falls.

The President's table, set for a formal
dinner, is accented in gold by this
candelabrum (above), the work of
early-nineteenth-century London
craftsmen, by a gold-on-sterling-silver
vermeil (right), and by a compote
(opposite) by the English silversmith
Paul Storr.

*Every First Family leaves its imprint on
the White House. The youth and élan of
the Kennedys charged the air with
excitement. At a state dinner, the guest of
honor is serenaded by musicians of the
Marine Band (above right) and the table
is set with gold service (above left). Mrs.
Kennedy would use casual garden flowers
with the finest gold setting (opposite).*

Mrs. Kennedy, in her search for authentic pieces to refurbish the White House, found a desk in the broadcast room, which she had moved to her husband's office. The paintings of early naval battles, the rocker, the desk-top mementos (carved whale ivory, World War II coconut shell, alligator desk set from President de Gaulle) all reflected the life and style of John F. Kennedy.

LOOK MAGAZINE PHOTO

he calls forth the urgent trumpets of change or the restful woodwinds of status quo. But Congress, predictably cacophonous, follows no score. In the best tradition of American jazz, improvisation is the style on Capitol Hill. With soloists one upon another demanding to be heard, it takes a maestro of rare talents to call from the dissonance a tune on which the country can unite.

The State of the Union pageant symbolizes what Washington and the country have come to take for granted, that the President is the leader to whom we look for national direction. Yet the pageant dates back only to Wilson, who revived the practice Jefferson had abandoned of going in person to the Capitol to place his legislative proposals in the palm of the legislature. The President's directive posture was further enhanced during the New Deal era when the legislative leaders of the President's party began making weekly visits to the White House for legislative strategy sessions.

Second only to the President in commanding the attention of the multitudes on this occasion of state is the doorkeeper of the House of Representatives, whose proud duty it is to announce the arriving notables by rank and station. This duty has been admirably and entertainingly performed for years by William M. "Fishbait" Miller of Pascagoula, Mississippi. "MISTER SPEAKER," bellows the doorkeeper from the rear of the chamber, "THE CHIEF JUSTICE OF THE YOU-NITED STATES AND THE ASSOCIATE JUSTICES OF THE SUPREME COURT." Then, at Fishbait Miller's command, the nine wise men, clutching their black robes about them, follow the doorkeeper down the center aisle amid a standing ovation to take reserved seats at the foot of the rostrum which the President is soon to mount. Senators have already filed over from the Senate side of the Capitol and been collectively announced, and joined their House colleagues. After seating each group, Fishbait scurries back to the door, peaks through its crack, does an about-face, snaps to a portly attention, and calls toward the rostrum in his drawling tenor to announce the ambassadors. And in they march, in order of longevity in Washington: Latins and Europeans, Africans and Orientals, counselors of state from the far reaches of the globe, nodding and bowing diplomatically to the applauding assemblage as they take their seats. When the Cabinet arrives, the stage is at last set with all the supporting players in the drama of Washington.

The public galleries above are jammed with the lucky bearers of visitors' cards good only for this occasion. Among them are the First Lady and her guests. When the President enters, behind a bipartisan escort of congressional leaders, the old chamber resounds in applause from both sides of the aisle, augmented by a chorus of hoorays and whoops of partisan joy from members of his own party. The only solemn spectators are the newsmen peering down from the press gallery and the Secret Service men who scan even this assembly for signs of a threat.

This assembly, to be sure, is brimming with men who threaten the President's program and his prestige, if not his person. It also includes those who aspire to his position and his power, from the Vice-President and the Speaker in their high-backed chairs behind him, to the freshmen congressmen in the last row. But in all the years of the Constitution under which they serve, none has gone to the unconstitutional weapons of violence to fulfill such ambitions. Constitutional weapons they have used aplenty – the acid tongue, the vote of defiance, the demand for his defeat, the call for his impeachment, even a trial of impeachment on one occasion – but never the dirk or the pistol, the not uncommon instruments of change in less stable realms.

What, indeed, sets the President apart from those men of high station who publicly applaud his entrance into the hall but privately aspire to his office? For what manifold duties must he qualify? By what sort of selectivity is he chosen and others rejected?

This man, the President of the United States, may be many things to many people; but the key to much of his performance is what he, as Mr. President, is to himself. The nature and power of the presidency is determined not only by law and custom but by the philosophy and personality of the man who holds the office. Woodrow Wilson once wrote, "The President is at liberty, both in law and in conscience, to be as big a man as he can. His capacity will set the limit..." Washington, Jackson, Lincoln, and the two Roosevelts were conspicuous believers in this "big man" view of the presidency. Others believed with William

Foreign guests of the President are received, and presented with gifts, in this second-floor parlor of the White House before descending to the State Dining Room. The saddle and blanket were gifts for a Latin-American chief of state.

Howard Taft that "the president can exercise no power which cannot be reasonably and fairly traced to some specific grant of power...either in the constitution or in an act of Congress..."

The Constitution is specific in conferring upon the President the authority to be commander-in-chief of the military, to issue pardons, to make treaties, and to appoint ambassadors, judges, and other civil and military officers, provided the Senate gives its consent, to recommend legislation to Congress, to veto acts of Congress, and to execute the laws of the land. In addition to these specific powers, the Constitution states: "The executive power shall be vested in a president of the United States." Therein lies the key to the philosophical dispute expressed by Wilson and Taft. The dispute has raged since Madison claimed that Washington had no specific power to issue the neutrality proclamation of 1793, but Hamilton defended the act as within the "executive power" of the presidency. This inherent power permits the President to do, as T.R. put it, "anything that the needs of the nation demanded unless such action was forbidden by the Constitution and the laws." This view, countered Taft, makes the President "a universal Providence."

Historians tend to rate presidents as "strong" or "weak" accordingly. When Harvard Professor Arthur M. Schlesinger asked fifty-five historians several years ago to grade the presidents in five categories from great to failure, they named Lincoln, Washington, Franklin Roosevelt, Wilson, Jefferson, and Jackson as the great presidents in that order of greatness. The near greats were Teddy Roosevelt, Cleveland, John Adams, and Polk.

Those rated as average were John Quincy Adams, Monroe, Hayes, Madison, Van Buren, Taft, Arthur, McKinley, Andrew Johnson, Hoover, and Benjamin Harrison. Six were graded below average: Tyler, Coolidge, Fillmore, Taylor, Buchanan, and Pierce. Only Grant and Harding were considered failures, inasmuch as corruption riddled their administrations. William Henry Harrison and Garfield were excluded because they died shortly after taking office. The more recent presidents must wait until the historians have gained the perspective of time before receiving their grades.

While it is significant that the great presidents all subscribed to the "big man" conception of the presidency, they were also, as Professor Schlesinger put it,

"lucky in their times" in the sense that they are all identified with some crucial turning point in our history. Washington got the constitutional government started, Jefferson expanded the country from the Mississippi to the Rockies with the Louisiana Purchase, Jackson prevented secession by South Carolina and broke the economic power of Eastern money over the agrarian South and West, Lincoln preserved the Union and emancipated the slaves, Wilson and Roosevelt introduced major social and economic changes, intervened in world wars, and fostered peacemaking efforts. By contrast to the greats who took timely action to achieve timeless results, most of the average presidents served in times that demanded little of them. The President, then, is the captive of both his philosophy and his time.

If the Constitution is not the last word on presidential powers, it offers virtually no word at all on the manner of selecting a president. It says nothing of political parties, nominating conventions, or presidential primary elections, which today provide the framework for the selection process. It provides only for the so-called electoral college, a group of electors from the various states who it was assumed would exercise their own judgment in choosing presidents, as when they unanimously elected Washington in 1789 and 1792. Electors still cast the votes that officially elect the President, but today they reflect the popular judgment of the voters in their respective states – a change that worked a transition from an aristocratic republic to a popular democracy.

The first five presidents – Washington, Adams, Jefferson, Madison, Monroe – were members of an educated political aristocracy dominated by Potomac Valley planters. When factions or parties developed after Washington, the aristocracy relied upon a caucus of each party's members of Congress to select the nominees. The man who received the nod from the majority party's caucus became President. This system lasted until 1824, when Andrew Jackson, Henry Clay, and John Quincy Adams ran without caucus endorsement; the inconclusive results threw the election into the House, where Clay's influence, as Speaker, assured the election of the aristocratic Adams. Four years later Jackson ran again, this time with the popular support of a number of state legislative caucuses and public meetings that had nominated him as their favorite. His sweeping election ended rule by the elite through King Caucus and opened the era of popular democracy. It led to the nominating conventions employed by both parties for the first time in 1832, and to all the festive trappings from torchlight parades to whistle-stop campaigning that were to follow.

As for the manner of the man chosen, Jackson's triumph began a trend among party politicians to promote a heroic general as suitable presidential material, especially if his record revealed no embarrassing incidents or views that might be held against him. In consequent desperation, the Whigs cloaked William Henry Harrison in the dubious heroism of an Indian fight at Tippecanoe, Indiana, and won the presidency in 1840, largely on the strength of his image as a hard-cider-drinking, log-cabin frontiersman, which was more fictional even than his military laurels. Thus, at any rate, began the most cherished of American legends, that of the self-made man, which has served many presidential candidates from Lincoln to Lyndon Johnson.

If presidential candidates and their political handlers have belabored the homely virtues in an effort to create confidence, they have also had to contend with public issues of varying description and with that intangible, the national mood. This mood may set in months before the election machinery begins to function, or it may be created or altered by the election campaign. Be it anxiety or complacency, well-being or discontent, it is a product of many events, none more compelling than the ferment of Washington. The yeast of that ferment is dissent. In Washington, dissent is the acknowledged right of many but the formal duty of no one. Unlike the British parliamentary system, the American system has created no office of chief dissenter.

Periodically, nonetheless, a strong figure emerges to mobilize resistance to a presidential proposal, say a Senator Lodge defeating Wilson on the League of Nations, or Senators La Follette and Walsh discrediting the Harding administration on the Teapot Dome oil scandal, or a Senator Wheeler wrecking Roosevelt's "court packing" plan, or a Senator Taft outflanking Truman to restrict labor unions. In confrontations as grand as these, Washington becomes noticeably polarized, pro and con. Men of influence and organizations of interests are drawn into the partisan struggle for supremacy. While the struggle is waged in the Congress for votes to pass or kill a treaty or a bill, a collateral struggle is waged in the country. It is, in essence, a struggle for favorable impressions on Main

Street. "I think the President is doing the right thing," is all the voter may say; but it's enough for any President. Unschooled in the finer points of the issues at stake, uninformed of all the implications, we, the people, nevertheless bow to no one in exercising the right to judge the fitness of our leaders.

Washington's intense interest in Main Street impressions is seen in the proliferation of public-opinion polling. Presidents, senators, and congressmen, when facing the electorate, increasingly engage opinion samplers so that they can better reflect or cater to the mood of the voter.

Out of a maze of impressions, variable as they are from one occasion or one citizen to another, a collective judgment is cast, a consensus reached. The quest comes down to a decision about which contender is the apparent possessor of the charismatic gift. Which one is more likely to have something of the specialness that set apart Washington, Jefferson, Jackson, Lincoln, the Roosevelts, Eisenhower, Kennedy. Thus one is chosen, another rejected. Leadership is bestowed by sovereign citizens upon that person in whom public confidence rests most firmly on the Tuesday following the first Monday of November every four years.

Generally the results of popular sovereignty have done honor to the Founding Fathers, the most radical visionaries of our history. We, the people, were to take control from a distant monarch and establish this representative government "in Order to form a more perfect Union, to establish Justice, insure domestic Tranquility, provide for the common defence, promote the general Welfare, and secure the Blessings of Liberty to ourselves and our Posterity." All this has been done, not perfectly, but to a degree that has convinced the most pragmatic doubters that the people might be trusted with decisions of state. As Will Rogers put it, "This country is not where it is today on account of any man. It is here on account of the real common sense of the big Normal Majority."

The vortex of American political life is the oval-shaped office (following pages) of the President, serenely adorned with flowers, books, mementos, and glass doors opening onto the garden. President Johnson tunes in on the turbulence swirling about him through a battery of telephones, two news tickers, a cadre of aides, and a succession of influential callers.

Will Rogers had put his finger on the question that divides freedom from authoritarianism: Is the real common sense of the big Normal Majority trustworthy? We say it is and function as a free society accordingly. But it's neither a new nor a revolutionary practice. The nomadic Israelites, a dozen centuries before Christ, periodically closed ranks behind a single leader when threatened by warring neighbors. United in a common faith, they believed God had bestowed His spirit upon one of their number to give protective leadership; and that this gift, or charisma, was evident in special leadership traits that inspired confidence. Israel relied upon charismatic leadership for several centuries, or longer than the still young life of the United States, until Solomon seized power by the more conventional means of a palace coup.

David, last of Israel's charismatic leaders, was the forerunner of the successful American leader. He had a private army, whose victories enhanced his prestige; he showed sagacity in setting out to succeed Saul; but he also had that extra personal quality that marked him as a charismatic leader. Like David, contenders for the presidency require an army of political supporters, an impressive succession of victories (at the polls or on the battlefield), a determined quest of the office, and that extra personal quality.

In contemporary America there is a disinclination to invest the elective process with a spiritual dimension. But politics after all has profoundly to do with religion. The whole idea of democracy – that is, the dignity of the individual – grew from the religious concept of man's perfectibility in the image of God.

Though private belief is secured against public meddling or coercion by the Constitution, the nation has formally asserted faith in Providential guidance. The Declaration of Independence confessed "a firm Reliance on the Protection of divine Providence." The national anthem declares: "And this be our motto – 'In God is our trust.'" All the coins of the realm and the one-dollar bills are stamped "In God We Trust." Only the higher denominations fail to carry this inscription, which may suggest that affluence inspires trust in more temporal powers.

The principle of charismatic leadership applies in lesser degree beneath the presidency in Washington's political community. Though only the President, Vice-President, and the members of the Congress must go directly to the people to secure the portfolio they seek, a President will seldom retain a Cabinet minister, or a lesser official, who has lost public confidence. Only the justices of the courts, appointed by the President for life terms, are personally secure against public criticism provided their conduct does not provoke impeachment proceedings. While judges represent a buffer against public whimsey, they, too, must prudently maintain the public's confidence in the courts in the interest of obedience to the court's view of justice in the land.

In this grand assembly before which the President stands in the House chamber there likely are a few misfits, or self-seekers or has-beens or never-wases or corrupted officeholders; but the filtration system of representative government tends to screen out these undesirables at some suitably low level, preventing those whose designs outreach their capacities from reaching the top. Granted that able men are occasionally filtered out with incompetents, the system tends to reserve highest leadership for those whose gift has become most apparent in the give and take of public affairs. This system of the free society, like Nature, occasionally aborts; but the species of free men survives and grows more numerous, hopefully even more mature. This is the strength and vitality of charismatic Washington, its example for the age.

The awesome, soul-burdening responsibility
of final decision makes the President the loneliest man
in Washington.

CHAPTER FOUR

The Lawgivers

The Congress, America's national town meeting, has been conducting the nation's public business on Capitol Hill in Washington since the autumn of 1800. President Washington had come down from New York to lay the cornerstone of the Capitol on September 18, 1793, initiating construction of a low-domed structure with two columned wings designed by William Thornton, an amateur architect who won five hundred dollars and a city lot for his design. When President Adams seven years later addressed the first joint session of the House and Senate in Washington, the lawmakers gathered in the single boxlike structure that awaited their arrival, the first unit in what was in time to become a magnificent marble-faced temple dominating the city's skyline. A second unit was finished in 1807, giving each house its own chamber connected by a low wooden walkway, where the dome was later to rise.

When the British burned the city in 1814, only the stone walls of the two boxes remained, their wooden interiors a charred ruin. Benjamin Latrobe, the architect who rebuilt the Capitol, used marble, brick, and metal for the artistic new interior, and won acclaim for his unique corn and tobacco motifs on the column heads. During this reconstruction, Congress met first in the Patent Office, the only government building to escape the British torch. Meanwhile local citizens, fearing that Congress might move the capital back to Philadelphia, hastily erected a "brick capitol" on the site of today's Supreme Court building as temporary congressional chambers. It was used from 1815 to 1819, and was the scene of the capital's first outdoor inaugural, that of President Monroe.

By 1824 the central portion of the Capitol, the Rotunda, was opened for a grand reception honoring Lafayette, who became the first foreign dignitary to address a joint meeting. The Rotunda was then covered by a low copper-sheathed dome. By 1850, as the number of states augmented the membership of both House and Senate, crowded conditions forced Congress to add enlarged wings containing the spacious chambers currently in use.

The great iron dome, painted white and capped by a statue of Freedom, was added during the Civil War. Lincoln ordered the work to continue uninterrupted as "a sign the Union shall go on." In this lasting form, the Capitol dominated the city and inspired the country. Many state capitols later were copied from it. After more than a century, the Capitol dome is old, yet forever new, glowing, and majestic. It symbolizes and stands guard over the grand town meeting hall of America.

The Capitol housed the Library of Congress until the turn of the century, when it was moved into its ornate building a block to the east. The Supreme Court also held sessions in the Capitol for 135 years until its marble temple opposite the Library of Congress was completed in 1935.

To cope with the thousands of citizens who storm the Hill daily, Congress has a force of over two hundred and fifty policemen, many of them working their way through law school, and twenty-four salaried tour guides to direct visitors through the building. Starting in the Rotunda the guide points aloft to the magnificent frescoes by Constantino Brumidi, an immigrant who fled political persecution in Italy in the 1840s. In Washington he spent twenty-five years, much of it lying on his back on an aerial scaffold, working his pigments and plaster art "to make beautiful the Capitol of the one country on earth in which there is liberty."

Passing on to Statuary Hall, which was the old House chamber, the tourists note that each state is permitted statues of two of its most distinguished

The powerful head of Lincoln by Gutzon Borglum dominates the sculptures lining
the Rotunda of the Capitol (right). Nearly all the statues are of American presidents,
by American artists. At the center of the great eyelike dome, 180 feet above the
Rotunda floor, is the fresco "The Apotheosis of Washington," executed in eleven
months by Constantino Brumidi. To create this masterpiece, the sixty-year-old
Brumidi often had to lie on his back on the scaffold. One enters the Rotunda from
the east portico through the bronze "Columbus Doors." Created by Randolph
Rogers, these depict scenes from the life of America's discoverer. In the panel above,
Columbus is shown at La Rábida friary before seeing Queen Isabella.
In the panel below, Columbus is shown returning in chains after his third voyage.
The links that originally joined the wrists have been stolen.

citizens. The selections have occasionally shown that national notoriety or popularity is equated with distinction by local admirers. Thus with Webster and La Follette stand Huey Long and Will Rogers. The grinning figure of the Oklahoma humorist was placed facing the House chamber in accord with his personal instructions so he could "keep an eye on the boys."

It would be desirable for visitors to the public galleries overlooking the House chamber to gain their first impression of Congress assembled on the day early in January following the biennial elections when each new Congress begins its two-year life cycle. As the noon hour for convening nears, newcomers and oldcomers mingle like legionnaires at a reunion, victorious comrades all, home from the campaign for approval by grass roots America.

Then, at the clatter of the Speaker's gavel, they form ranks, row upon row of spokesmen for every section and every segment of a vast nation, all solemnity now. It is always the same, yet always new and exciting, this ritual of democratic renewal. For this moment of the swearing in, when 435 pledging hands are lifted aloft like rows of uplifted swords, is a moment of majesty for all but the dead in spirit. In unison they state:

"I . . . do solemnly swear that I will support and defend the Constitution of the United States against all enemies, foreign and domestic; that I will bear true faith and allegiance to the same; that I take this obligation freely, without any mental reservation or purpose of evasion, and that I will well and faithfully discharge the duties of the office on which I am about to enter. So help me God."

In this moment every congressman, however prosaic his mind, however commonplace his manner, is

Through the office of a United States senator flows an endless stream of seekers, asking more than any one official, however well-staffed and energized, can possibly grant. In the relative calm of his inner office, Senator William Fulbright of Arkansas, chairman of the Senate Foreign Relations Committee, answers questions for a member of the press. The fate of controversial measures is strongly controlled by the chairmen of the standing committees. Whether a senator's constituency be rural or urban, so long as it returns him to office he retains by the rule of seniority his hold upon a well-defined segment of the nation's life. Whatever of importance takes place on Capitol Hill, the senators decide, individually or collectively, to allow to happen.

lighted for an instant by the immortal fires of his country's history and meaning. The buried nerve of the Ideal that lies somewhere in every one of them is touched and wakened. In his own mind, he himself takes on for a moment the heroic proportions of the famous figures whose bronze and marble statues line the corridors through which he has just passed: Washington, Franklin, Jefferson, Lincoln, and all the others.

Senators are sworn to uphold the Constitution by a quite different ceremony, which reveals a contrast between being a senator and being a representative. Inasmuch as senators serve six-year terms, only a third of the Senate stands for election every two years. On swearing-in day, those newly elected or re-elected are called individually by name, escorted in turn down the center aisle with all the attendant pomp of a visiting monarch. Gathered before the pedestal of the Vice-President, senators starting new terms take the oath, sign the book, and then turn to receive congratulations from colleagues who press forward to greet them with brotherly warmth.

In the symbolism of these ceremonies, the representative is a lawmaker in the mass, a legislative organization man, a member of a vast apparatus that waits upon no individual member in its own ongoing urgencies. But the senator, from the moment he assumes office, is regarded as a person, indeed a very important person of whom the group is aware and from whom it may even draw strength. Salaries at either end of the Capitol are the same, but the aura of individualism, of personal stature, that pervades the Senate makes it a place of wonder coveted by every representative whose pride is bruised by the relative anonymity of membership in the House.

Most tourists witness the Congress during routine sessions, which are disappointingly deficient in entertainment value. The floor below is often as desolate as the lone prairie, with one or two coyotes baying at the stars. Attendance increases as a vote nears, but the scene never comes up to the expectations of the tourist who has just visited Statuary Hall. If only a few congressmen would stand proud, heads high, shoulders squared, scrolls outthrust in the manner of those bronze and marble statesmen who line the outer corridor. Instead, the visitor encounters a mélange of slouching, shuffling, leaning, hands-in-pockets figures, an artistic catastrophe, not unlike the familiar home-town figures encountered in courthouses, lodges, city halls, union temples, veterans' posts.

Americans are curious sovereigns. Back home we traditionally feel comfortable electing such a familiar figure, often cinching the choice by declaring, "He's a nice guy." But upon visiting Washington we are disappointed to discover that Congress is adrift in waves of familiarity and informality. The tourist who troops through this grand temple of democracy in shorts and shirtsleeves secretly feels cheated that the lawmakers are not togged in silk knee breeches, lacy blouses, and powdered wigs. The last vestige of formal attire vanished with the death in 1954 of Senator Clyde Hoey of North Carolina, whose daily appearance in a brindle swallowtail coat and fresh boutonniere, his long silver locks brushed across his ears, rewarded visitors who expected nothing less grand from a United States Senator.

Looking down at the apparent disorder, one inevitably wonders how these men made their way in life before coming to Congress. In a recent Congress there were two clergymen, four physicians, five engineers, thirty-nine journalists, fifty teachers, sixty-one farmers, 157 businessmen, one labor official, and, always most numerous, 315 lawyers. A number rated themselves in more than one grouping.

More significant perhaps, 504 of the 535 members of Congress also listed politics as their profession. No longer the part-time public service of those who could afford to take time from their private pursuits, as it was when Congress met no longer than four or five months a year, national lawmaking for today's complex society has become a year-round occupation from which only the less conscientious members steal much time for private business or law practices. The most notorious of this latter class have been New York City congressmen, some of them the creatures or masters of unsavory political machines, whose devotion to Washington duties is squeezed into the middle of the week between four-day weekends in their home districts. This so-called Tuesday-through-Thursday Club accounts for the practice in the House of scheduling votes on major legislation in midweek.

Whatever the appearance of confusion to the visitor, the activity in either chamber is a unique form of professionalism in American legislating. Whether engaged in passing a hundred bills in an hour by common consent or wrangling for weeks, often jaw-deep in irrelevancies, over one contested bill, Congress works its will under rules and procedures that are so elaborate as to confound many members. Conse-quently, each body employs a skilled parliamentarian who sits at the foot of the presiding officer at all times to whisper authoritative advice to the chair when rulings are demanded to resolve disputes.

In performing its legislative function, Congress exercises the sweeping powers set out in Article I, Section VIII, of the Constitution:

The Congress shall have Power To lay and collect Taxes, Duties, Imposts and Excises, to pay the Debts and provide for the common Defence and general Welfare of the United States.

While there has been a long conflict of priorities between providing for the common defense and for the general welfare, between guns and butter, the Congress has made Washington the action center of the country because it has provided both in abundance. It has done this to assure a maximum of domestic tranquillity, that national goal set out in the preamble of the Constitution. For no circumstance of national life is more appealing, more reassuring to an incumbent of the White House or the Congress than domestic tranquillity. If the country is untranquil because of foreign troublemakers, boost the military forces. If the country is worried about a depression, prime the pump. If the country is angry about high taxes, vote for economy in government. If the country is indignant about corruption in high places, throw the rascals out. Or be thrown out. Domestic tranquillity is much to be preferred.

The last period of what passed for real domestic tranquillity was in the twenties. The war to end war was over, victoriously. Naval vessels were being sunk under a disarmament treaty. The market was rising. And Coolidge was saying that the business of America is business. Will Rogers said Coolidge was "the first President to discover that what the American people want is to be left alone." He was also the last. Hoover and Roosevelt discovered that when tranquillity vanished with the Depression, the people looked to Washington to be rescued. The New Deal, not the first attempt to legislate tranquillity back into being, was only the most far-reaching. Indeed, Americans have traditionally looked to their government for help. As Mark Twain put it many generations ago, "There is something good and motherly about Washington, the grand old benevolent National Asylum for the Helpless."

As a rule domestic tranquillity, to the extent that it

is ever a realistic goal in a nation that allows vocal dissent, is most readily achieved through measures to promote the general welfare, whether it be a Homestead Act or an old-age pension. But tranquillity is never static. One generation's sense of well-being is another's condition of poverty. The revolution of rising expectations that has swept the world has been an evolution in the United States for generations. Yesterday's cry for 640 acres of public land on the frontier is today's quest for a half acre in the suburbs, no money down.

Whatever is within the power of a congressman to give, he will give, hoping not only to tranquillize but to please. The Homestead Act served the western settlers of yesteryear, and federal housing loans serve the suburbanite of today, each a measure to promote the general welfare, courtesy of your friendly congressman. But popular expectations keep rising. "What have you done for me lately?" is the question he imagines his constituency is constantly asking. It is what keeps the Congress toiling away on Capitol Hill.

Compared to the Senate the House is a paragon of efficiency in disposing of bills – because it severely limits the length of time any member may debate the issue. In earlier days when the House allowed unlimited debate, its filibusters were as notorious for delaying action as those for which the Senate to this day remains notorious. In the spring of 1812, for example, New England Federalists who opposed war with England talked in day-and-night relays to prevent a vote on the war question. As a Federalist orator wearily held the floor, prowar Democrats burst into the chamber one night and created brassy chaos by tossing the spittoons about the chamber. In the confusion the Federalist stopped speaking momentarily and sat down. An alert Democrat promptly gained recognition and demanded a roll call vote. The filibuster had been broken, and the House voted to declare war. Another early filibuster ended in a pistol duel on the edge of Washington.

As the size of the House membership grew from the original sixty-five representatives to the present 435 with the addition of new states, the House necessarily tightened its rules to make legislating at all manageable. Today the precise amount of time allowed either side during debate on a bill is monitored by the clock and doled out to such speakers as either side wishes to recognize. A congressman can unwind on a pet subject by securing advance permission for a special order allotting him an hour or more if he wishes; but the special-order speakers rise in turn only after the main business of the day is ended and the chamber has been all but emptied of listeners.

As its work load increased, Congress finally indulged its members in private offices outside the Capitol after a century or more of performing all their desk chores in chambers. The crowded House in 1908 built the first of its three office buildings south of the Capitol; and five years later the old desks were removed from the House chamber and replaced with benches to make more seats. Senators enjoy large private offices in two buildings north of the Capitol. In the Senate chamber they retain their original schoolmaster desks, still outfitted with inkwell, dip pen, and a bottle of blotting sand crystals. Traditionally, senators fulfill the schoolboy yearning by carving their names inside the desk and thus identifying the seats of the mighty and the notorious for posterity.

Senators prefer to think they occupy the "upper house," a notion that infuriates the elders of the House, if not the younger congressmen who eagerly aspire to six-year Senate terms and the added prestige that a senator commands in Washington. The term, to set it straight, dates from the earliest period of the Capitol when the Senate chamber was one floor above the House chamber. In addition to the longer term, which frees them from re-election anxieties in two out of three elections, a senator has a larger staff of aides and a larger constituency. He is also entitled to free snuff, available in little lacquered boxes on either side of the rostrum in the Senate chamber and free mineral water, a beneficence that seems appropriate inasmuch as the Senate is literally a Roman term for a body of elders.

In recent decades a striking contrast has developed between the hurly-burly of the Senate's committee rooms in the Senate office buildings and the relatively quiet Senate chamber. It is all a piece of the electronic revolution, which has altered our politicians, if not our basic politics, just as noticeably as it has affected our singers. Today a throaty orator in the Senate, that historic scene of some of America's most crucial debates, is as rare as a great baritone on the American stage. The soft-voiced senator, like the crooner, is adequate, as long as the microphone doesn't go dead. In a Senate committee room, when the klieg lights, the cameras, and the mikes go on, a senatorial whisper may be heard across the continent; but in the Senate cham-

The congressional seniority system invests the power of committee chairmanships in the patriarchs. Few have wielded greater authority than Representative Carl Vinson of Georgia (above right), who served in the House longer than any other congressman—three decades as chairman of the House Armed Services Committee— and Representative Howard W. Smith of Virginia (below right), longtime chairman of the House Rules Committee.

A Senate committee, meeting in the old Supreme Court chamber at the Capitol in 1957 (following pages), draws cameras, klieg lights, newsmen (on right), and standing-room-only crowd as it questions United Mine Workers president John L. Lewis (shown in close-up opposite).

ber, still off limits to electronic amplification, his voice may not carry across the aisle.

Despite the decline of the oratorical splendor that echoed from the place in all the great debates over slavery, expansion of the Union, and acts of war, the Senate retains its solemn constitutional place as the highest realm for effective dissent. Here little Rhode Island is as strong as mighty California. Here every minority – be it sectional, racial, economic, religious, or simply an unpopular political view – can and must be heard if but a single senator rises and claims his right to speak in its behalf. The guarantee of audible dissent is the rule permitting a senator to talk as long as his strength or his sense of fitness permits. A squad of allied dissenters, of course, can abuse the guarantee by preventing the Senate from invoking its collective will when the talk has long ceased illuminating the issue. In recent years the filibuster has become the last line of Southern resistance to federal laws supporting the claim of Negro citizens to their just share in the Bill of Rights. But for all the talk, the Senate has in the ultimate hour passed reasonable and comprehensive civil rights bills without staining the chamber's crimson carpets with the blood of its impassioned members, one small tribute to the stability and workability of the American system and to the maturity and decency of those who make it work.

The Senate has always been conservative in the best sense of that abused term. Its deepest instincts are to conserve fundamentals of the past, to resist the tinkering alterations or sweeping changes proposed by the Chief Executive. It is often said it is easier to get a declaration of war than a change in the Senate rules. Presidents since Jackson have fought with the Senate. Indeed, much of the political history of the nation grew directly out of this ongoing contest for supremacy.

In a society in which speed and efficiency have become revered values in themselves, the Senate stands stalwartly, stubbornly against the tides of haste. Senators thrive on the description of the Senate as the world's greatest deliberative body, even those who protest that it might deliberate less and act more.

When all deliberation has ceased in either chamber, the final vote brings the moment of truth, the apex of tension that has been approaching for months through the long committee hearings, the backstage period of private persuasion exerted by lobbyists on either side, by the White House, by congressional

leaders nudging their men into line if they can. If the bill has been highly controversial, the public galleries are crowded, the walls of the chamber below lined with members of the little bureaucracy of Capitol Hill. And then the clerk begins his alphabetical cadence of surnames, recording each "aye" or "no" precisely. Whatever the result of that vote, the roll call suggests a deeper truth about this melting pot of a nation. The names themselves tell the story. Not those names long familiar to the public life of the republic – Fulton, Gray, Morris, Smith, Wilson, et al. – but the names of the later arrivals who have added the strength of diversity and proved out the merit of social democracy: Addabbo, Blatnik, Clancy, Daddario, Duncan, Farbstein, Fino, Gonzalez, Grabowski, Hébert, Holifield, Kastenmeier, Kluczynski, Lesinski, Libonati, Magnuson, Matsunaga, Nedzi, O'Brien, Olsen, Powell, Quie, Reifel, Reuss, Rodino, Rooney, Rosenthal, Schneebeli, Schweiker, Zablocki.

How long since they got off the boat? A generation or two for some, a decade or two for others – these black, brown, beige, and pink complexions, the face of a vital heterogeneous people, these Americans from Europe, from Africa, from Asia, from Latin America, these sovereigns of a warm and generous land. The very composition of the Congress is a living, speaking, self-renewing monument to that ennobling concept of We, the People.

If Toulouse-Lautrec had painted Washington, he would have set up his easel on Capitol Hill. Monet might have preferred the banks of the Potomac, especially the low arches of Memorial Bridge when the mist is on the river. Van Gogh might have gone into Rock Creek Park or into the slums, and Renoir would have been fascinated by the faces of the diplomatic set. But it would have taken a Toulouse-Lautrec to portray the color and smoke and emotion of an explosive congressional investigation. However, instead of the subjective artist's eye, the cool objective eye of the television camera brings us the scene from the Senate Caucus Room, of prancing witnesses kicking up their heels, of senators shouting them down, of the gendarme removing blatant bystanders. Here, by invitation or subpoena, there is more of the muck and grime and ignobility of American life than anywhere else on the public political scene. Here the politician can openly, safely sit down with harlots and tax collectors, racketeers and titans of finance, labor bosses and uncommon thieves in every conceivable line. The island of safety is that long committee table, which is presumed to divide the good guys from the bad, although occasionally mountebank faces mountebank across that oaken slab.

Congressional investigations are popular because they promise comforting patterns of black and white, a welcome break from the tension of legislative grays created by the complex of bills, amendments thereto, and motions to recommit for further study. A finding of right and wrong, good and evil is so much simpler in the hippodrome that investigates the past than it is in the forum which sets the course for the future.

The success of a congressional investigation is often measured less by the new laws it inspires, though this is ostensibly its object, than by its capacity to attract public attention or stimulate public indignation. On occasions the investigation offers brooding philosophical conflicts that would intrigue even a Jefferson, such as civilian vs. military suzerainty, or freedom to dissent vs. loyalty to the government. An investigation may also serve to dissipate unwelcome public indignation, as did the calm inquiry into President Truman's dismissal of General MacArthur.

But the most repeated theme, assuring wide attention, is the exposé of corruption in high places, such as the disclosure of the Teapot Dome oil scandal in the twenties. The explanation for this success formula is that most Americans have to make their own way in life without benefit of powerful family or political connections; and our popular literature is littered with plots in which the boss's son comes into the firm to face a most hostile reception from the employees. Yet if the theme is the same, the specific improprieties change. What strikes people as improper in one era and circumstance seems proper enough in another time and place.

In the Civil War, Army combat commissions were dispensed to politicians' sons and brothers, and even the saintly Lincoln didn't see much wrong in that; almost nobody did. He was a creature of his period, and the period creates the fashion in public morality as surely as in clothes. The worst periods are always those attended by war. "It is bad enough for us to have corruption in our midst but it is worse if it is to be condoned and accepted as inevitable," said Attorney General Bates during Lincoln's administration. "The demoralizing effect of this civil war is plainly visible in every department of life." Whether the war be civil or international, hot or cold, the effect is re-

markably the same. Perhaps it is war's uneven hand, the injustice, if you will, of wounds and death for some, fantastic profits for others; the end of some families, the start of fortunes for others; the unaccountable ennobling of some men and women, the subtle corrosion of others.

Whatever the period, the Puritan instinct is never quite extinguished. Congress is always quick to respond to this instinct to condemn moral laxity in others, if a bit deaf to critics of its own habits.

Rather than taking the form of a trial that might send the accused to jail, the congressional investigation is contemporary Washington's pillory. Whatever the questionable constitutional foundation for calling a citizen to answer for past offenses, this practice of shaming the accused before his peers has popular support.

Congress itself has given some personal ground to the Puritan instinct, notably in chasing whiskey dealers out of the Capitol and refining its own drinking habits. In the more boisterous days of the republic Congress reflected the heavy drinking tastes of the country. A Massachusetts congressman a half century ago recalled that congressmen guzzled many gallons each day of a beverage called "switchel," made of molasses, ginger, rum, and "water from the celebrated Capitol spring." When the idea of banning alcohol in the Capitol was first debated in 1866, a California senator defended spirits by claiming they "enable us to seize great facts, inspirations which once possessed are ours forever; and those who never go beyond the mere beastly means of animal support never lived in the high plains of life and cannot achieve them." The antidrinking resolution was defeated, and the senator's practice of carrying their drinks to their desks in the chamber went unmolested by law or changing custom until the turn of the century. In 1902 a rider on an immigration bill, banning the sale of alcoholic drinks in the Capitol, slipped through and still stands. But beer, ruled nonalcoholic, is sold in the House restaurant; and private cocktail parties continue apace, even in the old Senate chamber where the American Temperance Society was organized in 1833. Nevertheless, the accommodating liquor dealers (and

The congressional investigation (following pages), here conducted in the Senate Caucus Room, has created more villains and heroes than any other legislative function.

bootleggers during Prohibition) who once kept stores of whiskey in the Capitol basement for prompt deliveries to the lawmakers are long gone. Although a senator in his cups is not unknown to the chamber, the congressional rate of consumption has declined as surely as the level of splendid oratory.

Violence, physical and verbal, has also waned. The Constitution protects members of Congress from being haled into court for slander or libel for remarks uttered on Capitol Hill, but for years congressmen felt safer with a pistol tucked in their belts. Before the Civil War, a case of dueling pistols was a part of the outfit of a Southern or Western congressman. A number of American political leaders of the period survived duels, Andrew Jackson and Henry Clay among them, and some did not, Alexander Hamilton the most prominent. In those brawling frontier days volatile congressional debate was fueled not only by switchel but by epithets – liar, puppy, scoundrel – certain to impel an honorable man to challenge his adversary to a duel. But when a congressman from Kentucky killed a congressman from Maine in a duel with rifles at ten paces, Congress enacted the first federal antidueling law in 1839. Each house has since outlawed insulting language in debate, so that today one member refers to another as "the gentleman from New York" or the "distinguished senator from Illinois." Long after the antidueling act, however, pistols remained in vogue, and occasionally were brandished as tempers flared during debates or when the Speaker was pressed to maintain order in the rough-and-tumble House. In this quick-draw era a California congressman shot and killed a dilatory waiter in the Willard Hotel; and a New York congressman, Daniel Sickles, in 1859 shot to death in Lafayette Square the seducer of his wife, Philip B. Key, son of the author of "The Star-Spangled Banner." Sam Houston also took his cane to a House colleague on the street one day. The hapless fellow pulled his pistol only to have it misfire, sparing Sam for later glory at the Alamo. More serious, a South Carolina congressman caned Senator Charles Sumner of Massachusetts into unconsciousness in the Capitol. Canes have long ago vanished, and the last shooting in the Capitol was in 1954 when Puerto Rican nationalists opened fire into the well of the House from the public galleries, inflicting wounds on several members; a century earlier these gunmen would likely have been petrified by the mass of pocket artillery on the floor below.

As for wickedness of the flesh, we have the word of a newspaper correspondent of the 1880s, Frank G. Carpenter, that congressmen in that era gave gallery passes to their favored ladies of the evening, a brazenness we suspect will never be repeated by today's public-image-minded lawmakers. When Congressman Abe Lincoln observed a House colleague in the company of a commercial damsel he wrote: "He went home with her, and if I were to guess, I would say, he went away a somewhat altered man – most likely in his pockets, and in some other particular. The fellow looked conscious of guilt." For decades after the Civil War Washington's red-light district flourished along Pennsylvania Avenue until the suffragettes crusaded for a cleanup and the government reclaimed the area for its complex of office buildings known as the Federal Triangle. Since then sin in Washington has been more discreet. A case of congressional philandering is periodically exposed, or more often whispered about, but the incidence is probably less frequent than in the general population.

Pride, the deadliest of sins, shows no sign of comparable decline, despite the entreaties of the Senate's most popular chaplain, the late Peter Marshall, who used to open Senate sessions with prayers such as this: "We confess, our Father, that we know we need Thee, yet our swelled heads and our stubborn wills keep us trying to do without Thee. Forgive us for making so many mountains out of molehills and for exaggerating our own importance and the problems that confront us . . ." Forgiving exaggerated importance in Washington is no mean act of mercy. But exaggerators come and go with merciful rapidity while those truly important to the federal function linger with less need for the arts of political mendacity.

The Washington community polices itself with a cold eye for pretenders to the rank of VIP, but occasionally displays sentimentality toward a VIP emeritus. Such was the cushion to break the fall of Joseph P. Martin when he was unseated as Republican leader of the House, a position of importance whose most visible reminder is the chauffeured limousine which

From his inner sanctum in the Capitol and his front-row desk in the Senate chamber, minority leader Everett McKinley Dirksen of Illinois has advanced the art of bipartisanship by supporting the President on questions of civil rights and foreign affairs.

The Vice-President, traditionally chosen by the President to strengthen his party's ticket, was often forgotten after the election when he assumed his only constitutionally prescribed role, presiding officer of the Senate. Recent vice-presidents have been assigned additional duties by the President, often serving to bridge the executive and legislative branches. Vice-President Hubert Humphrey greets guests at a reception for an ambassador in the Senate Foreign Relations Committee rooms in the Capitol (opposite), is interrupted by an aide with urgent business (right), and returns to converse with Senator Albert Gore (below).

goes with the job. The House didn't shy from passing the party reins to younger hands but it blanched at the prospect of good old Joe losing his Cadillac; so, by order of the House, one additional chariot was ordered up to join that gleaming fleet that is drawn up hard by the marble archways of the temple at twilight to bear their proud possessors off to some sedate revel in the city below. Before affluence was so conspicuous, only the Speaker rated a car. Speaker Nicholas Longworth used to delight in offering his Democratic opposite, John Garner, a ride to and from his lodgings at the Washington Hotel; and at election time they would await the returns to see who got the car for the next two years.

If Congressional investigating tends at times to dominate the news from Capitol Hill, the less flamboyant town meeting flavor of Congress becomes evident when the Congress receives the President's legislative program and begins to exercise its constitutional authority "to make all laws which shall be necessary and proper..." The President's program assumes priority status with his party's leaders, but the new laws that it recommends are merely a small fraction of the eighteen thousand bills introduced in each Congress by its members. In the end most of these are ignored, but a thousand or more may be enacted. Generally, the fate of controversial measures is strongly influenced, if not controlled, by the dukes of Capitol Hill, the chairmen of the standing committees of the House and Senate. Each of them commands an independent duchy of legislative authority to which are referred new bills; and no bill emerges for full congressional consideration until it has received the approval of a majority of the members of the committee. Whether the chairman can govern the decision of a majority or not, he has the power to hasten or retard the progress of any bill deposited to his consideration. He needn't pass a civil service test of his qualifications for the chairmanship or even win the favor of his colleagues for this post, for the chairmanship passes to him the moment that he has served longer than all other members of his party on the committee. His constituency may be rural or urban, reasonably enlightened or not, but so long as it returns him to office he retains by the rule of seniority his hold upon a well-defined segment of the nation's life. Any day's events of substance on Capitol Hill are largely what these dukes decide, individually or collectively, to allow to happen. The late Speaker Sam Rayburn gathered with his favorites at dusk each day in a Capitol nook, passed the decanter, talked and listened, practicing the art of the possible, the essence of practical politics. It's not so much that this is the best way to run a lawmaking body, but all other ways seem a bit worse.

Looking at a day's activities in the congressional committees is like examining one of those glass-encased engines at an auto show. It reveals the mechanism that keeps America's autogovernment moving down the road of changing times. One day's hearing, like a single stroke of the piston, is followed by another and another, eventually impelling movement. Occasional efforts at overhauling this engine are proposed, to correct stalling or backfiring or to achieve greater speed. The only outward changes of recent decades have been to contract or expand the number of committees, which has approximately the same effect as altering the horsepower of an auto used only in rush-hour traffic. Congress moves at what it regards as deliberate speed and there's seldom any hurrying it.

But Congress does move. It does fulfill its high responsibility. It has been remarkably stable. Of all realms of government, it is most sensitive to the moods and opinions of the big Normal Majority. And what it does each day, each session, is the result of a complex, unseen interplay of advocate and opponent, legislator and lobbyist, orator and ghost writer, diplomat and journalist, society hostess and Cabinet officer, military and civilian, idealist and cynic, statesman and partisan hack, bureaucrat and private attorney. No one can measure the precise contribution of any one element in any given accomplishment; but there are days when the outcome ennobles us all, say the advancement of the Marshall Plan or passage of the Civil Rights Act of 1964. These are days when, by some magic of political alchemy, baser ingredients of partisanship are converted into golden consequences. There is no secret to the process – elective representative government of, by, and for the people – but thus far only a fraction of mankind has tried it.

Each day that the House or Senate convenes, the Government Printing Office goes to press with the Congressional Record, the verbatim account of the day's proceedings plus any related, or extraneous, material submitted for publication by members of Congress.

Congressional Record

PROCEEDINGS AND D[EBATES OF] THE 88th CONGRESS, SECOND SESSION

VOL. 110   WASHINGTON, T[UESDA]Y, OCTOBER 20, 1964   **No. 195**

Appendix

NOTICE

[The la]st [i]ssue of the daily Congression[al Record fo]r the second [session of the] Eighty-eighth Congress will be [published n]ot later than [Octo]ber 23, 1964. It is [sugg]ested [that a]ll proofs of [speec]hes [be] held for revision, o[r exten]sions, [if] as authorized [to u]se, be submitted to [the Gove]rn[ment Printin]g Office or to [the Nati]onal Record Clerk, [Room] M-112, [bef]ore that date.

[By ord]er [o]f the Joint Committ[ee on] [Pr]inting

[Omar] CAR[SON,] Chairman.

[An Era End]s, an Era Begins

[EXTENSION] OF REMARKS
OF
[HON. JOHN] W. McCO[RMACK]
[OF MAS]SACHUSETTS

[IN TH]E HO[USE] OF REPRES[ENTATIVES]
[Saturday,] October [17, 1964]

[Mr. McCORMA]CK. Mr. [Speaker, the second] [sess]ion of the 88t[h Congress has] [dr]awn to a close. It w[as]

[i]t has seen ma[ny]
[re]port brought
[S]oon its deeds w[ill]
recor[d] in the annals of
[wis]dom [of] its decisions and
[of] its actions will
[accompl]ishment
[i]t has given effe[ct]
[it] has prescribed wi[th]
[rea]ching. May I con
[b]oth sides of the
[as] a positive role i[n]
[of] the 88th Congres[s]
[contr]ibuted generously of
[its] foresight to the
[w]ill be given more
[mer]it[ed] attention in the hist[ory]
[of] the near and d[istant]

[the] same tried to convi[nce]
[Congress] was a dawdlin[g]
an[d] this in[st]itution, a "stopgap" [institu]t[ion]. The legacy we lea[ve]
[of the s]econd session is a

[pro]vocal
[a]lso a
[Pres]ident,
[st]rong
[pr]essor,
[wh]ereas
[begin],"
[con]tinue."
[and] we h[ave]
[rem]arkabl[e]
[in] doing [it]
[po]sition a [little]
[a] little

[t]his charge. It
[r]ecently deceased
[Donal]d Kennedy, and
[con]fidence" for his
[Lyndon] Baines Johnson.
[ha]d said, "Let
[tha]t we have begun
[an]d—thanks to this
[th]e 88th Congress.
[hel]ped to make our
[str]onger

[dai]ly session of Con-
[gre]ss is ul[t]
[pro]g[ress]
[i]s which
[i]nstrumental in
[pro]motin[g]
[gr]eatn[ess]
[determ]ined by the extent
which
[consc]ientiously and con-
[s]tently [m]
[e as a]re[t]he peo-
[wi]shes of the [p]olitical plat-
[f]orm of t[he]
[party] in power. With
[these] crit[eria]
[at] this g[reat]
[I] venture to say
[n]d the generations
[wh]ich con[gr]ess
[will] long remember
[this] Cong[ress]
[a p]articula[r]
[second] session in
[will] say that this
[Congress]
[i]n new era—an era
[w]hich, ar[e making]
[stri]king g[reat things]
[fi]elds of economic
[expansio]n
[opportuni]t[y]

[I] menti[on]
[ge]ntly discu[ss]
[thin]gs first and pres-
[s i]n which they
[w]ill move
[Nation] to hitherto
[un]attaine[d] [height of]
[progr]ess. I do so,
[because] [they accurate]ly represent the

determination of this Congress to come to grips with weighty problems crying out for solution in a crisis-ridden age.

ECONOMIC EXPANSION

Two of the most pervasive legislative measures acted on in this session which are benefiting our economic system are the tax reduction and revenue acts of 1964. In a landmark session for our economic system, this Congress imaginatively sought to make use of some of the tools put to its disposal in our capitalistic democracy by manufacturing a potent weapon against possible recession and by creating an appropriate stimulus to employment.

The entire impact of the tax cut is of course incalculable. Only time will reveal its full effect. However, facts and figures drawn up since its passage last February indicate an encouraging degree of measurable economic growth—growth which promises no sign of letup in the near future.

By enacting the most comprehensive program of income-tax reduction in our Nation's history, this session of Congress has given new and unprecedented vigor and buoyancy to our system of free enterprise. Because of it, approximately $11.5 billion annually has been added to the take-home pay of Americans in every income group and to business profits across the board.

In mid-August, the Council of Economic Advisers released these impressive figures on the economic gains that have been recorded since November of 1963: The gross national product, based on current prices, has increased [$30] billion, or 3.3 percent; industri[al produc]tion has gone up 5.2 percen[t; employ]ment in nonfarm occupatio[ns has in]creased by 1.4 million; the [unemploy]ment rate is down from 5.9 to 4.9 perce[nt;] the average weekly earnings in ma[nu]facturing is up $2.12, or 2.1 perce[nt;] personal income has risen $17 [bil]lion, or 3.6 percent; after-tax perso[nal] income has increased $20 billion, [or 4.5] percent; the after-tax personal inc[ome] for a family of four is up $360, or [7.4] percent; corporate profits—after tax[es—] have risen nearly $3.5 billion, or 12 [per]cent; and, in stock values, Dow-J[ones]

Unlike most great capitals, Washington has seldom experienced the clash of arms. The British set the government buildings afire in 1814. And Confederate forces during the Civil War attacked Fort Stevens, just north of town, but were beaten off as President Lincoln watched. Washington's parks, however, are filled with heroic military statuary. Some of it honors figures so obscure as to recall Will Rogers' irreverent quip, "Heroing is one of the shortest-lived professions there is." This memorial (below) to General U. S. Grant, at the east end of the Mall, is the largest equestrian statue in the country.

CHAPTER FIVE

Oyez! Oyez! Oyez!

In a softly lighted chamber of marble hung with crimson velvet a crier bellows, "The Honorable, the Chief Justice and the Associate Justices of the Supreme Court of the United States." An audience of a hundred and fifty or so rises almost in reverence from its red-cushioned pews as nine men robed in black file in to face the assemblage from the great long bench. The crier continues his traditional chant:

Oyez! Oyez! Oyez! All persons having business before the Honorable, the Supreme Court of the United States, are admonished to draw near and give their attention, for the Court is now sitting. God save the United States and this Honorable Court!

The visitor who observes this ritual, performed each day the Court is in session, has little doubt that the quiet dignity of the Corinthian-columned temple in which the Supreme Court sits was acquired from the justices themselves and the hallowed traditions their solemn demeanor serves. Even when the Court in 1809 met in Long's Tavern, one of several temporary "courthouses" used while suitable quarters were being prepared in the Capitol, one has no doubt that Chief Justice John Marshall and his associates imposed an uncommon air of honor and respectability upon that public house. After the Court finally secured quarters in the Capitol in 1819 it remained there until 1935, when its present building was completed. Its first Capitol courtroom was beneath the old Senate chamber; but after 1860, when the present Senate wing was added, the Court took over the old Senate chamber.

The mood of restraint that envelops the Court is

The Supreme Court weathers periodic storms of controversy more calmly than Washington endures the season's first snowfall.

its hallmark in Washington's otherwise unrestrained political community. Or, as Justice Stone once wrote, "While unconstitutional exercise of power by the executive and legislative branches of the government is subject to judicial restraint, the only check on our own exercise of power is our own sense of self-restraint."

Congress, to be sure, has the restraining power of impeachment to remove judges for "treason, bribery or other high crimes and misdemeanors." But only once has it exercised this power, in 1805 against Justice Samuel Chase for assailing President Jefferson, and he was acquitted.

Congress also holds the power to fix the size of the Court, a question that has occasioned assaults on the Court from both the executive and the legislative branches. When the Court was organized in Washington's administration, Congress fixed its size at six, a Chief Justice and five associate justices. Today it has nine. During the Civil War it was once increased to ten because the unfavorable attitude of several justices toward the war was thought to endanger the government's policies. After the war, Radical Republicans in Congress became incensed over the Ex Parte Milligan decision, which cast serious legal doubt over the military rule that the Radicals fastened upon the South. The result was an act to reduce the size to seven by denying President Andrew Johnson authority to fill vacancies until that lesser figure was reached. The Court reverted to nine under Grant.

The more famous attack from the executive by President Franklin Roosevelt came after the Court had struck down as unconstitutional several New Deal programs. Roosevelt's abortive "court packing" scheme for liberalizing the Court would have given him authority to appoint a new justice each time a sitting member of the Court reached the voluntary re-

The Solicitor General of the United States, an appointee of the President, defends the government. He goes to court wearing the traditional cutaway and striped trousers, once the costume of all attorneys appearing in court.

80

tirement age of seventy but continued to serve, so that the maximum size might be increased to fifteen. Congress killed the bill.

After both these assaults, the Court appeared to temper its decisions, leading to Mr. Dooley's famous observation, "The Supreme Court follows the illiction returns." More to the point, perhaps, was the observation of Charles Evans Hughes, before his appointment as Chief Justice, "We are under a Constitution, but the Constitution is what the judges say it is..."

The Court, indeed, exercises such vast, undefined powers over legislative acts, both national and state, that the social philosophies of presidential appointees to the bench are of prime consideration to the White House and to the Senate, which must confirm nominations. The Court's prevailing mood of "liberalism" or "conservatism," to the extent that those abused terms retain any meaning for the times, tends to be fashioned by a shifting alliance of philosophies within the Court and by the impress of changing national attitudes.

Changes in its outlook come only more gradually than in Congress or in the executive, where an election can revamp the composition of these branches overnight. Justices have lifetime appointments; although a few elect to retire or resign in favor of other pursuits, the average period of service has been fifteen years. Chief Justice John Marshall served thirty-four years, Chief Justice John M. Harlan thirty-two years, and Associate Justice Oliver Wendell Holmes thirty.

Nonetheless the Court does change. From the onset of the Industrial Revolution to 1937, the Court's opinions were strongly influenced by prevailing laissez-faire precepts. But after the philosophy of the New Deal at last penetrated the Court, it reversed numerous past decisions – Justice Stanley Reed counted fourteen reversals from 1937 to 1943 – because the majority alliance had shifted to a generally favorable view of government intervention in the economic life of the nation.

The Court has modernized itself in other respects as well. In 1955 it installed an amplifying system in the chamber to overcome its dreadful acoustics. And in 1964 it emancipated the page boys of the Court, those teen-age chaps who hustle off for law books at the snap of a justice's finger, from their black knickers. Since then the boys have worn long pants – like the congressional page boys who went modern two decades before.

One of the richest traditions of this country is that any citizen may take his grievance "all the way to the Supreme Court" in quest of justice. Within this tradition, Negro students from four states protested to the Court that racial segregation in the public schools is an injustice. Although the Court had ruled a half century before that "separate but equal" facilities were lawful, in 1954 it overturned this old decision and ruled in favor of the students, signaling the beginning of the end of the social structure of the Old South. Except for a handful of suits, the twenty-five hundred cases that reach the Supreme Court docket each year are brought on appeal from either federal or state courts below. State courts, ranging from a police court to a state supreme court, are limited to cases involving state law, but if their decision is based on the U. S. Constitution or involves a federal question, an appeal to the Supreme Court at Washington is permissible. The federal courts are organized on three tiers: District Courts, located in each state; Courts of Appeals, one for each of eleven circuits; and the Supreme Court.

Of these twenty-five hundred cases, the Court disposes of a vast majority by a simple order allowing the decision of the lower court to stand. The Court selects about two hundred to two hundred and fifty cases as the most important to review; and in about half of these cases, it listens to arguments by opposing counsel in the Supreme Court chamber. When the government is involved in the case, its arguments are presented by the Solicitor General or a subordinate attorney from the Department of Justice, who wears the traditional cutaway and striped trousers once required of all lawyers appearing before the Court. Attorneys still wear dark suits but the court once tolerated a Kansas attorney wearing a tweed suit, pink shirt, and tan shoes to argue his appeal in behalf of a druggist convicted in the lower courts of selling liquor to an Indian. He won his case.

Like the House of Representatives, the Court is averse to long-windedness. The Chief Justice, with the aid of a time clock, imposes a strict time allotment on each counselor, a cause of evident frustration to the hapless attorney whose time for making brilliant points of law is pre-empted by questions from inquisitive justices. Instead of deciding each case on the spot before undertaking another, the nine justices in a single day may listen to arguments in numerous cases raising issues of corporate mergers, or civil rights, or

From this row of black-leather chairs (opposite above) facing the courtroom, the
nine Supreme Court justices listen to arguments in cases appealed from lower courts.
A decision may affect but a single citizen or, by interpreting the Constitution anew,
reshape the course of American history. Printed copies of an appellant's brief must
be submitted to the clerk of the court for distribution to justices, opposing counsel,
and the press prior to arguments in the courtroom. Each member of the Supreme
Court performs most of his work in his private chambers, reviewing precedents—as
Justice Arthur Goldberg is doing above—and writing decisions assigned to him by the
Chief Justice. The chambers, secluded from public view at the rear of the Court
building, include a private bath and dressing room, which Justice Oliver Wendell
Holmes bewailed as an unfortunate departure from the communal men's room,
which Holmes said was the only place he could meet his brethren frequently to
discuss cases.

labor relations, or criminal justice. Decisions subsequently are reached in what must surely be the most fascinating ceremony of the Court, which is off limits to all but the nine wise men. It takes place every Friday from October to June around a green-covered table in an oak-paneled sanctuary. The Chief Justice presides, and the most junior justice serves as doorkeeper to preserve the secrecy of the conference when messages are passed to and from the outer world.

Marshall used to initiate the proceedings by serving his colleagues a drink on rainy days, presumably for medicinal purposes. After the custom set in, it was difficult to keep the bottle corked on sunny days, so Marshall ruled that, rain or shine in Washington, drinks be served on grounds that it was surely raining somewhere in the Court's vast jurisdiction. But when Congress gave up public boozing in the Capitol, so did the Court.

Today the justices initiate the proceedings by jolly handshakes all around. Then, case by case, they thrash out their decisions. The Chief Justice leads off, followed by each justice in order of seniority. When the vote is taken, the most junior member casts his lot first and so on up the seniority scale to the Chief Justice. One justice is then assigned to write the majority opinion. Those in the minority may concur in one dissenting opinion or write individual dissents. The task of writing a decision may take months; for drafts are circulated until each justice agrees to the final wording. The Court is the only household of the government whose virtue has been unsullied by the anonymous masters of prose, the ghost writers.

Completed decisions are printed in secrecy in a print shop in the basement of the Court, unlike almost all other government publications, which are produced at the huge Government Printing Office on North Capitol Street. Even classified military material is printed at the GPO in a guarded section whose eight hundred workers have had security clearance; but not the decisions of the Supreme Court. The integrity of the Court has thus been self-protected, providing an unexampled record of no advance leaks on momentous decisions in over a century, since a gabby justice gave President Buchanan advance information on the Dred Scott decision.

Decisions are made public by the author justice reading his opinion aloud in open court. As he begins, printed copies are handed to newsmen, who swiftly scan its pages for key phrases and start the transmission belt that carries the news to daily newspapers and broadcasting stations the country across before the justice has finished reading his opinion.

A half million visitors annually pass through the massive oak doors of this temple of justice, many of them standing in line for their turn in the pews. But millions who have never seen the words "Equal Justice Under Law" carved into the marble lintel have nonetheless experienced its consequence in their workaday lives, simply because the Supreme Court has stood like a rock – and will go on standing – for the idea that every citizen's rights and freedoms under the laws of the land must be protected.

A petition for a writ of certiorari, seeking a Supreme Court review of a lower court decision, in this instance was denied and then stamped with the official seal of the Supreme Court.

CHAPTER SIX

The Diplomats

If Washington at large is the all-American city, reflecting the ever shifting images of this immensely varied land, its Embassy Row is splendidly un-American, a succession of reflecting pools casting up images of faraway lands and peoples. In its many moods Embassy Row by day is charming, sedate, businesslike, polite but a trifle reserved; and by night it is charming, gay, inviting, hospitable, intoxicating, irresistible.

The diplomats who inhabit this region of the city are Washington's cosmopolitan night people. Whether transported from one embassy to another in the quiet certainty of a chauffeured Rolls-Royce or behind the wheel of a chattering Volkswagen, they know exactly where they are going and why. With spidery unobtrusiveness, they form invisible webs of personal contacts, spinning gossamer strands of goodwill with a handshake, an embrace, an exchange of pleasantries, a whispered confidence, a raised glass, ingratiating themselves throughout the diplomatic, military, and political communities, snaring choice morsels of intelligence for the home office.

To the outsider driving along Massachusetts Avenue at dusk, observing the limousines depositing gowned ladies and jacketed gentlemen at the doorsteps of mansions alive with light and laughter, Embassy Row is a world of fascination and intrigue, a scene of absolute splendor and social glamor where common cares vanish in the presence of Very Important People and the abundance of liquors and exotic foods. To the insider who observes this ritual with a nightly sense of duty to his government, it is an enervating way of acquiring (skillfully concealed) aches in the stomach, head, and feet. Or, as one European ambassador's lady said plaintively when asked about her social schedule, "Ah, there is no peace."

Embassy Row is not the tidy row that L'Enfant had in mind when he suggested that it be located along the Mall between the Capitol and the Washington Monument on deep building lots "which are best calculated for spacious houses and gardens, such as may accommodate foreign Ministers, etc." Instead, most of the 115 embassies in Washington are scattered buckshot through a vast urban triangle between Sixteenth Street and Massachusetts Avenue north and west of their intersection at Scott Circle. Many of them occupy old residences built a half century or so ago for wealthy families who were attracted to Washington's winter social season. The Russian Embassy, just outside the triangle below Scott Circle on Sixteenth, was the palatial home of the widow of the railroad-car maker, George Pullman, who is said to have blown three million dollars in an abortive attempt to crash society here in the Wilson era. The Brazilian Embassy far up Massachusetts occupies the handsome manse built for the wife of Colonel Robert R. McCormick, the isolationist owner of the Chicago *Tribune* and the old Washington *Times-Herald*. The Indonesian Embassy just west of Dupont Circle was built in 1903 by a Colorado mining tycoon, Thomas F. Walsh, whose widow married the owner of the Washington *Post*, and, as Evelyn Walsh McLean, became famous as one of Washington's most lavish hostesses and owner of the Hope diamond.

If the income tax eroded an opulent way of life and forced the capitalists to abandon their mansions to some of the world's most radical governments, ironically these homes have been spared destruction by virtue of their foreign ownership. The reason is simply that the embassies are tax-free; so, foreign governments can afford the luxury of charm and Old World elegance found in these mansions on Embassy Row. Indeed, one of the contributions to the enduring handsomeness of Washington is this diplomatic pres-

Lord Harlech, formerly chief of the largest foreign mission in Washington, at breakfast with Lady Harlech in the British Embassy (left) on Massachusetts Avenue. They are going over a day's schedule that includes tea for the "Tuesday Afternoon Girls" (above) and a late-afternoon family game (right) before a black-tie dinner.

ervation of buildings of character which, if left to commercial judgments, would soon fall before the wrecker's ball to clear this valuable land for more profitable towers of mortar and glass.

A number of embassies were designed specifically for diplomatic use and as a national advertisement. The British have a red brick country house set on six acres of shaded grounds. Built in 1928 to serve both as the ambassador's residence and offices or chancery, it was augmented in 1960 by a modern office building of utilitarian design to accommodate the expansion of the chancery staff. Italy constructed a handsome Italian Renaissance embassy facing Sixteenth Street, with the chancery connected at the rear, complete with a walled garden accented with sculpture from ancient Rome. The Danes have a new embassy that is Danish modern from its sweeping horizontal exterior to the inverted martini-glass chandeliers. Iran, Saudi Arabia, and Kuwait have new chanceries that call up visions of Arabian Nights.

Japan decided against Oriental architecture and built an embassy in 1932 whose colonial style would do a Virginia planter proud. But behind is a ceremonial Japanese teahouse, a showpiece for visitors. Germany's new chancery is a modern architect's delight of exposed steel and Oregon Douglas fir, snug against a residential hill on Reservoir Road.

This is one of the few new chanceries to be applauded rather than protested by nearby residents. Russia received the reverse treatment in vainly seeking permission to build a huge chancery in residential Chevy Chase. Neighborhoods used to vie for new embassies a few decades ago; today they fight them off. Fearing the twin devils of the motor age, heavy traffic and no parking space, they resist the inexorable spread of commercial development into the fine old residential streets northwest of Dupont Circle.

This understandable aversion extends to foreign governments because diplomacy has become a major business in Washington. A chancery, like any nerve center of a bustling organization, generates much coming and going. The staff of a Washington chancery is generally the largest each government maintains anywhere in the world. It ranges from fewer than a half dozen for a new African state to more than five hundred for the British. The size varies with the involvement of the government in world affairs and the extent of the political, economic, information, military, and cultural interests that that government

For a formal dinner on Embassy Row, the placement of flowers about the drawing room is a matter of the hostess's taste but the placement of VIPs at her dinner table is predicated on rank.

Washington's cosmopolitan night people make it a city of perpetual conversation. Here they meet at a leading social event of the fall, the International Ball in the Sheraton-Park Hotel.

shows in the United States. Indonesia, to cite a new and important state, has subdivided Evelyn Walsh McLean's old top-floor ballroom into offices that accommodate part of an embassy staff of more than seventy-five – fifteen military attachés, thirteen political, ten economic, nine information, six education, and the rest administrative. A new small African state, Malawi, opened its diplomatic headquarters in a hotel suite with an ambassador and two aides.

Whatever their size, embassies have standard functions: issuing travel visas, looking after the interests of their citizens in this country, gathering and transmitting information that will benefit the home government politically, economically, diplomatically, or militarily, spreading goodwill, and negotiating issues of state. Britain's miniature Whitehall on Massachusetts Avenue executes these functions with a bureaucracy comprising a hundred and fifty diplomatic staff officers, two hundred military, and seventy-five civilian attachés. Some are experts on the politics of the Middle East, with its complex of American oil and Arab feudal baronies, or a dozen other sensitive areas of the globe. Others represent Her Majesty in secret military councils at the Pentagon as a result of the NATO alliance. Others promote trade in British manufactured products, and some simply promote a new British image in America. While always cheered by favorable reviews for new British films shown in the United States, the British cultural attaché was ecstatic when American youngsters sent birthday cakes to the ambassador so that he might celebrate the birthday of Ringo, the Beatles' drummer. "This is corrosive of the old staid image," he observed cheerfully. "We're not all stuffy beefeaters, you know."

One of the more important persons at every embassy is not a foreign diplomat at all, and often an American lady. She is the ambassador's social secretary, the keeper of the lists of VIPs whose friendship the ambassador is bound to seek. Ambassadors come and go but the social secretary stays on and on, busily keeping track of the constant changes in political, military, and diplomatic posts throughout this transient town. Each year she may issue ten thousand or more engraved invitations requesting "the pleasure of your company" to celebrate the home government's independence day, the monarch's birthday, the arrival of a prime minister, the departure of anyone worthy of a party. An ambassador regards the cocktail and dinner parties he attends each evening as an extension of his working day. His entertaining style varies with his personality and his representation allowance, the diplomatic term for the liquor-and-food expense account he receives from his government. Whether he personally prefers dinner for twenty or cocktails and canapés for three hundred, he must fit it into his budget as well as his schedule. The British allow their ambassador over one hundred thousand dollars annually, the French over eighty thousand dollars to meet the cost of high living on Embassy Row.

The costliest single event for each ambassador is his country's national holiday party. The British ambassador invites some three thousand for strawberries and Devonshire cream in the embassy garden to celebrate the Queen's birthday, not on her birthday but in early June when the garden and Washington's spring weather are most likely to favor the celebrants. The French celebrate Bastille Day, July 14, and both Algeria and Vietnam celebrate their independence from the French on November 1. Russia celebrates her revolution for two days, November 7 and 8. So it goes, from January 1, when Cameroon, Haiti, and Sudan start the new calendar year's soirees, to December 24, when Libya winds it up.

The busiest American diplomat on the party circuit is the chief of protocol, who represents the President or the Secretary of State when, as is usually the case, they are too busy to attend. When the chief is inundated with invitations, he attends two or three functions and dispatches his deputies to the others. The Secretary does well to find time from his absorbing responsibilities for official social functions. In one year recently his social calendar showed that he had attended or given fifty-five dinners, usually for a hundred guests each, fifty-three luncheons, and nine receptions for as many as a thousand persons each. He entertains in a handsome suite of paneled rooms on the top floor of the State Department's new annex.

Though entertaining is a necessity of protocol, the Secretary subordinates it to the constant urgencies of America's deep involvement in every region of the world. Whether he is conducting a secret staff meeting, scanning the latest cables from the ambassador

In the tea house behind the Colonial-style Japanese embassy, the traditional tea ceremony is occasionally performed.

The high point of the social season for most embassies is a reception marking a popular holiday. Of all the receptions, the one to which invitations are most coveted is the June garden party (above) at the British Embassy celebrating the Queen's birthday. To the sari and kimono native dresses long familiar to the Washington scene, has been added the boubou (below left), worn by wives of diplomats from Mali in the embassy's garden. Tea is served at the Moroccan Embassy (below right)

in a trouble spot, conferring with a visiting foreign minister over a delicate dispute, or briefing the President on last-minute overseas developments, the Secretary must exercise adroitness in negotiations, breadth of understanding of complex foreign politics, and calm decisiveness in advising the President. At his beck and call is a vast organism composed of regional bureaus within which are specialists on each country and every international problem. His staff meeting with his bureau chiefs has been likened to a king holding court of his feudal lords – the Prince of Europe, the Duke of Africa, the Baron of Latin America, the Lord of the Orient, the Earl of the Near East – each zealously seeking the king's favor for his realm. The king must view the whole kingdom before declaring his policies. Then, virtually every public word he utters is flashed around the world by the foreign correspondents. States that are hostile to one another, say Israel and Egypt or India and Pakistan, examine his statements for indications of favoritism. Leaders of over forty nations analyze his remarks for implications affecting the alliances they have with the United States. Communist powers search his comments for phrases to be damned in the continuing war of words.

Ever since President Washington signed the act creating the Department of Foreign Affairs in 1789, promptly renamed the Department of State, and appointed Thomas Jefferson his Secretary of State, the primary duty of the Secretary has been to conduct our foreign affairs "in such manner as the President of the United States shall from time to time order or instruct." Jefferson began his duties with five clerks and a dozen emissaries overseas. So long as America remained isolated behind its oceanic borders, State remained a minuscule bureau. As late as 1869 the departmental staff numbered only thirty-one. And in 1939 a photographer posed the entire State Department staff in Washington behind Secretary Cordell Hull on the front steps of the old State, War, and Navy building next to the White House. State had two thousand employees here and 4,300 abroad in that year of the Neutrality Act of 1939, America's last affirmation of its isolationist tradition. Thereafter followed the rapid escalation of the United States into a world power, first as the arsenal of democracy when Britain was besieged by Hitler, then as a partner in the war, and more recently as leader of the Free World against Communist expansion.

Twenty-five years after the Neutrality Act, in 1964, State had 11,500 employees overflowing its modern headquarters in Foggy Bottom and 30,500 more scattered around the world. In addition, the U. S. Information Agency, whose diplomats of communications articulate the Voice of America and distribute books, films, and informative articles, has grown to twelve thousand employees since its postwar birth. Though the expansion of American activities and personnel in foreign affairs has been spectacular, State and USIA combined still employ only half as many persons as the Department of Agriculture.

The President, of course, is America's principal diplomat. As President Kennedy once put it, "I do not think there is any responsibility placed upon the President of the United States, even including that of commander-in-chief, which is more pressing, which is more powerful, which is more singularly held in the executive (as opposed to so many other powers in the Constitution, which are held between Congress and the executive) than that which is involved in foreign policy." The expansion of State is a direct response to this presidential responsibility, yet the growth hampers as much as it helps the President and his Secretary of State. "The trick here in decision-making," one White House specialist in foreign relations has said, "is to make use of the resources of the bureaucracy without letting it strangle you." The bureaucracy is indispensable for routine administration involving some three hundred diplomatic and consular posts, handling everything from passports and visas to treaties and trade. But each new team of policy-makers, after eagerly reorganizing the bureaucracy in the name of efficiency, ends up bypassing it in a crisis in the interest of decisiveness.

Because of the multiplicity of crises confronting U.S. decision-makers, in 1961 State established an Operations Center, the diplomatic equivalent of a war room, which points up the fusion of diplomatic-military responses to trouble. Located a few steps down the corridor from the Secretary of State's seventh-floor suite, the Operations Center is manned twenty-four hours a day by foreign service and military officers trained to evaluate fast-breaking developments, to alert the appropriate policy-makers at any hour, to prepare the regular morning top-secret summary of latest advices from abroad for the Secretary and his subordinates, and to relay instructions quickly to U.S. diplomats out on the firing line. Special "hot lines," secured against wire tapping, con-

*The Mexican Embassy (above left) features
native murals. Italy's embassy (above right),
reminiscent of the Renaissance, is one of the
few originally designed for diplomatic life.
The largest Communist embassy (opposite),
Russia's, occupies an ornate mansion on
Sixteenth Street built by the capitalist
railroad-car maker, George Pullman.*

nect the Operations Center with the White House, with the Pentagon's National Military Command Post and with the Central Intelligence Agency's situation room. Diplomatic-military fusion is further illustrated by the foreign service officer assigned to nearly every American military base around the world to act as a political advisor to the base commander, and by the Pentagon's "little State Department" under an Assistant Secretary of Defense for International Security Affairs, who doles out millions of dollars in military aid where it is considered politically expedient to do so.

The standing complaint of diplomats throughout the world is niggardly support by the home office. As Dr. Henry M. Wriston, president of the Council on Foreign Relations, puts it, "While lavish funds are voted for the military, the agency designed to keep the peace is kept on starvation rations." This attitude accounts in part for appointment of wealthy men to ambassadorial posts, particularly in Old World capitals where it is thought necessary for the ambassador to spend more on entertaining than Congress ever appropriates. The expense account allowed the American ambassador at the Court of St. James's, for instance, is about half what the British allow their ambassador at Washington. The tradition of presidents rewarding wealthy political supporters with prestigious ambassadorial appointments continues, but with greater regard for their professional qualifications than was the case during the twenties, when Ambassador Dawes rated the job as hard on the feet and easy on the brain.

There is also increasing reliance upon the professional diplomats. Since creation of the foreign service officer corps in 1924, the proportion of professionals serving as chiefs of missions abroad has doubled, from 35 to 70 per cent. Democratization of the American diplomatic corps proceeded more rapidly than in countries with royal traditions and titled privileges. President Roosevelt even opened the ambassadorial ranks to women by his appointment of Ruth Bryan Owen, the daughter of William Jennings Bryan, himself a Secretary of State under Wilson, as minister to Denmark in 1933. Today, of America's more than nine thousand diplomatic officers, some twenty-five hundred are women. Each year State processes several thousand foreign service applications from some of the nation's brightest college graduates. In this most highly competitive field in government, only

Some of the capital's most handsome town houses have been converted
into embassies. Baron and Baroness Scheyven and their daughter in the
library of the Belgian Embassy on Foxhall Road (above left).
Ambassador and Madame Menemencioglu in the solarium
of the Turkish Embassy on Sheridan Circle (above right).
Washington's most influential diplomat, the Secretary of State,
entertains in the new State Department reception room (opposite above).
The stand-up cocktail party is an especially useful social device on
Embassy Row for honoring visiting dignitaries, in this instance the
British Prime Minister (opposite below).

two hundred are accepted annually. The rise of African nationalism prompted State during the Kennedy regime to enlist more Negroes, largely through campus recruiting and a summer intern program to help prepare them for the foreign service exam.

The recruit may be sent to the Foreign Service Institute in Washington for special training in African dialects or Arabic or the stern language disciplines of the Orient before being assigned. His assignment may take him to Marseilles or Bangkok as a vice-consul, where he starts up the long career ladder by stamping visas or helping stranded Americans. Later he moves on to an embassy in Beirut or Stockholm or Accra, specializing in political or economic reporting of local conditions or promotion of American cultural affairs. Between embassies, he will serve in the Department at Washington, in the bureau of his geographic specialty if he is lucky, in time perhaps becoming the desk officer for a given country. The desk officer, as the contact man at State for that country's ambassador at Washington and for the American ambassador in that country, correlates developments on both ends of this diplomatic pipeline.

Since the Second World War, Washington has become headquarters for yet another type of diplomat, the specialist in international finance. The Bretton Woods (New Hampshire) Conference of 1944 led to the creation of the International Monetary Fund and the International Bank for Reconstruction and Development, popularly known as the World Bank. Their offices are back to back at Eighteenth and H, two blocks west of the White House. The Fund, containing some sixteen billion dollars in gold and currencies of its more than a hundred member countries, facilitates freer world trade by meeting its members' obligations during deficits in their balance of payments. The Bank has loaned over seven billion dollars for economic development projects, largely electric power, transportation, industry, and agriculture, in some sixty-five countries, ranging from a fertilizer plant in Iceland to widening the Suez Canal. The Inter-American Development Bank, a more recent creation, specializes in loans for Latin America.

These and other international agencies headquartered here – the Organization of American States, Export-Import Bank, International Finance Corpora-

tion, International Development Association, Pan American Health Organization, Inter-American Social Progress Trust Fund, and Inter-American Defense Board – have greatly augmented the cosmopolitan character of Washington. The Fund alone has a staff of six hundred drawn from fifty-nine nations.

The diplomat is proud of his calling, generally broader of view and interest than the members of Washington's other specialized professional communities. He recognizes, rather defensively, that many Americans still possess an isolationist residue of wariness and impatience with foreign entanglements. He is hurt by general indifference to the hardships often incurred in foreign duty – a fact of life faced by every diplomat, which is called to mind at the diplomatic entrance to State by a plaque naming seventy-three diplomats who died under heroic or tragic circumstances on foreign soil. He is understandably disdainful of those who remain dubious of State, the one department of government that lacks organized support of vested interest groups such as farmers or workers or teachers to bolster its programs.

The diplomat, from the President down through the ranks of State and along Embassy Row, must confront his countrymen with the unwelcome obligations that accompany the pursuit of international harmony and peace in our age. Schooled in world history and practical experience, he knows that in the pursuit of peace the odds are still against him. His job essentially is to reverse these odds.

Lights burn around the clock at the State Department (opposite), nerve center of America's world-wide diplomatic corps.

The diplomatic courier (below) is a vital link in the paper chain that connects America's State Department with its embassies around the world, or any of the foreign embassies in Washington with their governments at home. One of hundreds who fly in and out of the city each week, this courier, an American, waits for all other cargo to be loaded before his pouches are locked into the hatch of the jet. The last passenger to board and the first to debark, he resumes his watchful custody when the hatch is opened at his destination. It matters not whether the pouch contains routine immigration papers or top-secret intelligence; he guards it with his life.

CHAPTER SEVEN

The New Warriors

As one approaches Washington from the south, a rise in the road suddenly brings into view that modern concrete and glass fortress on the clay and grassy banks of the Potomac. From this vantage point the Pentagon takes on a new perspective, neither pentagonal nor linear but curving, its cement arms reaching out to enclose within their grasp the Capitol dome and the Washington Monument on the horizon. They enclose and grip all of Washington in a defensive embrace. If this is an optical illusion, it is no political illusion to observe that the rest of government has been half swallowed, half blotted from one's sight by the moving, mountainous glacier of the military.

Since the onset of the cold war we have witnessed a palace revolution, a revolution by consent. From that fortress on the Virginia shore, the government across the muddy moat is held in fee, governed, negotiated with, and protected by nameless commanders who cross and recross the drawbridge in their olive-green limousines.

The grant of power by which they rule is not spelled out in phrases but in figures. The royal seal they hold, their momentary constitution, is that four-pound document, the federal budget. It is therein stated and set down that all of us, we of the fief, hereby grant and provide to the rulers of the fortress a portion of our future harvests and wardrobe, our iron beasts of burden and articles of pleasure, a portion of our finest young men, and other diverse things to the sum of half the annual tax collections of the realm.

All the domestic needs of the fief must be compressed into this other half. There is no certainty that the fortress needs so much, but the commanders say

The Pentagon, headquarters of American military might.

that a man in full armor requires thus and so against this particular foe. And what yeoman, or what burgher speaking for the yeoman, will say the fortress Nay?

The consent for this revolution stems from national security consciousness and the very incomprehensibility of today's military establishment. A citizen may comprehend such annual defense requirements as thirty thousand tons of coffee or five hundred million aspirin, or even that the Defense Department employs more civilians than live in all of Norway; but his mind reels upon entering the robot realm of computers talking to computers by telephone beeps to determine the strongest deployment of forces available to a field commander, of missile guidance systems capable of directing atomic rockets from beneath the oceans to targets anywhere on the globe, of bombers lazing through the skies carrying more explosive power in one bomb bay than was set off by all the Allies in World War II. To most Americans it is enough to accept the word of the Commander-in-Chief that this awesome range of weaponry is necessary insurance, no matter the cost.

Americans, after all, have always been antimilitarist but never antimilitary. We insist that military commanders know their place in the constitutional scheme because war is too serious a business to be left to the generals, but we are absorbed with tales of battlefield glory. We loathe aggression but will go to the ends of the earth to defend a shaky ally. It is in this latter context that the United States military complex has become the world's most titanic enterprise. Because of alliances with over forty nations from the North Sea to the South China Sea, American naval vessels patrol all the oceans and American military garrisons operate from some seven thousand global bases.

The pentagonal ring design of the world's largest office building is wholly visible only from the air, in this instance from an Army helicopter coming in for a landing. Built in 1943, the unique structure houses twenty-five thousand employees, more of them civilians than members of the armed services.

Ever since the Great War, the brain center of this mightiest military force in all history has been the Pentagon. Built in 1943 on 583 acres formerly occupied by dumps, shacks, pawnshops, and rendering works, this structure designed to absorb all the scattered offices of the burgeoning War Department cost eighty-three million dollars, a figure then considered astronomical. The War Department originally was called the Board of War and Ordnance, created by the Continental Congress to raise an army for General Washington. With only a paid secretary to manage its affairs and no resources or authority, the War

Board sought troops from the Colonial militia but remained powerless to stem the ebb tide of desertions that inevitably followed enlistments. Washington complained that before each battle he had to recruit a new army. From 395,000 enlistments during the Revolution, the Army's greatest strength at any one time was 89,000 and at the time of Yorktown it had dwindled to 29,000. When the War Board became the War Department in 1781, it acquired broad powers that later were divided among the Army, Navy, and Interior Departments and the President himself. Maritime troubles with France inspired a separate Navy Department and six navy yards, one at Washington, for construction of warships. Frontier troubles with the Indians kept the Army busy as the nation pushed westward.

The need for coastal defenses prompted creation of the Army's Corps of Engineers, whose varied works since have included completing the Washington Monument, the Panama Canal, and great hydroelectric dams from Muscle Shoals to Bonneville. And the advance of the airplane as a major military weapon more than a century later brought on the Army Air Corps, which emerged as the third service, the Air Force.

The defenses of the city of Washington originally were centered in Fort Washington eleven miles south of the city on the Maryland shore of the Potomac across from Mount Vernon. George Washington suggested the site, a monumental bluff with a commanding advantage for gunners firing on the river below. In the War of 1812 the British Navy discovered that this defensive outpost was indeed a monumental bluff; when His Majesty's ships sailed up the Potomac, Fort Washington's commanding officer blew up his own fortress. The British squadron sailed unmolested upriver to Alexandria, exacted tribute in cotton, tobacco, sugar, flour, and wine, and dropped safely back downriver to continue harassing American ships in the Chesapeake. Washington city was spared naval bombardment only because the target had been destroyed three days before by British troops that had bypassed Fort Washington, approached the capital via Bladensburg to the northeast, routed the hapless defending militia on the afternoon of August 24, 1814, and set the capital afire.

There is irony in this act of foreign troops chasing Congress and burning the Capitol. For the idea of establishing the capital in a remote Federal District originated when Congress in 1783 sought to escape domestic soldiers who had badgered the lawmakers at Philadelphia demanding long-overdue pay.

Had the English arsonists not shown such regard for private property in burning chiefly public buildings, the capital would likely have been removed to another city and Washington would have become a political ghost town in its fourteenth year. Congress debated a removal bill several weeks until Washington business interests, fearing loss of the city's main payroll, offered the government a half-million-dollar loan to finance reconstruction. Congress accepted. Washington was saved not by guns but by dollars.

The jittery townsmen, nonetheless, insisted on rebuilding Fort Washington. The war ended before it was finished but for over a century its parapets, moat, and drawbridge gave the city a sense of security. Today the old fort, manned by the obliging rangers of the National Park Service, is a favorite picnic spot. So are a dozen or more of the sixty-eight small forts and batteries built in a protective ring around Washington during the Civil War, one of the most elaborate networks ever created to protect a city in the cannonball age. Confederate General Jubal Early made the only direct attack on the capital at Fort Stevens and was repulsed as President Lincoln watched from the barricade, part of which has been reconstructed at Piney Branch and Quackenbos Street, N.W.

Today's military posts that ring the capital, garrisoned by more than sixty thousand uniformed and seventy-five thousand civilian personnel, are not combative but administrative, technical, and ceremonial. They include such renowned posts as Fort Myer and the Marine Barracks, which supply spit-and-polish buglers and rifle bearers for Washington's rites and pageants; Andrews Air Base, home field for the President's aircraft; the David Taylor Model Basin, where new ship designs are tested in simulated seas; Fort Belvoir, headquarters of the Army Engineers; Fort McNair, the campus for military eggheads; and the Naval Observatory, which keeps the nation's clocks synchronized with the stars.

The fortresses that actually protect Washington are scattered around the globe, on land, sea, and air, sheltering oceans and continents in their embrace. As the GHQ for this protective ring, the Pentagon is as disarming as it is powerful.

Its ramparts are manned by neither grenadiers nor

artillerymen. Its sally port and passageways, save for certain secret sanctuaries, are open to the public. In fact, the visitor is greeted not by armed sentries but by a smiling lady receptionist. Her duty is to help him find his way through seventeen miles of corridors, rings, bays, and color-coded tiers with the aid of a floor plan on which she traces the shortest route to the office he seeks.

This is the world's largest office building, having triple the space of the Empire State Building. It has its own restaurants, banks, libraries, chapels, barber and beauty shops, bowling alleys, gyms, and stores selling everything from clothing and pastries to wedding rings and tranquilizers. It operates its own printing plant and repairs its own twenty thousand typewriters. It is served by its own bus terminal, heliport, and dock, generates its own power, conditions its own air, treats its own sewage, converts its own wastepaper into pulp, and provides medical and dental treatment for those in pain.

Mail is delivered by messengers pedaling tricycles. To each of two and a half million U.S. servicemen this mail carries the word by which his life is ordered – his transfer, his promotion, orders for his unit, the endless regulations that govern his attire, his family's allowances, his re-enlistment, his very behavior up to retirement or his interment in a national cemetery. To every defense contractor, this mail carries the word by which his plants are tooled and retooled, shut down or operated around the clock. To every state, foreign or domestic, in which an American military base is maintained, it carries word of expansion or contraction with its consequent local prosperity or distress. No American office has ever issued so many orders affecting the lives and fortunes of so many.

The Pentagon bureaucracy, composed of about eleven thousand military and fourteen thousand civilian personnel (plus another two thousand charwomen, cooks, and guards), is dominated by civilians in terms of authority as well as numbers. At the apex sits the Secretary of Defense, in a sense the most powerful Cabinet minister of all time. His authority, vested in several postwar acts of Congress, makes him the President's deputy commander-in-chief, exercising unified control over military services and their respective civilian secretaries. Intense rivalry persists among the Army, Navy, and Air Force for assigned missions and use of new weapons systems in the over-all defense pattern, just as it has since the

invention of grenades several centuries ago and the airplane in this century. Faced with lobbying on behalf of each rival service by its senior officers, its retired but vocal alumni, and its political friends, the Secretary of Defense must make decisions for creating a workable balance of offensive and defensive forces that provide maximum national security with the fifty billion dollars a year being expended.

Achieving this basic objective requires hardware and forces suitably deployed by each service, lightning communications to and from the Pentagon, and a high degree of co-ordination in the nine geographical or functional commands that are linked through the Pentagon: the Pacific, the Alaskan, the Caribbean, the Atlantic, the Eastern Atlantic and Mediterranean, the European; the Strategic Air Command (SAC), the Continental Air Defense Command, and STRIKE, a mobile force ready for instantaneous deployment to areas of fresh trouble. Should the order be issued to propel this global force of inconceivably destructive energy toward a provocateur, it would be flashed from the President to the field commanders via a short chain of command – the Secretary of Defense and the chiefs of staff of the three services are its central links – bypassing the bureaucracy.

Each day, deep in the bowels of the Pentagon, an Air Force colonel places a call to one of fourteen major air command posts throughout the world and asks to speak to the commanding officer. As he waits for the commander to come on the line, the colonel watches the second hand of a wall clock. The conversation that ensues is cool and brisk: "This is Commander So-and-So," says the voice from the distant outpost. "Commander, it took you twenty-two seconds to come on the line. Have you any comment?" "No comment." "Very well, this is the Air Force Command Post. Over and out." If the distant commander tarries longer than thirty seconds in answering the Pentagon, no excuse – no matter what the hour of day or night, whether he is asleep or in the shower or on the golf course or inspecting his forces – will save him from receiving a letter from the Air Force Chief of Staff telling him, in effect, to shape up. Every second counts in today's military strategy.

It is this sense of immediacy that gives the Command Post its war-room atmosphere. A staff of 360 personnel maintains watchful readiness here (and at a secret alternate site outside Washington) around the clock, receiving reports of military or political developments that may cause trouble for the United States, alerting Washington's top officials as necessary. By depressing one button, the colonel in charge can ring eighty key telephones simultaneously throughout the Pentagon to relay an important communiqué. By another instrument, electronically guarded against wire tapping, he can reach the President or any lesser Washington decision-maker important enough to rate an aide carrying a Minuteman mobile phone, a wireless black box that is his constant companion to afford instantaneous communication as far as seventy-five miles away from the Pentagon on the ground or several hundred miles in the air. By glancing at a panel of green and amber lights, he can tell the approximate location of a nuclear explosion anywhere in the world. Watching a missile scoreboard overhead, he knows the anticipated time of impact in seconds of an unfriendly missile. By fingering the keyboard of a teletype apparatus in which war plans are locked, he can instantly transmit these plans and orders to every field commander on the circuit. By addressing the console of a giant computer capable of containing two billion bits of data, he can flash upon a television screen in microseconds virtually any known military data – from the location and condition of all airfields in the Congo to any of five hundred complex allied war plans designed to meet any international contingency. Moreover, he can direct his computer to talk with computers at various field command posts to provide instant calculations effecting the most powerful deployment of forces to meet an aggressor.

The computer is symbolic of changes confronting the new warriors. Officials throughout government, of course, regard it as an indispensable servant of this age of automation. Already more money has been invested in computers for the military than it cost to build the Pentagon itself. Three of them, costing thirty-seven million dollars, are assigned to the Air Force Command Post. The visitor who spies upon this thinking man's robot, watching its jerky manipulations of magnetic tapes, listening to the eerie humming of its electronic brains, noting the incomprehensible speed of its calculations, cannot escape the haunting sensation that the machine has at last gained the edge on man in Washington.

The computer is also a bureaucratic status symbol. The agency that employs computers feels that it is keeping pace with this revolutionary age. It may be as heartless and prosaic as the Internal Revenue Service using computers to check the veracity of a hundred million taxpayers. Or it may be as sophisticated as the Goddard Space Center using computers to evaluate a fantastic quantity of scientific-mathematical data received via microwave transmitters from Cape Kennedy to determine within ten seconds whether a newly launched space flight is on course or must be brought down prematurely to save an astronaut from landing in a trackless jungle.

More important, the computer symbolizes the educational revolution forced upon the military. Automation, miniaturization, rocketry, and nuclear weapons systems have stretched the military mind in recent years far beyond any technological advances in all the past history of warfare. The professional soldier must still, as in Napoleon's day, have the instinct to march at the sound of guns, to confront threats to his country, and safeguard its borders. But today's new warriors find the battlefields of the cold war mined with social problems. His training must sweep past the classical stratagems of battle and the logistics of supply to the horizons of international politics in all its economic, sociological, psychological, ideological, and scientific aspects. In the main, this is a post-Korea phenomenon. Since then the United States has sent military missions to most nations outside the Communist sphere of influence. As part of the American "country team" headed by the ambassador to that country, the task of the military has been to integrate his skills with those of the diplomats in helping that country resist Communist domination. To meet this challenge his knowledge of foreign cultures and languages or the economics of village life is far more important than his expertise in the manual of arms.

The Pentagon, consequently, is producing the best educated military force in history. Enlisted men in World War I had, on the average, a fifth-grade education. Today 85 per cent of enlisted men have a high school diploma, 65 per cent of all officers have a college degree, and 25 per cent of the officers have advanced degrees. These percentages continue to rise because the Pentagon each year sends several thousand officers to some four hundred colleges and universities for a year or two of full-time study; in addition, the government pays half the costs of off-duty college work undertaken by a quarter million servicemen each year. Most of this study is in the physical sciences but in the past decade the social

NOTHING CLASSIFIED ON THIS PHONE

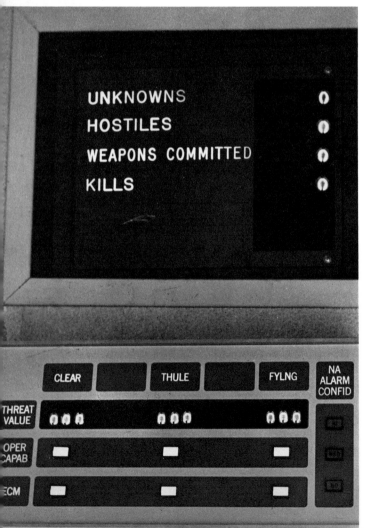

UNKNOWNS   0
HOSTILES   0
WEAPONS COMMITTED   0
KILLS   0

CLEAR		THULE		FYLNG	NA ALARM CONFID
THREAT VALUE					
OPER CAPAB					
ECM					

Instantaneous, secret communications between Washington and all field commanders constitute the "button" in this age of intercontinental rocketry. When command-post officers telephone distant Air Force posts from the console (above), commanders are expected to answer within thirty seconds. They do. Like an electric football scoreboard ready for the game to start, this missile scoreboard (left) on the wall of the Air Force Command Post is kept prepared for a contest that Washington hopes will never occur. The Air Force Command Post, in the Pentagon basement (opposite), maintains a twenty-four-hour global watch. At the height of a crisis, specialists gather about the conference table to lend expertise to decision-making.

sciences have taken on an order of importance never before dreamed of by the military mind.

Among the in-house courses conducted by each service at bases all over the country, the most broad-gauged are taught at the National War College and the Industrial College of the Armed Forces located at Fort McNair in Southwest Washington. These two schools are operated by the Joint Chiefs of Staff for the most promising officers, average age forty-three, and civilian policy-makers. The War College offers a year's work on such meaty topics as the components of American power, formulation of national security policy, counterinsurgency, studies of the Communist states and the other geographic regions and strategic areas. The Industrial College presents a ten-month course geared more to the economics of national strength and world affairs, from industrial mobilization at home to the population explosion abroad.

This age has greatly raised not only the sights of the new warriors but their numbers. In the past generation the American officer corps has increased tenfold. The nation's military profession has become comparable in size to the medical or the legal professions, each of which has about a quarter million practicing professionals. To some minds this expansion of the military, and its stranglehold on the national budget, raises the immense question of whether our society can remain free of military domination.

Certainly one of the tests of the soundness of the American political system of checks and balances is whether, under these unprecedented conditions of year-in and year-out preparedness for war, the nation can prevent the subtle transfer of all decision-making from the White House and the Capitol to the Pentagon. This is not to suggest any increased risk of a military coup in Washington. The American military mind is too preoccupied with the new horizons of this age and too steeped in the constitutional tradition of civilian rule, as one Pentagon official put it, "to be worrying about taking over the government or starting world wars." In a world in which the military coup is still a common instrument of political change, this enduring faithfulness of the American military in the role of the submissive partner in the democratic marriage with civil authority is reassuring. The politicians have occasionally turned to a general to lead the country, but never in nearly two centuries has a militarist forced his way into the White House at gunpoint.

If the astonishing changes in modern militarism confound the Pentagon, they evoke a popular longing for the good old days when military feats were at least comprehensible in human terms. Washington responds to this sentiment by perpetuating one stirring military program that hasn't changed since the days when Fort Washington guarded the capital. It is performed by the branch of the American military establishment with the highest reputation for glory and personal heroics, the United States Marine Corps. For thirty years the Marines have buttoned on their scarlet jackets and ice-cream pants, strapped on silver bayonets, slipped into white gloves, taken down polished bugles and red field drums to perform the traditional Friday Evening Parade in the quadrangle of the Marine Barracks. This is the oldest post of the Corps, established by Jefferson in 1801 at Eighth and Eye, S.E., near the Navy Yard. Once a sunset ceremony, the parade has been performed in recent years beneath spotlights with dazzling effect – troops and musicians emerging from the shadows at the bugler's call of assembly, silver sabers and golden horns glistening, officers and their ladies sauntering over from the commandant's house, the Marine Band striking a martial air, the silent drill platoon astounding the bleacher crowd with intricate precision marching and magical variations on the manual of arms, the lowering of the colors, the Marines' Hymn and "Anchors Aweigh," the haunting notes of taps as night enfolds the last bugler in a far corner of the quad.

Today the Friday Evening Parade is probably Washington's most popular anachronism. It is like a costume ball that leans to Strauss waltzes and evokes nostalgia for a Vienna of the past. The costumed Leathernecks recall not the anguish and blood of the dying, only the legendary glory, the feats of personal courage of American fighting men from the halls of Montezuma to the shores of Tripoli, the reefs of Tarawa to the beaches of Normandy. The parade evokes a deep nostalgia for a vanishing era of foreign legions and gunboat diplomacy and national saber rattling, of an age when tidy little wars fulfilled man's deepest combative instincts instead of threatening the very extinction of the human race. Washington, the capital of the new age, flocks to the Marine Barracks, as it flocks to the Smithsonian, to experience something of the past, trying hard to forget that the rocket and the bomb have nudged the passing parade into the recesses of memory and national sentiment.

CHAPTER EIGHT

The Bureaucracy

"The population of Washington," observed Mark Twain, "consists pretty much entirely of government employees and the people who board them." This image of Washington as a company town remains true today even though the city is expanding more rapidly than the federal establishment. The nearly quarter million federal employees in Washington comprise half the city's labor force. These are the white-collar battalions who rumble in from the outer city each morning and evacuate by night. This is the Washington of nine to five and don't keep the car pool waiting. This is the special world of bureaucracy where the civil service inhabitants speak a language all their own, recognize their own pecking order, and practice nonviolent resistance against all those who threaten the bureaucracy with virtuous talk of economy through reductions in force.

As one enters this world through the doorways of any of the great departments, observing the government girls in perpetual motion over their typewriters or trays of coffee cups from the cafeteria, it is hard to recall that bureaucracy was once exclusively a man's world. It was not until the 1850s that a few women performed government work, and that was on the sly. They received their assigned work by mail at home, usually paperwork involving patents or land warrants, and it was always sent in care of a male relative so that no woman's name would appear on the federal payroll. Once, the Treasury Department

The chauffeured limousine is a bureaucratic status symbol of a high order. A Cabinet member rates one, senators and judges don't. Status seekers who rent a limousine are set apart by telltale license numbers that begin with LA. Low-numbered District of Columbia tags, from 1 (for the chairman of the D.C. Board of Commissions) to 999, denote the city's upper-level residents.

surreptitiously broke the sex barrier by allowing a woman to take over the job of her husband when he fell ill. When he returned to work, she was retained – but in the name of her brother.

The era of the government girl began during the Civil War when the shortage of able-bodied men impelled Congress in 1864 to authorize the bureaus to hire women. But after the war ended, a movement to oust the girls began. Treasury Department girls, it was alleged, stole currency on the job and evaded detection by hiding it in their hoopskirts. Today's G-girls, over a half million strong, owe their careers to these brave innocents who indignantly squelched this allegation by removing their skirts and shaking them out before the eyes of the Treasury guards before leaving for home each evening.

Six decades later Franklin Roosevelt appointed the first woman Cabinet member, Secretary of Labor Frances Perkins. Though a fourth of all federal workers are now women, they hold only 2 per cent of the top positions.

Whatever their civil service ratings, the government girls who have come to Washington from virtually every state are one of the most conspicuous attractions of the city's life. Munching their luncheon sandwiches on the benches of Lafayette Park or the Pentagon's inner court, or sunning themselves weekends on the banks of the Potomac or the "P Street beach" overlooking Rock Creek parkway, the government girls add a dimension of delight to the dominantly masculine world of politics. Some G-girls in their respective haunts suggest a self-contained community akin to the diplomatic, military, congressional, or other fractional social communities in Washington. The community spirit is strongest among the loneliest. It shows in the newcomer who is drawn to the YWCA or a women's hotel or the rooming houses around Dupont Circle. A later manifestation is the sharing with other girls of an apartment or a house, most fashionably in Georgetown. Marriage is more common than not among G-girls; but two thirds of those who do reach top government positions have only the bureaucracy to love, honor, and obey.

For either sex, the bureaucracy may be impossible to love for its plodding sameness, and difficult to honor for its internal rivalries, but it must be obeyed if one aspires to move upward through the ranks. The bureaucrat's code is cluttered with "thou shall nots" that collectively demand conformity and caution. The average bureaucrat is a stable nonrebel who obeys the code because he values slow but sure advancement, leisurely coffee breaks, generous vacations and sick leaves, the security of government insurance and retirement benefits.

Bureaucracy, then, is cautious conformity compounded. Its army of occupation makes no pretense of traveling on its stomach; it swivels on its derrière.

The bureaucrat who survives every RIF (reduction in force) to reach the higher altitudes of the government grade and pay scale suddenly acquires the behavior pattern of the corporation man, and the status symbols. He cannot aspire to a private lavatory or an office refrigerator or a key to the private elevator or a chauffeured limousine, for these are the spoils of Cabinet members and their assistant secretaries. But once he has reached GS-15 he is entitled to "Executive-Type Office Furniture and Furnishings," as set out in Section 204.03 of the General Service Administration regulations. Executive-type furniture, costing 60 per cent more than standard common-use items, includes upholstered chairs and davenports, smoking stands, lamps, and rugs. In the game of executive upmanship at the subcabinet level, each player scrounges for "in" furnishings. Oriental rugs, once a hot item, gave way to wall-to-wall carpeting. Water carafes were a mark of distinction until they became so common the G-girls fetched coffee in them. In season and out, however, a parking space in the departmental basement garage retains such high value that, as the saying goes, it is harder to get than a two-grade promotion.

The care and feeding of bureaucracy is the special responsibility of the President's auditors at the Budget Bureau, housed across a private driveway from his office in the Executive Office Building. The federal budget, which annually is proposed by this office, can

trim, fatten, or starve an agency; but in all matters financial, Congress has the last word. The budget goes to Congress in January, thus beginning the bureaucracy's only period of real vulnerability; for Congress takes this responsibility with much-publicized seriousness. As individual congressmen load the Congressional Record with speeches favoring economy in government, the members of the Appropriations Committees call in the bureaucrats to cross-examine.

In recent years the federal budget, topping one hundred billion dollars, has become not only decisive for the government's varied programs but a factor of vast influence in sections of the private economy which depend upon subsidies or a steady flow of government contracts. Inasmuch as only about 15 per cent of the budget is devoted to civil service salaries, the bulk of federal spending goes for government procurement – military items (thirteen billion dollars), paper clips and pencils (one million dollars), surplus crops (one and a half billion dollars), mimeograph paper (two and a half million dollars); or it goes for public improvements – highways, dams, post offices, harbors, irrigation projects – for which most congressional districts compete. So, against the pressure for economy there are counter pressures for spending.

Significant as federal spending has become, the spending of private enterprise and the local and state government agencies continues to provide the meat and potatoes of America's needs. The federal budget provides only the salt. However, there is scarcely a community, rural or industrial, left in the land that remains on a salt-free diet. The effective congressman is adept at extracting every ounce he can from the Washington salt mines. His accomplishments are considered certain credits back home at election time, even as he calls for economy and less government elsewhere.

When President Washington took office there were three hundred and fifty civilians on the federal payroll. Today one of every seventy-five Americans works for the federal government—a total of two and a half million in all parts of the country and the world. Of every 130 bureaucrats, the Defense Department employs fifty-two, the Postal Service thirty, the Veterans' Administration nine, the State Department and related foreign operations fewer than three, and the other domestic agencies the remainder.

If there is one single explanation for the proliferation of the bureaucracy, it is the security-wish of this anxious age. The Pentagon dominates the scene because of the manifest requirements of military security in a world made horribly insecure by modern weaponry. Americans also want the security of government-inspected meats and drugs and processed foods. They want their mortgages and savings accounts insured and their securities guarded against fraud. They want bigger dams, wider highways, more national parks. They want assurance that kidnapers, counterfeiters, and dope peddlers will be caught and imprisoned; they expect air travel to be safe; they want strikes prevented, railroad and airplane rates controlled, gas and electric companies regulated, and their mail delivered swiftly and inexpensively. They want the farmer protected against nature's uncertainties, the unemployed worker insured, the veteran given free hospital care, the Indian schooled and paid his just claim against the white man. And if their Social Security check is late, the government had better do something about that too.

Americans want all this and the conquest of space besides, while surrendering none of their rights to criticize bureaucracy's legendary wastefulness and bigness. Whether the federal clerical mills are any more prone to waste time shuffling papers than are large insurance companies or mail order houses is problematical, but there is no gainsaying the bigness of the federal establishment, or the fact that it is here to stay.

The New Deal and the Great War stimulated not only the proliferation of government but an influx of remarkably varied talents. No longer an army of clerk-typists, the civil service covers fifteen hundred job categories, virtually the entire range of the professions and vocations. Indeed, engineers, scientists, and technicians in government outnumber typists by more than two to one. A typical government bulletin today advertises openings for speech pathologists, plant quarantine inspectors, oceanographers, teachers, auditors, farm credit examiners, psychologists, engineers, policemen, social workers, dietitians, bookbinders, radio technicians, librarians, fish biologists, astronomers, and printers, as well as urban planners.

If the American civil service has not yet been granted the respect paid the British civil service, certainly it has gained esteem and attracted an increasing number of bright young men and women into its most challenging positions, partly because the civil service today bears no resemblance to its predecessor, the spoils system. This practice of rewarding political hacks with jobs in Washington is as old as the republic but it gained its greatest impetus in Jackson's identification with the common man. By the time of the Grant administration, corruption was rife; graft and influence, not personal qualifications, were the keys to becoming a bureaucrat. The spoils system not only handicapped government effectiveness but burdened the President, whose house was constantly besieged by job hunters. Lincoln, once ill with smallpox, told an aide: "Tell all the office-seekers to come in at once, for now I have something I can give to all of them."

Calls for reform went unheeded in Congress until President Garfield was assassinated by a disappointed office-seeker in 1881 only a few months after his inauguration. The National Civil Service Reform League, capitalizing on public outrage at the President's murder, pushed through Congress the basic civil service act in eighteen months. It required that certain positions be filled through competitive examinations and barred blanket dismissals by new administrations. The coverage of the law was scant at first but today it extends to 86 per cent of government jobs. Spoils, if that term can be used any longer, are limited to about fourteen hundred top positions at the Cabinet and subcabinet level, where it is generally agreed a President is entitled to install men whose views coincide with his own.

A civil servant is entitled to vote and express his political convictions but not to become active in partisan political endeavors. In general he plays it safe and remains aloof from the ongoing struggle between the political parties. If he feels a little bit outside the mainstream, he is compensated by the knowledge that presidents and Cabinet officers come and go but the civil servant stays on and on.

The Washington Correspondents

Four years before he became President, Thomas Jefferson gave the American press an unexampled place of importance in the free society when he said: "Were it left to me to decide whether we should have a government without newspapers or newspapers without a government, I should not hesitate to prefer the latter." During his sixth year in the White House, Jefferson, the wounded politician, declared: "It is a melancholy truth that a suppression of the press could not more completely deprive the nation of its benefits than is done by its abandoned prostitution to falsehood. Nothing can now be believed which is seen in a newspaper. Truth itself becomes suspicious by being put into that polluted vehicle."

Jefferson's divergent views are those that frequently divide the world of the Washington insider from the world of outsiders everywhere. The outsider reads his newspaper to learn what is going on inside, and the more revealing the better; but the insider, warily scanning these same columns, betrays hypersensitivity when press criticism strikes at his weaknesses or when newspapers expose what he would prefer to be kept from public view. The doughboys

The correspondent's interview with an informed source is indispensable to his craft. In the Senate reception room, just outside the Senate chamber, veteran Associated Press correspondent Jack Bell questions Connecticut Senator Abraham Ribicoff. Though the bust of Vice-President Garner in the foreground appears to be casting a watchful eye, lobbyists and constituents sitting on the benches wait, unheeding, to see other senators. The wall panels, left vacant by the artist Brumidi, were filled by the Senate in 1959 with portraits of its choice of the five greatest senators: Henry Clay, Daniel Webster, Robert M. La Follette (all showing), Robert A. Taft, and John C. Calhoun.

who traverse the no man's land between these two worlds, belonging to neither, are the Washington correspondents.

If Jefferson had carping partisan editors to contend with, he at least was not troubled by Washington correspondents, for there were none in those early days. Even the story of the transfer of the capital from Philadelphia to Washington brought no reporters to cover the story. The new capital itself had no newspapers, although both Georgetown and Alexandria did. Jefferson, indeed, was fortunate in persuading a Philadelphia friend to establish the capital's first newspaper, the triweekly *National Intelligencer,* which became a semiofficial organ for Jefferson and for Madison and Monroe.

Washington's leading contemporary newspapers, the *Post* and the *Evening Star,* reflect the transition through which capital journals have since gone. Down to the Civil War it was customary for the administration in power to throw printing contracts to favored editors in return for editorial approval of their policies. Newspapers frequently were as transitory as political regimes. They were nonetheless widely read outside Washington, for until the advent of the telegraph in 1844 these journals were the prime source of political news for the rest of the nation. The *Evening Star* was launched in 1852 to aid the presidential bid of General Winfield Scott, the Mexican war hero nominated by the Whigs. Scott's defeat by Franklin Pierce impelled the *Star*'s editor to foresake partisanship and to convert the paper into an authoritative news organ. It was acquired by Crosby S. Noyes in 1867 and has been in the family ever since.

The *Post* was launched in 1877 as a Democratic organ, became nonpartisan after the turn of the century under John R. McLean, backed Harding and Coolidge, was sold to Eugene Meyer in 1933 and began its rise in strength and prestige as a liberal independent newspaper.

The newspaper of greatest circulation after World War II was the *Times-Herald*, a merger of two Hearst papers bought by Colonel Robert R. McCormick, owner of the Chicago *Tribune*. It was an amalgam of McCormick anti-New Dealism and Hearst sensation. Next in circulation came the *Star*, cautiously moderate and the favorite of old-family Washington, trailed by the *Post*, favored by intellectuals attracted here by the Roosevelt social revolution. This symbolic editorial struggle for ideological supremacy came to an astonishing climax in 1954 with the outright sale of the organ of isolation to that of internationalism. The *Post* thus eclipsed its rivals to become the city's number one journal. A new Noyes generation subsequently modernized the *Star*. Today Washington has two of the most responsible and readable newspapers in the country, plus a better-than-average tabloid, the Scripps-Howard *Daily News*. Because their readers include Washington's movers and shakers, the influence of these three journals is highly magnified.

The first Washington correspondents, quite literally, were visiting editors who came to Washington and wrote letters back to their newspapers. James Gordon Bennett, upon reading a book of Walpole's

letters at the Library of Congress, adopted their style for his communiqués to the New York *Courier* concerning society and political gossip. In 1841, after Bennett had gone to New York to establish the New York *Herald*, he set up a Washington bureau with regular pony express courier service to New York until the advent of the telegraph a few years later. In the 1820s and 1830s other newspapers, published in New York, Boston, and Portland (Maine), had assigned correspondents to Washington, but it was not until the Civil War that Washington came into its own as a national news center. The Associated Press, founded in 1848, assigned Henry Villard to cover Lincoln, setting an early pattern for today's White House correspondents. Also, a precedent was established for press vigilance against government wrongdoing when some of these Washington correspondents prompted Lincoln to dismiss War Secretary Simon Cameron for alleged graft.

The early editors' correspondence from Washington was largely partisan propaganda. Bennett's letters, however, sparkled with nonpartisan items about the lives and activities of Washington officials. By his adherence to the news value of events, he is credited with undermining party organs.

After the Civil War, forty-nine reporters stayed on

President Johnson's press secretary, George Reedy (above), in conducting daily briefings for White House correspondents, walks a tightrope balancing the demands of the press for information against his desire to protect the President's public image. The practitioners of the relatively new art of visual journalism, from still photographers to television cameramen (below), covering an inauguration ceremony at the Capitol, have greatly expanded the size of the Washington press corps. If a journalist, as it is said, is a reporter who keeps his jacket on, Congress makes journalists of those who report its proceedings. It has outlawed shirt sleeves for correspondents (opposite), who pass from these working-press rooms through the doors at the right to the press gallery overlooking the House chamber.

as accredited Washington correspondents. The technology of the industrial revolution that gave the publishing industry advanced machinery now brought the correspondent the most indispensable instrument of his craft, the telephone. Washington's first telephone directory of 1878 listed more telephones in newspaper offices (thirteen) than in all government offices (eleven, including one at the White House and another at the police station).

The great growth of the Washington press corps occurred in the twentieth century. With the New Deal, the correspondents, who previously had concentrated largely on Congress, shifted their attention to the White House and the executive departments. It is said that the day Roosevelt took the country off the gold standard in 1933, the press corps was forced into a new era – the era of the specialist. The better news bureaus were obliged to employ more college-trained reporters to decipher the mushrooming complexity of federal activities. This trend was accelerated during and after World War II, and today there are well over a thousand accredited correspondents in Washington, the most thoroughly covered capital in the world.

Foreign correspondents stationed in Washington represent some sixty-five newspapers or news agencies in nearly thirty countries, including Russia's *Pravda, Izvestia,* and *Tass.* Their beats take them primarily to State, the Pentagon, Embassy Row, and to the White House for that uniquely American institution, the President's news conference, which symbolizes, among other things, the accessibility of government officials to reporters in Washington. In Europe, by contrast, reporters are treated less like professional men than like tradesmen, seldom having opportunity to question presidents or prime ministers.

Ever since Teddy Roosevelt added the West Wing to the White House and invited reporters in out of the rain to interrogate visitors to his office, newsmen have dogged the President. Let him fly to the other side of the globe; they are off in jet pursuit. Their plane departs after his, but lands ahead of his so that even the contingency of a presidential plane crash can be instantaneously covered by eyewitness reporters. Let him stick to his oval office; they lounge about on the leather couches outside his press secretary's office, waiting for that aide's twice daily briefings, which offer the ingredients of the day's news about the President. Or they wait for appointments with White House officials or to interview the President's visitors, some of whom avoid this encounter by slipping out a side door.

Woodrow Wilson, ever the political scientist, inaugurated the presidential news conference because he thought it should prove as useful as the question period in the British House of Commons for illuminating or clarifying official policy. Today it is a hallowed institution that no President would dare abolish. Harding, Coolidge, and Hoover continued it but with minimum effect; for after Harding blundered on a foreign policy question, newsmen were required to submit their questions in writing in advance, and all three of these presidents tended to respond only to the easy or trivial ones.

It remained for Franklin Roosevelt, taking full advantage of the press conference to communicate with the reading public, to transform it into a significant institution. F.D.R. invited newsmen into his office twice a week, permitted spontaneous questions, and enjoyed the repartee with the scribes. He allowed them to quote him directly or to attribute the information to the President unless he specified that it was off the record or for background.

The postwar expansion of the press corps ended the intimacy of these conferences. When the President's oval office became overcrowded, Truman in 1950 shifted the conference to the Indian Treaty Room in the old State Department building next door. Thus began the more formal conference, with reporters arriving ahead of time to take seats, rising when the President enters the room and not sitting down until he motions them to do so. Eisenhower continued news conferences in the same manner and place but set two precedents when he allowed motion picture cameramen to film the conference from the rear of the Treaty Room and a stenotypist to make a transcript of all questions and answers. Both changes advanced the art of leadership by publicity. Filmed excerpts became a feature of television news programs, and the complete text was published after each conference in the New York *Times* and other large newspapers. Kennedy shifted the conference to the more commodious new State Department auditorium and went one step farther to dramatize the proceedings: he permitted live television and radio broadcasts. President Johnson prefers the intimate Rooseveltian news conference around his desk, or a strolling question bee in the garden, limited to the regular White

House correspondents by virtue of its spontaneous scheduling.

Whatever the format, the President's answers send reporters scrambling for their telephones as soon as the traditional "Thank you, Mr. President" signals the end of questions. Moments later crisply written news dispatches covering major pronouncements are chattering through the network of teleprinters to newspapers and broadcast studios around the world.

The literate world receives most of its news from Washington via the two major wire services, Associated Press (AP) and United Press International (UPI). They deploy their reporters strategically to monitor the bureaucracy's principal moving parts, the courts, Congress, and those peripheral agents of change from Embassy Row to the labor temples. AP has more than eighty staffers in its Washington bureau, and UPI more than sixty, yet they are spread so thinly along the lengthening news front that they can scarcely do more than cope with the daily barrage of mimeographed press releases. Overworked but never overpaid, the wire service reporter is not infrequently looking for a better job.

The New York *Times*, with some thirty reporters, maintains a larger Washington bureau than any other single newspaper. The *Wall Street Journal* is close behind. Strong bureaus have long been operated here by the Baltimore *Sun*, New York *Herald Tribune*, St. Louis *Post-Dispatch*, Chicago *Daily News*, *Christian Science Monitor*, Chicago *Tribune*, and the Hearst and Scripps-Howard chains. The Los Angeles *Times* and the Newhouse chain recently entered these ranks. Many other newspapers have one or two capital correspondents or are represented by bureaus that cover for more than one paper, the most durable of which was created by Bascom Timmons in 1919.

The phenomenal growth of the news magazines added a host of specialists in group journalism. Writing anonymously, in some instances having no voice in the slant the story acquires as it moves through the editorial assembly line, they are at odds with the long tradition of the signed column for which the Washington correspondent takes full responsibility.

Electronic journalism on a grand scale is a by-product of World War II. The Columbia Broadcasting System established a radio news service in the 1930s but at the time of Pearl Harbor had only three men in Washington. The postwar advent of television

brought a multitude of technicians and more correspondents and commentators to swell the news corps. For example, the smallest of the three networks, the American Broadcasting Company, jumped from a half-dozen-man bureau operating out of WMAL a decade ago to a staff of some eighty-five in a modern office on fashionable lower Connecticut. CBS has over a hundred news and technical personnel in a new headquarters on M Street.

Television has engendered hostility within the press corps with its clutter of cameras and cables and the magnetic attraction of its klieg lights. Television's show-business aspects complicate the task of covering Washington developments truthfully without warping them with synthetic drama, for almost any VIP would prefer a moment's exposure on the nightly TV news to front-page prominence in the nation's press. Reflecting this recognition of the public impact of TV, the White House has arranged with the networks to maintain a camera crew in the Fish Room, a few strides from the President's office, to permit the Chief Executive to go on the air at any hour to address the nation.

Some events particularly lend themselves to TV coverage and some do not. Sessions of the House and Senate and the Supreme Court are closed to cameras of all types, so TV correspondents are reduced to standing on the steps of the Capitol or the Court to lend on-the-scene authority to their reports. But TV coverage of national conventions, election-night vote tabulations, inaugurations, or special dramas such as the Kennedy funeral events or the Army-McCarthy hearings have been memorable landmarks in its short history of Washington reporting.

Since 1908 the most prominent watering grounds of the Washington press corps have been the National Press Club, which for years had the only stand-up bar in town. It is more noted for its luncheons addressed by world leaders and for its policy of excluding women during working hours, a point of friction with newswomen who demanded (and finally in 1964 received) equal privileges in covering newsworthy luncheon speakers. Older and so exclusive that it has only fifty correspondents as members is the Gridiron Club, whose chief *raison d'être* is an annual dinner to which members invite the President and Washington's political elite for an evening of satirical hilarity at the politicians' expense.

The enduring power of the Washington correspondent, whatever his medium, lies largely in his power to decide what is "news" and to dismiss what is not. In exercising this power of selectivity, the correspondent sets the boundaries within which his audience forages for thought and opinion – and TV and the news magazines necessarily narrow these boundaries much more than the newspapers.

The Washington correspondent not only records the first rough draft of history but functions as a participant in the ferment of a free society. H. L. Mencken once said that reporters love their work because "they get front row seats." They also thrive on their involvement in shaping the course of public affairs affecting the lives of their countrymen.

Every Washington correspondent savors the heady wine of power as an effective image-maker or image-shatterer. He also recognizes that the privileges of the full feast are reserved for the syndicated political columnist. The publication of a column several times weekly in as many as several hundred newspapers magnifies the columnist's influence on public opinion and enhances his prestige among Washington officials, especially if his column appears in one of Washington's daily papers. It is a demanding calling, trying to encapsulate the world or even Washington in five hundred to seven hundred words without missing a deadline; but those who succeed are the most independent, most highly opinionated, most feared, most envied, and most highly paid of the Washington correspondents.

The most durable of Washington columnists has been David Lawrence, a pioneer of this journalistic form in the 1920s as a correspondent for the New York *Evening Post*. Later his stoutly conservative opinions were syndicated to newspapers at large and published as an editorial column in the magazine he founded, *U. S. News & World Report*, published in Washington.

The most sensational of the political columnists has been Drew Pearson, who, with Robert S. Allen, pioneered the "inside dope" column after anonymously writing a 1929 book in similar vein. From his home in Georgetown, Pearson works mainly by telephone with the aid of several legmen, intensively cultivating a garden of talkative sources whose names periodically are dropped favorably into the columnist's account of the latest battle between good and evil in the capital. Pearson is read fearfully by the politicians; his muckraking exposés of actual wrongdoing have sent four congressmen to jail.

The most celebrated of the columnists has been Walter Lippmann, whom Arthur Krock of the New York *Times* said the other correspondents regard as "their foremost clarifier of complicated issues and their acknowledged master of the prose of interpretive journalism." One of the founding editors in 1914 of the *New Republic,* the liberal weekly journal today published in Washington, an aide to Wilson at Versailles, later editor of the New York *World*, Lippmann began his column from Washington in 1931 for the *Herald Tribune.* Twice a week in the quiet of his home on Woodley Road opposite the Washington Cathedral, Lippmann writes his column in longhand, makes editorial changes as he dictates it for typing, confers with a research assistant over the final draft, and then is off to lunch, usually at the Metropolitan Club. Later in the afternoon, after hiking along the canal or taking in a movie with his wife, the columnist settles down at home with the foreign newspapers before dressing for dinner or an evening of entertaining friends.

Lippmann's enduring influence is incalculable. Presidents not only read him but call on him. And he has given the Washington correspondents "a wider vision of our duty," says James Reston, Washington columnist of the New York *Times.* "He has shown us how to put the event of the day in its proper relationship to the history of yesterday and the dream of tomorrow."

Speaking of the special responsibility of the correspondent in this free society, Lippmann has said: "If the country is to be governed with the consent of the governed, then the governed must arrive at opinions about what their governors want them to consent to." The manifest responsibility of the correspondent is to provide the relevant informational linkage. "In this we do what every sovereign citizen is supposed to do, but has not the time or the interest to do for himself. This is our job."

Jefferson would undoubtedly agree. Apparently fully recovered from the sting of editorial rebuke suffered in his White House years, the philosopher overcame the politician in later years to say, "The only security of all is in a free press."

Freedom of the press comes gradually to life in the hands of Herblock. His stinging political cartoons on the editorial page of the Washington Post *delight or infuriate, depending on the partisanship of the reader.*

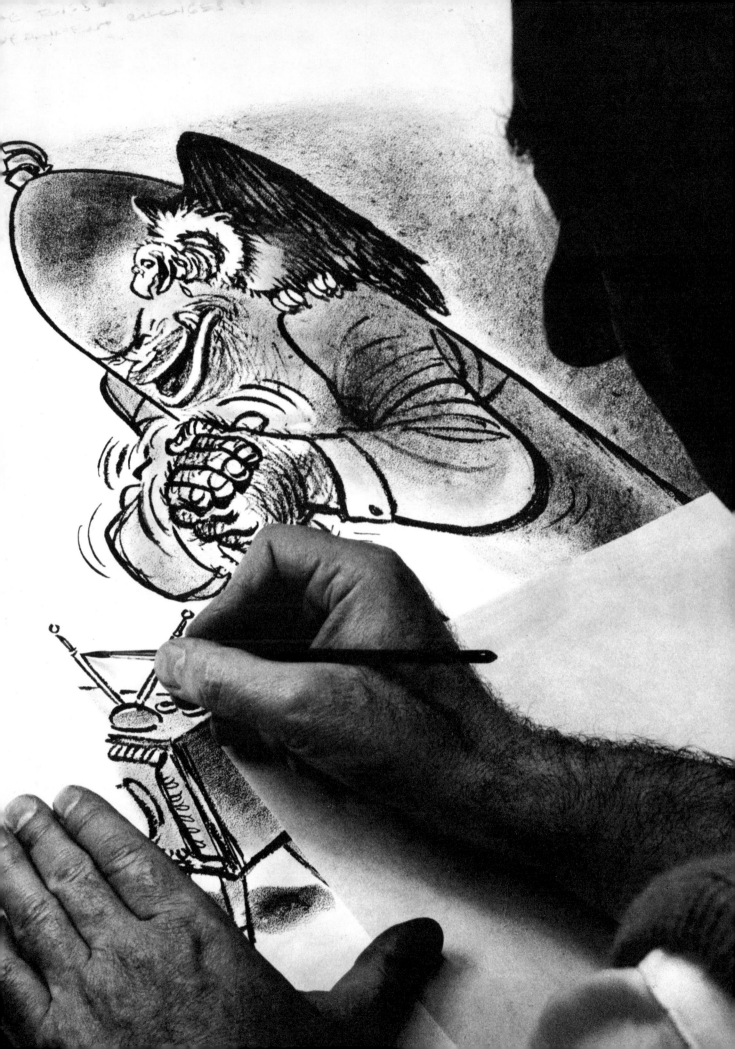

The once all-male capital press corps today includes many women.
Here Mary McGrory, gifted political writer for Washington's Evening
Star, questions former Cabinet member Arthur Flemming (at left) after
he has testified before a Senate committee.

CHAPTER TEN

The Persuaders

Ever since Walt Whitman inveighed against "bribers, compromisers, lobbiers, spongers...lousy combings and born freedom-sellers of the earth," the lobbyist has been cast as the villain in the drama of Washington politics. Being publicly regarded as a crafty fellow who thwarts the public good in behalf of the special interests by intimidating and obligating congressmen with the Devil's own temptations is an occupational hazard of his trade.

Not all who qualify as lobbyists uphold this legend of notoriety, certainly not the prim crusaders of the National Woman's Christian Temperance Union, or the numerous do-good causists who come and go with each congressional session. There are, however, hundreds of others who do.

Although low on the scale of public esteem, lobbying is high on the scale of income in this city of modestly salaried politicians and civil servants. Consequently it is one of Washington's most flourishing professions and a not insignificant source of the city's business income through the expansive magic of the expense account.

Active lobbyists outnumber congressmen two and three to one and are becoming more numerous. The building boom in downtown Washington of recent years was stimulated in part by the demands of lobbyists for more office space. Most conspicuous have been the new labor temples, notably the Teamsters' marble palace a block from the Senate office building and the modern AFL-CIO building on Sixteenth Street a block from the White House. Gone are the days when a labor baron took the day coach to Washington; today he and the secretariat of his union are headquartered here. The most evident business lobby is the United States Chamber of Commerce, which has its own building across Lafayette Square from the White House. Others inhabit handsome suites in the new buildings in the neighborhood, particularly along H, I, and K streets, lower Connecticut Avenue, and lower Fourteenth, Fifteenth, Sixteenth, and Seventeenth streets. Countless landlords and restaurants in this area would go broke if the lobbyists were driven out of the city.

The well-paid persuaders fall into two broad groups: those who are salaried heads of the Washington office representing a large organization such as the unions or the National Association of Manufacturers or American Farm Bureau Federation; and those enterprising free-lancers who represent a changeable multiplicity of clients, from domestic oilmen to foreign dictators. Both types command influence in accord with their skill in the fine arts of persuasion. But the organization lobbyist tends to reflect the weakness or the strength of his organization in the constituency of the congressman or senator he seeks to influence; the United Auto Workers lobbyist pulls more water with Michigan senators than with those of New Mexico, just as the American Petroleum Institute lobbyist stands higher with Texas than with Maine congressmen.

The free-lance lobbyist, by contrast, lives by his wits. His political contacts are as intensively and delicately cultivated as a Japanese garden. He may be a former officeholder himself. And, likely as not, he is of that special breed, the Washington lawyer.

Corporation law is more profitably practiced in New York, and divorce law is more profitably practiced in Los Angeles. But Georgetown and Spring Valley and Chevy Chase are populated by Washington lawyers earning two, three, and four times the salaries of senators and Cabinet members. The surest stepping stone to such a lucrative private practice, ironically, is a Cabinet post. Thus one finds an ex-Secretary of State who represents a foreign government or two; an ex-Secretary of the Interior who represents a few mining companies; an ex-Attorney General whose clients include corporations that are allergic to the Justice Department's antitrust division.

Or a term on the Federal Power Commission, Interstate Commerce Commission, or Civil Aeronautics Board opens splendid opportunities for the ex-commissioner-turned-Washington-lawyer if he has no hesitancy about working for the utilities, railroads, or airlines he had been duty bound to regulate. Ex-senators usually do better than ex-congressmen when, retired from Congress, they turn to lobbying.

All these former officeholders, along with lesser civil servants who take up private pursuits, possess a distinct advantage: they know their way through the federal labyrinth. Among Washington's ten thousand or more lawyers, several thousand are recognized specialists in every area where government touches private interest, be it taxes, communications, transportation, patents, Indian claims, antitrust, agriculture, maritime, or defense contracts. They gained their specialized knowledge as bureaucrats. This inside experience is a prime asset to the Washington representative trying to stop one bill and promote another, pressing for this executive or regulatory agency decision and against that, at all times seeking sympathetic treatment for his client, be it business or labor, farmer or teacher, doctor or a thousand other specialized groupings of citizens with a common interest. The lobbyist in this sense is a figure to be reckoned with because he receives his mandate from clients who are citizens and, as such, have a right to lay their needs before their government. For in a democratic society the government must always remain within public reach.

Lobbying gained notoriety in the nineteenth century largely through the insistent generosity of the railroad tycoons who had become the country's most expansive entrepreneurs, and the most dependent upon favorable land grants and other privileges from Washington. "I think this coming session of Congress will be composed of the hungriest set of men that ever got together," Collis P. Huntington reported to his Southern Pacific partners, Mark Hopkins, Leland Stanford, and Charles Crocker. "I believe that with $200,000 I can pass our bill...I stayed in Washington to fix up the R.R. Committee in the Senate. The Committee is just as we want it." Other industrialists were not far behind in exerting pressures on Washington

for high protective tariffs and monopolistic patent rights, so much so that by the close of the century the lobbyists were often regarded as the third house of Congress.

Compared to those primitive specialists in direct action, today's lobbyist is a sophisticated practitioner. Samuel Colt once paid a congressman ten thousand dollars to secure an extension of the patent on the revolver that bears his name, and he engaged a lobbyist to indulge receptive congressmen in all the delights of the flesh they might desire in downtown hotels. Today he would hardly be so crass as to bribe or enrich a congressman with cash, but instead would contribute to his re-election campaign fund to help pay for lapel buttons, bumper strips, television and radio announcements, newspaper ads, and the like. The congressman who faces a tough challenger often runs a deficit; but if he has an easy race, a surplus of contributions might enhance his personal affluence. Another respectable form of rewarding officeholders is the speaking fee, often a thousand dollars or more, for addressing meetings of the lobbyist's organization – and if the speech is ghost-written, as it usually is, this is just another part of the charade.

Both political parties hijack the lobbyists shamelessly in election years with a festive form of larceny, the fund-raising dinner. Tickets go for a hundred dollars, or in some instances a thousand dollars, per plate for the benefit of the party's pet charity, electing its candidates. The important lobbyist who fails to purchase tickets for a table of ten political cronies may find them less than charmed on his next request for assistance. He has to take care of the other party, too, coolly hedging his bets against the uncertainty of election results.

But money is not all that talks to a politician. Public opinion counts high, and the complete lobbyist today is something of a public-opinion molder. By stimulating newspaper and magazine articles or editorials, by publishing house organs for their members, many organizations take the indirect route of public relations to influence government decisions. A variation on this approach is the organized letter-writing campaign directed for or against a pending bill. It is rather easily detected by congressional secretaries because of stock phrases and arguments planted by the organizing pressure group.

A more advanced technique is the attempt to reach key congressmen through their closest friends or relatives, family doctor, lawyer, or fraternity brothers. This requires painstaking research and legwork but those with the patience and resources to use it make great claims. A lobbyist for a large national organization who engineered just such an invisible campaign against a major bill claimed that success stemmed directly from influencing a key lawmaker through his dentist.

Large-scale lobbying for foreign governments is a postwar phenomenon. Much of it is performed by public relations firms, some in New York as well as Washington. Its chief aim is to win generous treatment by the Pentagon, State Department, and Congress in the manifold decisions involving billions of dollars in military and economic aid. The theory is that Americans employed by foreigners can reach deeper into the American pork barrel than any foreign ambassador, inhibited by diplomatic niceties, would dare to try. Occasionally a skillful foreigner has succeeded. Take the case of Philippe Bunau-Varilla, the imaginative French engineer who dissuaded Congress from choosing Nicaragua for the Isthmian canal that he was promoting for Panama. Instead of employing a high-powered publicity campaign in behalf of Panama as might be done today, Bunau-Varilla fostered a nagging doubt about Nicaragua. After the House had already voted in favor of the Nicaraguan route, Mont Pelée in Martinique erupted with a loss of thirty thousand lives. Subsequently a Nicaraguan volcano, Momotombo, became active. Realizing that Momotombo was engraved on Nicaraguan postage stamps, Bunau-Varilla made the rounds of Washington stamp dealers "to find there ninety stamps, that is, one for every Senator, showing a beautiful volcano belching forth in magnificent eruption," he later wrote. "I hastened to paste my precious postage stamps on sheets of paper...Below the stamps were written the following words, which told the whole story: 'An official witness of the volcanic activity of Nicaragua.'" The Senate revised the canal bill in favor of Panama with but eight dissenting votes, the House fell into line, and the rest is history. Even in this case the French promoters were not without American lobbying help. They wisely engaged a prominent New York lawyer, William N. Cromwell, who had contributed sixty thousand dollars to the Republican campaign chest to prevent the party from going on record in favor of the Nicaragua route. It was no coincidence that the pro-Panama forces were led by Senator Mark Hanna, grateful chairman of the GOP National Committee.

This invisible financial link between lobbyists and politicians periodically prompted congressional investigations and finally the passage in 1946 of the federal act that requires those who deal with Congress to file a quarterly report. As the Supreme Court later interpreted the law, Congress (and the public) "wants to know who is being hired, who is putting up the money, and how much." The reports are filed with the clerk of the House. Because no one was charged with enforcing the act (a convenient congressional oversight), the total five to ten million dollars reported in annual expense reports is generally regarded as less than candid. The only court case against a lobbyist since then involved two oil company representatives who carelessly reverted to nineteenth century form while lobbying in favor of a natural-gas bill. They left twenty-five hundred dollars in the office of Senator Francis Case, a South Dakota Republican who felt honor bound to broadcast this incident from the Senate floor. The crusty old Senate unflinchingly passed the bill but President Eisenhower vetoed it because he felt it had been "tainted" by this illegal approach.

The perennial big spenders – oil, sugar, truckers, unions, utilities – have periodically been joined by the American Medical Association, in opposition to Medicare legislation, by savings and loan associations and insurance companies seeking favorable tax legislation, and by the Farm Bureau, which opposes high price supports and crop control farm bills.

In the main, long-established lobby groups such as these are considered reliable, if predictable, in the arguments they advance. Congressmen who tend to agree with their general point of view, be it liberal or conservative, prolabor or probusiness, often ally themselves with their favorite lobbyists. They freely accept prepared material or ghost-written speeches and proposed bills from them on the presumption that the material can withstand assaults on its reliability. To this extent, many lobbyists have gained limited respectability, a status they earnestly crave to replace the legend of notoriety that haunts their trade. At all events, the lobbyist has become a cog in the Washington machinery, and the big wheels of government would have difficulty turning without him.

CHAPTER ELEVEN

Washington after Five

The gateway to the inner circles of Washington society is tended by four anonymous guardians selected by Mrs. Carolyn Hagner Shaw, the social arbiter for the nation's capital. Each autumn Mrs. Shaw brings out a new edition of The Social List of Washington, the green felt-covered bible of the town's prominent persons. "It lists the bluebloods and those who make the wheels go around in Washington," she explains. This elite corps, which numbered some two thousand at the turn of the century, now exceeds seven thousand. The central fact about it is that the wheels vastly outnumber the bluebloods.

Washington society thus is a traitor to class and tradition. Real Society, the kind found, for example, in Philadelphia or Boston, exists to sanctify blood relationships, to perpetuate a social status quo created by these families, and hence to exclude outsiders. Spawned primarily by political relationships, Washington society is perpetually changing. Every other winter after an election, Mrs. Shaw rushes into print with a supplement to her green book. Any cow-county congressman who has garnered a plurality is automatically listed. Every politician or businessman who has wangled a presidential appointment is added to the Social List, and there he stays so long as he doesn't offend too many hostesses.

The identity of those who judge his behavior is a secret. Mrs. Shaw divulges only that one is a club-woman, two are social gadabouts, and the only male member is a retired government official. Moreover, she stoutly claims even she can't influence them when they sit down each summer to the delicious task of determining who is "in" and who is "out" for the coming social season. What criteria are applied? Unpleasant notoriety, such as a nasty divorce case or a government scandal, and you are out. Pleasant notoriety, such as associating with the right people and having money enough to throw elegant parties, and you are in, or on your way.

Having survived twenty-five years of society's peculiar anxieties, Mrs. Shaw is impervious to pressure. Anyone dropped from the Social List who starts to show that hell hath no fury like a matron (or her ambitious husband) scorned, is urged to speak to Mrs. Shaw's attorney. None ever has. Any gifts from aspirants to the social heights go back with a form letter. "I tell them it's against my policy to accept gifts. I don't tell them, 'This is one strike against you, old boy.'"

Mrs. Shaw is friendly and unaffected and a bit bemused by the power attributed to her. She lives in one of Georgetown's attractive alley dwellings with a dog, a cat, and an unlisted telephone that connects with her office a short distance away. Her mother, who loved parties, started the green book in 1930. Mrs. Shaw, who admits to being "practically antisocial," has successfully carried on. Though her board members compile the Social List, Mrs. Shaw is the town's unofficial authority on etiquette and protocol. For years she wrote a daily column on the subject for the Hearst syndicate; now the column appears weekly in the Washington Star.

If Washington society ever has the sensation that mother is watching, the feeling is well founded. As archivist of its improprieties, Mrs. Shaw keeps a card file, insured for twenty thousand dollars and locked in her safe, in which she notes the position, family background, and social idiosyncrasies of each member of society. A green book subscriber who calls her office seeking advice on a dinner party is likely to be forewarned that Admiral So-and-So is an O.D. (old drunk) and it would be advisable to seat him between Mrs. What's-Her-Name, who talks too much, and Miss You-Know-Who, an S.C. (social climber), but

All is not pursuit of power in Washington (right).
A leading patroness of the symphony, Mrs. Jouett Shouse
(left), enters on the arm of the Vice-President, led by
Mrs. Humphrey. Washington society dines at the
annual National Symphony Ball (below).

for heaven's sake be careful with Senator Such-and-Such, who is a notorious F.P. (fanny pincher).

"We don't have as many fanny pinchers as we once had," observes this chronicler of social sin. "Times have changed."

In the formative years of Washington society there was considerable overlap of bluebloods and government leaders. Jackson's era of the common man brought on the first sensational clash between commoners and aristocrats. The beautiful, vivacious wife of Jackson's Secretary of War, and daughter of a Washington tavern keeper, Peggy O'Neale Eaton, was ostracized by ladies more gently bred, including the wife of Vice-President Calhoun, who refused to receive her. When Jackson's minister at Second Presbyterian Church remonstrated against Mrs. Eaton, the President rebuked him and quit the congregation. The rift in society was not healed until Eaton left the Cabinet.

By the end of the century, official Washington had outgrown its rough-and-ready frontier ways and taken on sophisticated Continental manners in keeping with the emergence of the United States as a great power. Senators began wearing high silk hats and frock coats. Foreign diplomats no longer regarded Washington as a hardship post. And the new American capitalists who wanted a taste of Washington society flocked to the capital. The subsequent expansion of government and the diplomatic corps, adding officials by the thousands, relegated the elite residents, the cave dwellers, to a tiny minority.

Peggy Eaton would be accepted today, probably cultivated, and her parties would be crowded and well publicized. Washington's most publicized hostesses of recent years have demonstrated that wealth invested in parties attended by high-ranking officials is a sure-fire formula for social success, no matter how new the hostess is to Washington. Mrs. Perle Mesta of Oklahoma, widow of a Pittsburgh steel magnate, became the town's "hostess with the mostest" during the Truman-Eisenhower years. She receded into relative oblivion during the Kennedy years but regained social prominence as an intimate of the Johnsons, to whom she had sold her Spring Valley house before he became President. Her rival was Hungarian-born Gwendolyn Cafritz, whose late husband's fortune made in Washington real estate underwrote the lavish parties at their Foxhall Road home. Another contemporary contender was Mrs. Marjorie

Merriweather Post of Illinois. Heiress to an estimated two hundred sixty million dollar breakfast cereal fortune, Mrs. Post entertains in the grand manner at Hillwood, her magnificent estate at 4155 Linnean Avenue.

The rivalry between Mrs. Cafritz and Mrs. Mesta was exaggerated by the society writers, according to Mrs. Shaw, and was bland compared to that of the grand dames of a generation ago, Alice Longworth, Cissy Patterson, and Evelyn Walsh McLean. Alice and Cissy began competing as debutantes for the most eligible bachelors in town. Alice married a young congressman from Cincinnati, Nicholas Longworth, and the other married a dashing Polish cavalryman, Count Joseph Gizycka. One night at the Longworths' after dinner Cissy monopolized a young nobleman in an upstairs library. The following day she received a note from her hostess:

"Dear Cissy: Upon sweeping up the library this morning, the maid found several hair-pins which I thought you might need and which I am returning. Alice."

Cissy said she replied:

"Dear Alice: Many thanks for the hair-pins. If you had looked on the chandelier you might also have sent back my shoes and chewing gum. Love, Cissy."

In those days the party of the year was Mrs. McLean's all-night New Year's Eve levee. It especially taxed the ambassadors who were obliged to attend the President's annual New Year's Day reception for the diplomatic corps the next morning. The President moved from this event to the north portico at noon, where he shook hands with any citizen who came in off the street. New Year's Day entertaining was discontinued by Hoover.

Another change in social intercourse here has been the abolition of card-calling days. For over a century wives of officials were obliged to hold open house for one another on designated days each week. Wives of congressmen received on Tuesdays, Cabinet wives on Wednesdays, senators' wives on Thursdays, wives of Supreme Court justices and ambassadors on Fridays, and the First Lady on Saturdays. Usually the receiving lady served tea and sandwiches for her afternoon guests. But the growth of Congress and

The strains of public office are relieved by the natural exuberance of the professional politician. When he erupts, tensions dissolve.

the diplomatic corps made this practice unwieldy.

Protocol also dictated that officials leave their cards at the homes of all other officials who outranked them, a tedious practice sometimes expedited by chauffeurs congregating on appointed days behind the Supreme Court to exchange their masters' cards. Wartime rationing during the early 1940s made abandonment of this archaic practice both excusable and patriotic. Calling days were conveniently forgotten with the advent of peace and the cocktail party.

Alcohol has always been a favorite lubricant for the masculine wheels of Washington society, but tea sufficed for the ladies for generations. When President Hayes' wife inflicted her W.C.T.U. principles upon male guests, she was privately ridiculed as "Lemonade Lucy," and the Secretary of State grumbled that "water flowed like champagne" at the White House. In the pre-cocktail party era a gentleman stopped at his club, the Metropolitan, the Cosmos, the Army-Navy, or the University, to imbibe with his friends before going home to dress for dinner. In those days debut parties and receptions were non-alcoholic; today they are glorified cocktail parties.

This change is deplored by those who wistfully recall the halcyon days. "A cocktail party is like a Shriners' convention," snorts Alice Longworth. The socially active wife of a ranking congressman, Mrs. Hale Boggs, defends the cocktail party as invaluable to congressmen for making "downtown" contacts. She notes that while most executives can do this over luncheon, congressmen usually devote lunch hours to entertaining out-of-town constituents at the Capitol.

Washington society normally finds excuses, not reasons, for throwing a party. An arrival or departure from Washington is one of the commonest. There are some six hundred catered parties every month from September to May; and throughout the year, there are countless other soirees ranging from elaborate feasts thrown by lobbyists in hotel ballrooms to intimate dinner parties in the city's best salons.

All this mingling is not without its serious and useful purpose. The need to communicate is as compelling here as the drives of hunger and thirst. "This is the only city in the world," observed the late Eric Johnston, "where sound travels faster than light." A Washington hostess, faithful to the American idea that if people talk long enough any problem can be solved, takes pride in bringing together men of state from all over the world. Her success is measured by the publicity value of her guests. Washington society news perforce is mostly about men. A woman's social prominence generally depends upon the position of her husband. Justice Holmes once ungallantly remarked that "Washington is full of great men and the women they married when they were very young."

Since much of the energy that drives the social carrousel issues from the same dynamo that runs politics (a quest for power or the desire to bask in its presence), personal relationships tend to last only as long as individuals hold offices that serve one another's interests. The only thing that remains reasonably permanent is protocol, or the rules of etiquette. Some VIPs have been known to become unpleasant over a violation of protocol. The French ambassador has walked out on a hostess who seated him improperly. Most take the view of Carolyn Shaw, however, that "protocol is not social affectation; it makes things simpler."

Washington's etiquette schools attract parvenues by the dozens – wives of congressmen and agency heads – taking the hundred-dollar course in how to find your dinner partner at a big embassy affair, or the three-hundred-dollar course that includes "the creation and maintenance of a social position in Washington." One social engagement the uninitiated attend with greatest trepidation, dinner at the White House, usually turns out for the fortunate few who are invited to be as pleasantly easy as it is memorable. Arrangements differ with the size and occasion of the party, as well as the personal touch of the First Lady. Jacqueline Kennedy's extraordinary creations included a sunset cruise down the Potomac for 138 guests, a floodlit lawn party at Mount Vernon, a ball for Nobel prize winners in the White House. Most White House dinners are structured on orthodox plans. As a guest, you would enter via the south portico beneath the Truman balcony and be ushered into the Diplomatic Reception Room. After checking wraps, you would be escorted by a White House aide up one flight to the main floor, where the red-jacketed Marine Corps musicians play for the arriving guests. The aide shows the lady a table seating chart. He gives the man a card with the name of the lady he is to escort into dinner; on the back of the card is the seating chart. As you enter the East Room, another aide announces you as though you were a titled lord arriving at court. You are told where to stand when the President arrives and introduced to those who

Alice Roosevelt Longworth serves tea in her Massachusetts Avenue town house. She deplores the cocktail party as subversive of the refined taste that prevailed when she was the capital's reigning hostess.

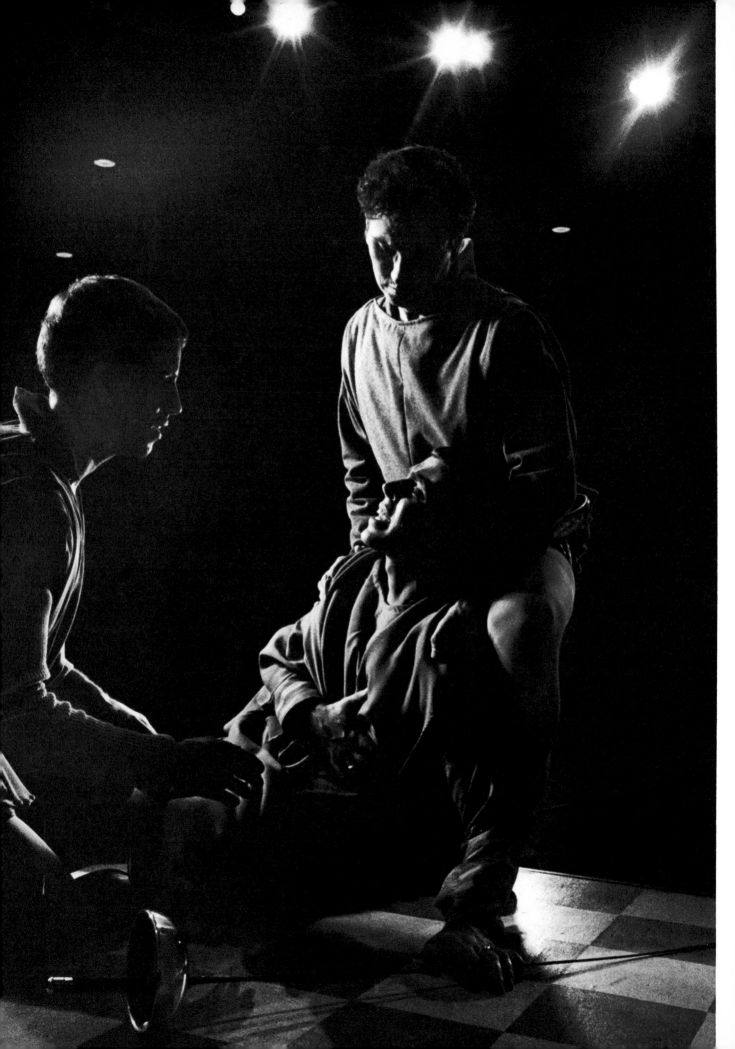

Catholic University's drama department, its students playing Romeo and Juliet (opposite), is justly praised for its consistently good theater. Washington's excellent repertory company, Arena Stage, born in an old burlesque house, reared to maturity in an abandoned brewery, now has a modern theater (right) in the new Southwest section.

Although Washington imports most of its entertainers, it proudly exports the talent of its own Charlie Byrd (left). When he is not appearing in other world capitals, he plays at the Showboat, a small, unpretentious night club. Backstage at the government-owned Carter Barron Amphitheater in Rock Creek Park, African diplomats seek autographs from American jazz trumpeter Louis Armstrong (below). An African dancer performs (opposite).

will be standing next to you. Then the martial tones of "Hail to the Chief" bring the assembly to attention and the President enters with his guest's wife on his arm, followed by the First Lady and the guest of honor. The four principals lead the guests to the dining room and are seated in high-backed chairs at the U-shaped table. After dinner the men usually congregate in the Green Room for coffee and liqueur, the women in the Red Room. They meet again in the East Room for entertainment and champagne.

Preoccupied with its party circuit, Washington has not had a vigorous public night life and for generations has been regarded as a cultural desert. The flowering of culture in the country at large has brought bloom to the capital as well. The capital still lacks night clubs or restaurants to compare with New York's; theatrically, it is more like New Haven than Broadway; and musically, it is no better than half a dozen other American cities. But most cosmopolitan palates can be satisfied in its growing number of good restaurants. From spring to autumn its new sidewalk cafés are delightful. A younger generation, restless and affluent, has inspired a profusion of new little night spots – folk music cellars, discothèques, strip joints, coffee houses.

Arena Stage, the city's permanent theatrical company, is famed beyond the District. Founded by a

drama student and one of her teachers at George Washington University, Zelda Fichandler and Ed Magnum, Arena was financed by forty persons, including a policeman and a vice-president of the World Bank. It opened in 1950 in the Hippodrome, an old burlesque house on Mount Vernon Square, moved in 1956 to the Heurich brewery in Foggy Bottom in order to double the seating capacity to five hundred, and a few years ago built its own modern theater-in-the-round just off the Maine Avenue waterfront.

The lone survivor of numerous legitimate theaters here is the National, which opened in 1835 with the radical departure of moving "the more boisterous section of the audience from the pit to the upper gallery, and the reservation of the lower floor for more exclusive patrons." No theater has ever had more exclusive patronage. It was gutted by a fire in 1845. Five years later the President, Vice-President, Cabinet, and Supreme Court were out front when it reopened as New National Hall with Jenny Lind on stage. Two years later a wall collapsed. It was rebuilt as New National Theatre, only to burn four more times before the present theater was built in 1922.

Washington's most famous theater was Ford's, where Lincoln was shot in 1865. A Baptist church on the site had been converted into Christy's Opera

House in 1861, remodeled into Ford's Atheneum the next year, and then burned. Rebuilt of brick, it opened as Ford's Theatre in 1863 and was considered one of the finest in the country, with a seating capacity of seventeen hundred. The night of the assassination the President and Mrs. Lincoln had taken Major Henry R. Rathbone and his fiancée to enjoy a comedy, *Our American Cousin*. Near the end of the third act, John Wilkes Booth entered the President's private box and fired his single-shot derringer before anyone noted his presence. As Lincoln slumped in his chair, Major Rathbone sprang at Booth, but was stabbed in the arm. Dagger in hand, Booth leaped to the stage below, fracturing his left leg. He galloped off on a horse and eluded his pursuers for twelve days.

Three doctors who broke through the terror-stricken audience to reach the President recognized that the wound, above the left ear, was mortal. Rather than risk a carriage ride to the White House over the cobblestone streets, they ordered him carried across the street to the Petersen house, where he died the following morning in the bed of a government clerk. Ford's Theatre never gave another performance.

Between the Civil War and the early twentieth century, theatrical development flourished on a number of other stages, attracting the country's leading entertainers. Today the National books tryouts en route to Broadway and touring hit shows. In recent years Washington has had a wider choice during the summer when straw-hat stages at Olney and Shady Grove are active. In addition the town has many amateur drama groups, notably the Little Theatre of Alexandria, which has brought Gadsby's Tavern to life every summer for the past two decades, and Catholic University's drama department.

The oldest and best-known musical organization in Washington is the Marine Band. It made its White House debut at President Adams' New Year's Day reception in 1801, and has been playing for White House parties – and for public enjoyment – ever since. John Philip Sousa, a native Washingtonian, led the Marine Band from 1880 to 1892, wrote marches and light operas, and organized an eighty-five-piece orchestra of local musicians. Washington had difficulty, however, launching a permanent symphony. The

Constitution Hall, the center of good music, where the National Symphony performs regularly.

city's musical life for years revolved around its churches. The organist at the Congregational Church, J. W. Bischoff, wrote "When You and I Were Young, Maggie." The Army and the Navy bands were organized during the 1920s. (All three still give regular free concerts on the Capitol steps, at the Watergate, and at military bases between their national tours.)

Next, the Library of Congress, which houses the greatest music collection in the country, began holding chamber music concerts in its Coolidge Auditorium, featuring the Budapest String Quartet and other ensembles. Finally the National Symphony Orchestra was organized by Hans Kindler, cellist of the Philadelphia Symphony, and opened in 1931 in Constitution Hall, where it has been performing ever since. Under the direction of Howard Mitchell since 1948, it has brought the world's greatest artists to Washington as guest soloists. In recent years the capital has acquired its own ballet and opera company.

As a government, the United States has not patronized the arts. Politicians have generally agreed with the painter Larry Rivers, who told the Woman's National Democratic Club that "Government taking a role in art is like a gorilla threading a needle. It is cute to watch, the heart is in the right place, but it is clumsy and, above all, impossible." The occasional bill to provide federal grants to subsidize the arts never received serious attention in Congress until recently.

The Kennedy Center for the Performing Arts represents a crack in the wall. In approving a cultural center as a memorial to the fallen President, Congress authorized up to fifteen and a half million dollars in federal funds, to be matched equally by private donations, to underwrite construction of the thirty-one-million-dollar center. In breaking ground, President Johnson said, "The opportunity we give to the arts is a measure of the quality of our civilization. It is important to be aware that artistic activity can enrich the life of our people, which really is the central object of government."

Long before, the nation's second President, John Adams, had envisioned what is now happening in Washington: "I must study politics and war, that my sons may have liberty to study mathematics and philosophy. My sons ought to study mathematics and philosophy . . . in order to give their children a right to study painting, poetry, music, architecture, statuary, tapestry and porcelain."

Ballet performed under the stars at Carter Barron Amphitheater is an incomparable summer evening's delight.

Disquaire at the Whisky a Gogo (opposite above). Native African dancers stir a VIP audience at the State Department auditorium (opposite below). Greek music and Arabic dancing enliven Port Saïd, a downtown café (above right). Josh White sings at The Shadows (above). Washington's many pretty girls are evident before and after five, publicly and privately, as here at the Gaslight Club.

Pennsylvania Avenue seen across the National Gallery fountain.

CHAPTER TWELVE

The Inner City

A new city, reflecting the spirit and appetites of a world capital, is swiftly emerging along the river Potomac. George Washington would be dazzled by the city's commercial success and astonished that it came not by the river but in large part because of those dreadful entangling alliances. L'Enfant would be gratified that it is taking on fresh aspects of his original plan for a capital of sweeping vistas, public gardens, broad boulevards, fountains, squares, and parks.

The new Washington hugs its monumental core. It includes new museums along the great Mall, plans for landscaping the Mall itself, the creative accommodation of the new and the old around Lafayette Square, the beginnings of Pennsylvania Avenue as the grand axis of the nation, the magnificent John F. Kennedy Center for the Performing Arts rising in redeveloped Foggy Bottom, the restoration of Capitol Hill, and the utter transformation of Southwest Washington from the city's worst slums to America's largest venture in urban renewal.

These invigorating changes in less than a decade have been complemented by the demolition of rows of ugly "temporary" government buildings strewn along the Mall and on Constitution and Independence avenues, some of them dating from World War I. In the private sector there has been rapid replacement of squatty old structures in the western end of the downtown business district by modern office, hotel, and apartment towers, many of uncommonly good design. If Washington still has many urban problems to solve, it shares this condition with all capitals, with all great cities. No other city has moved so quickly from small-town physical plant and isolated state of mind to a world metropolis – and done it with more attention to good taste.

The city in which Washingtonians live and play and love and die reaches well beyond the working core. Its outer fingers will soon touch those of Baltimore on the north and Richmond on the south. Within the District of Columbia, the inner city is gradually losing population as old residential neighborhoods surrender to commerce. More than 800,000 persons lived in the District in 1950, only 760,000 in 1960.

Geographically the District is divided into four unequal quadrants that meet at the Capitol. The arrangement of streets is so orderly – north-south streets by the numbers, east-west streets by the alphabet, diagonals named for states – that only the traffic circles baffle the newcomer and threaten his bearings.

The largest quadrant, Northwest, has traditionally been *the* section in which to live, although now there are many "good addresses" in other sections because of sweeping changes in the old town. In Washington, moreover, a man's street address offers no reliable measure of his power or prestige. Unlike New York, where money is the key to both and a man's Manhattan address marks his status, Washington tolerates the diverse lodgings of its power elite. Because powerful men in Washington often have only modest means, they live in oddly separated sections. Some live in suburbia, adjusting their schedules to miss the lemming run of commuters. Most live in the inner city, in fashionable row houses on Capitol Hill, or sprawling clapboard homes in Cleveland Park and Chevy Chase, or suites in older hotels – the Sheraton-Park, the Shoreham, the Mayflower – or new elevator apartments in Southwest or upper Connecticut Avenue with a switchboard to screen incoming calls. The greatest concentration of power and wealth is in a single square mile of outrageously priced real estate known as Georgetown.

A distinctive silhouette on the capital's skyline, rising from atop Mount
St. Alban, the Washington Cathedral (above) has been under
construction since 1907 and will continue to be for decades to come.
The magnificence of its Gothic style is emphasized by the carved
figures on the high altar (below). The traditional cathedral floor plan,
in the shape of a cross, shows stunningly in this picture (right),
taken from a scaffold high in the vaulted ceiling.

*Octagon House (opposite), on New York Avenue, is where
President Madison lived after the British burned the White
House and where he signed the Treaty of Ghent (below), ending
the War of 1812. The signatures include those of Henry Clay
and John Quincy Adams, leader of the group that negotiated
the treaty in France.*

Georgetown

For a century after Georgetown was founded in the 1750s, it dominated the Maryland shore of the Potomac as a tobacco and wheat port, receiving clipper ships and schooners from the seas and dispatching cargo inland through the Cumberland Gap, up the Chesapeake and Ohio Canal. Washington's leaders lived in Georgetown while the new capital city took form. A stagecoach, the Royal George, set out over its cobbled streets for the Capitol each day and returned at nightfall. One can imagine the wealth that came to Georgetown by strolling through the magnificent estate at 3101 R Street, once the home of John C. Calhoun, and known today as Dumbarton Oaks, a place of contemporary historic note for the 1944 conference held there to draft the United Nations Charter. Its exquisite public gardens are unequaled in Washington. Built about 1800 of late Georgian architecture, the house has been altered over the years but retains the regal air of an eighteenth-century château. Another grand old mansion that is open to the public is Dumbarton House, the headquarters of the National Society of Colonial Dames of America at 2715 Q Street. Built around 1747, it has been restored and furnished with antiques of the 1790-to-1810 period when Georgetown flourished. Tudor Place at 1644 Thirty-first Street is still in the same Peter family that built it in sections from 1794 to 1816. Lafayette, Lee, and other statesmen were entertained here, and the Peter girls are said to have devised a petticoat semaphore code to signal their cousins at the Lee mansion on Arlington heights. The Park Service has preserved the Old Stone House on M Street, built around 1763, for public inspection. Most other historic houses in Georgetown are privately owned and subject to public scrutiny from the sidewalk only, including the former home of President Kennedy at 3307 N Street.

The coming of the railroad, strangler of canal towns, all but destroyed Georgetown. From the Civil War to World War I its shipping vanished. From a pre-Civil War population of 6,798 whites, 1,358 free Negroes, and 577 slaves, Georgetown's population had grown to 17,300 but half these residents were poverty-stricken Negroes. The port had become a commercial backwater, the town a musty curiosity, its shops selling secondhand articles, main streets still cobbled and lined with fading Georgian splendor, alleys choked with tiny dwellings that lacked either plumbing or electricity.

This supine Georgetown of moneyed aristocracy was quite defenseless, then, when the New Deal intellectuals stormed Washington and became enchanted with her lingering charm. With more nerve than money, they moved in with their books and their social ideals, managed to pay the grocer and landlord, and began an absorbing affair that lasted through the war. After the war, her bohemian period over, Georgetown demanded diamonds. The most dilapidated houses were transformed into fashionable digs and sold for large bundles of cash. Social elegance, once again, became her manifest destiny.

Contemporary Georgetown is obsessed with her appearance. Georgian or Federal period is the style. The town's merchants do a brisk business in decorative eagles, brass door knockers, carriage lamps, shiny black shutters. The harmony of this architectural fashion is zealously protected by the Commission of Fine Arts, seven citizens appointed by the President to view the changing city with an artist's eye. The Commission vents an artist's rage at such utilitarian monstrosities as the Roosevelt Island Bridge (it recommended a tunnel) and the uninspiring design of some of the new federal buildings, which economy compels it to accept. Within the immediate confines of Georgetown, the Commission rules more effectively—indeed, absolutely. A window or doorframe facing the public street may not be altered without its consent. Any passion for modern design must, like a secret vice, be indulged in the privacy of parlors and boudoirs. This authority to dictate public taste was granted by Congress in a law declaring the town from R Street south a national monument, a neat legal device for creating a unique living monument to the past.

Secure within its legal and natural barriers—the Potomac, Rock Creek, Dumbarton Oaks Park and Archbold Parkway—the tiny kingdom of Georgetown attracts denizens of class, cash, prominence, and ambition. Sufficient cash will get anyone past the real-estate mercenaries who guard the kingdom from their pastel forts along Wisconsin Avenue, but position alone assures the coveted invitations of the town's stellar hostesses and the attention of the society columnists.

Georgetowners speak fondly of their little village,

of walking to the stores, of knowing and being known by shopkeepers, of taking dinner with friends up the street. In their quest for privacy, however, Georgetowners betray their urban tastes. Everyone walls up his garden to gain seclusion no village ever afforded. No hanging on the fence to chin with the neighbors. The Georgetowner waits to be invited over for a drink.

Much of Washington views the place with interest or envy. On designated days each spring, suburban matrons pay several dollars each to pass through a a few of society's favored salons on the Georgetown house tour. More frequently they poke through the shops on Wisconsin Avenue, Washington's most delightful shopping district, or return with husbands to mingle with the college crowd along the new night club strip on M Street.

Georgetown University stands on the town's fringe, secure in its own historic identity as "the alma mater of all Catholic colleges in America," as Pope Pius put it. It was founded as a men's academy in 1789. Run by Jesuits but not financed by the Church, the university today has a coeducational enrollment of some seventy-five hundred students, three-fourths of whom are Catholics.

The university's Healy Tower, built of solemn gray granite in Flemish Romanesque style, is a fixture of the Washington skyline. It was named for a nineteenth-century president of the institution, Father Patrick F. Healy, the mulatto son of a white sea captain and a Negro slave woman, whom he married upon purchasing her freedom.

Those who lament Washington's lack of a great university acknowledge that Georgetown has attained academic distinction with its School of Foreign Service, established in 1919, the first school in America devoted to formal training in the arts of diplomacy and foreign commerce. Nearby is Georgetown Visitation Convent, founded in 1799, the oldest Catholic girls' school in the original thirteen states. It has about four hundred students on the high school and junior college level.

The most obvious paradox of Georgetown is that it tolerates the ugliest section of the city's long waterfront. River barges heavy with gravel feed the monstrous dockside concrete mixers; they in turn suckle broods of elephantine cement trucks that rumble off in all directions to help build the new city. A rendering plant fouls the air. A flour mill next door posts a sign disclaiming responsibility for the odor. A George-

towner in his expensive townhouse above the waterfront learns to look beyond to the river and Roosevelt Island or to enjoy the old Chesapeake and Ohio Canal, which separates the town from its industrial compound. The canal is favored by hikers and bicyclers and sedentary nature lovers who take the mule-drawn barge, a tranquil four-hour voyage twenty-two miles up to Seneca, Maryland, and back.

Foggy Bottom

Southeast of Georgetown lies Foggy Bottom, a section whose future is brighter than its past. As the location of the State Department since 1947, it has achieved international currency with the Quai d'Orsay and Whitehall. Originally an eighteenth-century hamlet called Hamburg, later Funkstown, it gained its moniker from "miasmic vapors" rising from swamps where the Lincoln Memorial now stands. After Washington absorbed it early in the 1900s, this became the capital's gas house and brewery district, populated by German, Irish, Italian, Jewish, and Negro working people. Foggy Bottom's transition from gas-house shabbiness to town-house elegance began after State moved in and the gas company switched to natural gas. Apartment houses rose from the site of the old gasworks along Virginia Avenue and Arena Stage moved into the cavernous Heurich brewery before building its present theater in new Southwest. Now the city's first formal cultural center is going up in Foggy Bottom. Located on the river, this magnificent memorial to President Kennedy is a cubicle complex of theater, concert, and opera houses designed by Edward Durell Stone. Next to the cultural center are Washington's most luxurious flats, where a penthouse overlooking the panorama of the city beautiful sells for a quarter of a million dollars. Farther down Virginia Avenue near State is the new Pan American Health Organization headquarters, a handsome edifice of Uruguayan design.

Foggy Bottom also has its academic enclave, the sidewalk campus of the city's largest college, George Washington University. Enrollment exceeds twelve thousand. President Washington suggested this section for a national university. At his death he left fifty shares in the old Potomac Canal Co. to help finance it; but the stock became worthless after the canal ceased operations in 1816, and neither Congress nor private interests took up the cause. John Quincy Adams, Calhoun, and other statesmen contributed funds after the University, originally called Columbian College, was chartered in 1821 at the request of Baptists. President Madison, accompanied by Lafayette, addressed its first commencement. After the turn of the century, it cast off its sectarian ties, later moved several times from its original campus near what is now Meridian Hill park, and finally settled in the blocks bounded by G, E, Twenty-first, and Twenty-second streets. George Washington offers both day and night classes to accommodate the many government workers, even members of Congress, who are advancing their education after office hours.

Lafayette Square and Pennsylvania Avenue

The old residential quarter between the campus and the White House will soon be completely commercial. Fortunately the historic Octagon House at Eighteenth and New York has been preserved for public visits by the American Institute of Architects headquartered there. President Madison lived here until the White House was rebuilt following the fire. The nineteenth-century atmosphere of Lafayette Square, facing the White House, was nearly destroyed when Congress suggested tearing down the old homes around it to clear the land for new federal buildings. President and Mrs. Kennedy intervened and adopted a plan by architect John Carl Warnecke for restoring the homes and setting the office buildings behind.

The first structure on the square after construction of the White House was St. John's Episcopal Church, built in 1816. President Madison paid rent for Pew 54 and the next five presidents continued to use it. Since then Pew 54 in "the Church of Presidents" has been set aside for presidential use, rent free. Every President has attended services here, if only to preserve this tradition.

The best of the private residences on Lafayette Square is Decatur House, built in 1818. Stephen Decatur, naval hero of the Tripolitanian war, lived here for fourteen months between his marriage and his death in a duel. After his young widow retired to seclusion in Georgetown, the house was occupied by Henry Clay, Martin Van Buren until he became

President, and various Old World ambassadors. Its garden served as a slave market around 1844. Today this example of late Georgian architecture is preserved for the public by the National Trust for Historic Preservation. On the opposite side of the square is the house in which Dolley Madison, as one historian put it, spent "a triumphant widowhood" as social leader until her death in 1849. The Cosmos Club occupied the building after 1886 and later expanded into the adjacent Tayloe house, nicknamed the "little White House" when Mark Hanna lived there during McKinley's administration.

The most important house in the Lafayette Square neighborhood is Blair House, cater-cornered from the White House on Pennsylvania Avenue. The Blair family owned the place for over a century until the government acquired it during World War II as a guest house for foreign dignitaries on state visits. Cabinet members have lived there and presidents have frequented its parlors. Robert E. Lee came to Blair House to receive from Colonel Montgomery Blair President Lincoln's offer of command of the Union army at the outbreak of the Civil War. When President Truman lived there in 1950, during reconstruction of the White House, two Puerto Rican nationalists tried to shoot their way through the front door in an assassination plot.

Pennsylvania Avenue, grand axis of the nation, is marked for sweeping improvement from the White House to the Capitol. In addition to serving as the inaugural parade route, Pennsylvania Avenue was the city's busiest promenade for over a century. Lined with hotels, rooming houses, markets, taverns, dry-goods stores, ice-cream parlors, newspaper offices, theaters, gambling halls, and bawdy houses, it attracted the high and low of society. That it was dusty and often rutted or flooded slowed its pulse not a bit. A wooden boardwalk was laid before the street was paved. Slaves were auctioned at Center Market, where the National Archives, repository of the Constitution and its Bill of Rights, now stands. Inaugural balls from John Quincy Adams to Buchanan were held in Carusi's Assembly Rooms, a public ballroom on the site of today's Internal Revenue headquarters. Two vice-presidents, John Tyler and Andrew Johnson, were living in hotels on the avenue and there sworn in as presidents upon the deaths of Harrison and Lincoln. Clay died in still another avenue hotel, and Walt Whitman rented a room overlooking the avenue.

By mid-twentieth century Pennsylvania Avenue had lost its social magnetism. The Federal Triangle, that great wedge of granite government buildings, had cleaned up the appearance of the south side but deadened it after twilight. Harvey's restaurant had moved to Connecticut Avenue, leaving the Occidental the only recommendable dining room on the entire avenue. The *Star* and the *Post* had built modern publishing plants elsewhere. New hotels farther uptown had eclipsed those that remained on the avenue. And commercial sin had been outlawed. The old promenade was dying and no one seemed to care.

In the mid-sixties the Kennedy and Johnson administrations produced a bold plan for fashioning Pennsylvania Avenue into the grand thoroughfare L'Enfant had intended. Gimcrack store fronts along the north side would be replaced by a new triangle of handsome private and public buildings, starting with the new Federal Bureau of Investigation headquarters opposite the Justice Department. The monumental proportions of the boulevard would be accented by a huge reflecting pool at the foot of Capitol Hill and a national square at the other to be used as a ceremonial entrance to the White House.

Capitol Hill

Capitol Hill's recent alterations recall Daniel Webster's admonition, "What is valuable is not new, and what is new is not valuable." Perhaps nothing new could match the magnificent crown of this summit, the Capitol itself, but the Supreme Court building radiates its own splendor and the old congressional office buildings are in sedate good taste. In jarring contrast to these pleasing adaptations of Corinthian and Ionic architecture, the new office buildings of the House and Senate are classic forms of "American ironic" — monuments to expensive tastelessness.

The private sector of Capitol Hill is undergoing a "Georgetown restoration" movement that is converting the Hill's old working-class neighborhoods into a highly desirable and highly priced residential area. Legend has it that L'Enfant envisioned this as the principal residential section of Washington when he faced the Capitol to the east but that Daniel Carroll and his neighbors overpriced the lots carved from their estates and thus influenced the westward growth of the city. In fact, early residents found it more sensible to settle near the new government buildings downtown or in thriving Georgetown. For a time, only boardinghouses sprang up around the Capitol to accommodate the lawmakers; Congressman Abe Lincoln lived in one of them where now stands the Library of Congress.

There are few houses on Capitol Hill more than a hundred years old. Friendship House, a community settlement house at 619 D Street, S.E., is thought to be pre-Revolutionary in origin. Its first known occupant was a tobacco planter who went broke entertaining free-loading VIPs. Francis Scott Key bought it in 1815, the year after writing "The Star-Spangled Banner," and moved from Georgetown. On G Street, S.E., between Sixth and Seventh is Christ Church, built in 1807, where presidents Madison, Jefferson, and John Quincy Adams attended services. President Lyndon B. Johnson has attended services at St. Mark's Episcopal Church at Third and A streets, S.E. An authentic Georgian period mansion, Belmont House, is at 144 Constitution Avenue, N.E., a block east of the Senate office building. Secretary of the Treasury Gallatin reputedly formalized the Louisiana Purchase in this house. It was burned by the British in 1814 but restored and given by Alva Belmont, a suffragette, to the National Woman's Party for a headquarters.

Most of the other row houses on the Hill are post-Civil War. Many of its alleys and courts are lined with tiny dwellings built for ex-slaves. When builders "restore" these houses they often reconstruct all but the outer shell, redecorate with an elegance far surpassing the original, and attach Federal period trimmings.

This improvement effort began on the Hill after World War II and gained fashionable status in 1949 when Supreme Court Justice Douglas bought a house behind the Court. Since then the area has attracted members of Congress and their aides, who value the rare experience of walking to work in the heart of a metropolis, and a stimulating group of professionals in diplomacy, education, military, bureaucracy, and private pursuits. Capitol Hill's new village will likely reach to the Anacostia River in another decade.

East of the Capitol Hill section there is one graceful symbol of the new city and the primary focal point of sports-minded Washington: D. C. Stadium. A concrete bowl with an undulating rim, it was built with federal funds to replace creaky Griffith Stadium

Among the renowned organizations headquartered in Washington, the National Geographic Society exhibits artifacts from its expeditions in its handsome building on Seventeenth Street (opposite), one of the many new structures that have transformed much of the western end of the downtown business district. Washington is giving up the ease and charm of a small Southern city and swiftly becoming a metropolis. Its mixture of modern and historic is typified by this hotel at Thomas Circle with an all-weather swimming pool (above). From it one can view the classic steeple of National City Christian Church, attended by President Lyndon B. Johnson.

159

as the home playing field of the Washington Senators baseball club and the football Redskins. The President traditionally launches the baseball season here in April by ceremoniously tossing out the first ball from a front-row box filled with his political pals. Despite this high-level rooting, the town hasn't had a pennant winner since 1933; it resignedly accepts the crack that Washington is first in war, first in peace, and last in the American League. The cavernous Armory near the stadium is used for such political festivities as thousand-dollar-a-plate fund-raising dinners and inaugural balls, plus the usual run of nonpartisan horse and flower shows.

The Congressional Cemetery nearby on Potomac Avenue probably bears more early history-book names than any in the country. Originally it was the burial ground for Capitol Hill's Christ Church. In 1816 Congress paid the church to reserve a section for Washington officials. Until the advent of the railroad made preferred home-state burials feasible, the death of a VIP in Washington meant burial in Congressional. President Zachary Taylor, dead of typhus fever after a year in the White House, and Dolley Madison and Calhoun were interred here but later buried elsewhere. John Philip Sousa, the march king, was one of the last famous men buried here, in 1932. For about forty years Congress took care of its own with a quaint government-issue cubicle sandstone tomb capped by a squat cone. There are eighty-five of them in long rows, each with its legend of stereotyped brevity: name, age, state, and years of service in Congress. The inscription on the tomb of John Quincy Adams is a classic example of mindless adherence to bureaucratic regulations; the stonecutter recorded that Adams had been fourteen years in the House but not that he was the sixth President of the United States. Like the tombs of twenty-one other congressmen, this merely memorializes Adams; he is buried in Quincy, Massachusetts. Congress quit issuing tombs in 1877 after a Massachusetts senator complained that the prospect of interment beneath one of these atrocities added a new terror to death.

Historic Landmarks

The unwelcome price of newness in the inner city has been the destruction of many landmarks. Since the Depression about half the five hundred and fifty buildings regarded as historic have vanished. The Fine Arts Commission and the National Capital Planning Commission are trying to preserve some three hundred remaining buildings and places. These include, in addition to the obvious landmarks, such diverse points of interest as handsome old Union Station, which the railroads want to tear down as they did Pennsylvania Station in New York to sell the rights for a more profitable office building over the tracks; the Carnegie Library in Mount Vernon Square, ironically the scene of the Know-Nothing riot of 1857, when it was a public market; the Custom House, one of Georgetown's finest but unnoticed structures; the city's old markets, which have been closing one by one; old City Hall at 451 Indiana Avenue; Commandant's House at the Marine Barracks, and the nearby Navy Yard, which once built ships for the infant post-Revolution Navy; the Chesapeake and Ohio Canal, which Congress once considered "improving" with an adjacent superhighway; Old Soldiers' Home, which presidents Lincoln, Hayes, Arthur, and Buchanan used as a summer residence; and Gilman's Drug Store, 627 Pennsylvania Avenue.

A search for the homes of some of yesteryear's VIPs reveals a melancholy aspect of the growth of this small town into a big city, the telling transition from the personal to the impersonal.

At 1501 Massachusetts, where Elihu Root, Teddy Roosevelt's Secretary of State, once lived, there is a modern office building. A motor lodge has replaced the residence of Gifford Pinchot at 1615 Rhode Island Avenue. Characterless apartments rise where once lived William Gibbs McAdoo, Henry A. Dupont, Hamilton Fish, and Lincoln's son, Robert, who was Secretary of War under Garfield and Arthur. The Brookings Institution's modern headquarters stands where the elder Henry Cabot Lodge lived. Alexander Graham Bell's home site on Connecticut just south of Dupont Circle is now a parking lot. Office buildings have supplanted the fashionable homes facing Farragut Square where once lived Admiral Dewey, Governor Alexander "Boss" Shepherd, Vice-President Fairbanks, and Leland Stanford. Just west of Connecticut on I Street, a garish drugstore has replaced the home of Jefferson Davis; and peddlers of coins, jewelry, eyeglasses, and real estate have subdivided the former Oliver Wendell Holmes house in the same block.

There are a few notable exceptions. The handsome

John Russell Pope-designed home of Vice-President Levi Morton at 1500 Rhode Island has been preserved by its trade association occupant. James G. Blaine's red gingerbread house at 2000 Massachusetts, later occupied by the air brake inventor George Westinghouse, is appropriately the headquarters of a railroad association. Across the street is the town house of House Speaker Nicholas Longworth in which his vivacious widow, Alice Roosevelt Longworth, has lived for some forty years.

In this Dupont Circle area, private clubs and foreign governments have saved many of the better mansions. The fashionable Washington Club occupies the salons of Eleanor (Cissy) Patterson at No. 15 on the Circle, where President Coolidge lived in 1927 while the White House underwent repairs. The intellectual Cosmos Club has Sumner Wells' château at 2121 Massachusetts. The Society of the Cincinnati has Anderson House across the street, scene of many formal dinners honoring foreign dignitaries before the State Department reception rooms were added.

Dupont Circle itself, a lovely shaded park at the intersection of Massachusetts, Connecticut, New Hampshire, Nineteenth, and P, has changed personality but not its essential character as one of the city's most inviting rest stops. Once a gossip center for nannies sunning the children of the neighborhood elite, it now attracts embassy employees, students from many lands, and other young people who inhabit the boardinghouses and apartments nearby. Summer twilight habitués typically gather at the feet of a bearded guitarist or drape themselves over the graceful fountain erected by the rich descendants of an obscure Civil War admiral, Samuel Francis du Pont.

Kalorama

Kalorama Heights, a few blocks northwest of Dupont Circle, has uniquely retained its intended character as an elegant residential quarter interspersed by embassies, notably the French, which has occupied the palatial John Hays Hammond home at 2221 Kalorama for thirty years. Originally the estate of Joel Barlow, a literary figure who purchased the heights at Jefferson's suggestion for fourteen thousand dollars, Kalorama takes its name from the Greek word for "beautiful view." The view of the city has since vanished behind hotel and office buildings; but Kalorama has resisted commercial incursions and gained distinction as the youngest of the city's sections with a legitimate historic claim: the only neighborhood in which five twentieth-century presidents have lived. Fortunately, their homes and those of other prominent figures remain intact. Wilson lived his last years at 2340 S, now a public museum. Hoover lived a few doors away at 2300 S while he was Secretary of Commerce. Franklin Roosevelt, as Assistant Secretary of the Navy under Wilson, lived at 2131 R. Taft lived at 2215 Wyoming after he left the White House to serve as Chief Justice. And Harding, as an Ohio senator, lived at 2314 until he moved to the White House. Also, Chief Justice Charles Evans Hughes lived at 2223 R, and Justice Louis Brandeis at 2205 California.

The oldest house in Kalorama is "The Lindens," a handsome Georgian residence built in 1754 for the British colonial governor of Massachusetts. It was uprooted from its original site in Danvers, Massachusetts, and reconstructed at 2401 Kalorama Road in 1937 by George Maurice Morris, whose widow lives in it. Virtually every Kalorama town house shows individuality of design and a spaciousness rarely attainable in Georgetown and other old sections of the city.

At the western tip of the Kalorama triangle is the section's newest and most elaborate structure, the Islamic Center, popularly called the Mosque. The Mosque is a house of worship for Washington's three thousand Moslems. They are ceremoniously called to prayers from the Mosque's graceful minaret each Friday shortly before or after noon, the precise time being determined by the calendar. An institute, consisting of library and classrooms for study of Islamic culture and languages and located in the two wings of the center, is dedicated to promoting better understanding between America and the Moslem world.

The Islamic Center, which cost over two million dollars, is a joint undertaking of the twenty-one Moslem countries, whose ambassadors at Washington all serve on its board of directors. Its rich furnishings were gifts from all parts of the Moslem world: the luxurious Persian rugs on which worshipers kneel and visitors may walk in stocking feet came from Iran; the pulpit, made from twelve thousand pieces of ivory and wood, came from Cairo; the grand chandelier was donated by Egypt; and the Turkish tiles were installed by artisans sent from the Middle East.

Designed by the Egyptian Ministry of Wakfs (re-

Blair House (left), facing Pennsylvania Avenue cater-cornered from the White House, comes to life as quarters for visiting heads of state. At the President's guesthouse, a gourmet's buffet (opposite) awaits the dignitary and his entourage at any hour. Recently refurbished with antiques (below), the house dates from 1810. It takes its name from the second owner, Francis Preston Blair, who built the adjoining Lee house for his daughter just before the Civil War. The Truman family lived here during renovation of the White House. A plaque at the front entrance commemorates Leslie Coffelt, the White house guard who was killed protecting President Truman from two gunmen on November 1, 1950.

From the first crocus and forsythia in March through cherry blossoms, dogwood blooms, and azaleas, to chrysanthemums in October, the nation's first city is in flower. In Rock Creek Park the dogwood leaves (left) have turned color and the blossoms have given way to berries. Visitors relax in the park amid riotous fall colors (below).

Washington, the city of trees, owes much of its beauty to the District's Governor Shepherd, who had seventy thousand saplings planted in the 1870s. The shaded parks (opposite) and tree-lined avenues make the capital's sultry summers bearable, its springs and autumns breath-taking.

The Washington zoo in Rock Creek Park, operated by the Smithsonian Institution, houses some three thousand animals, including this simian (opposite left) and several tigers, of which the one to the left is a rare white specimen from India. President Teddy Roosevelt set the style for fording Rock Creek (below) when he used to hike through the park. Two fords remain in use, at the north and south ends of the zoo.

ligious endowments) and constructed of Alabama limestone, the Center was dedicated in 1957 in a ceremony attended by President Eisenhower. Within its outer walls that face squarely on Massachusetts Avenue, the Mosque is set slightly askew so that worshipers face the Holy Kaaba at Mecca in far-off Saudi Arabia.

Northwest

Upper Connecticut Avenue, north of Kalorama, is swiftly becoming a canyon of tasteless apartment houses all the way to Chevy Chase, seven miles from the White House. West of Connecticut lies the Cleveland Park section, named for the President who once lived there in a house since torn down. Cleveland and three other presidents – Van Buren, Tyler, and Buchanan – used the magnificent Woodley mansion at 3000 Cathedral Avenue (now the Maret School) as a summer White House before the days of air conditioning.

This section of town is dominated by the Washington Cathedral, one of America's great ecclesiastical structures. Erected on Mount St. Alban, it vies with the Washington Monument and the Capitol for prominence on the city's skyline. Work on the cathedral began in 1907, when President Roosevelt laid the cornerstone, brought from Bethlehem. After more than half a century, work on its towering fourteenth-century Gothic spires continues. Over sixteen million dollars has been spent and a like sum is expected to be spent completing the cathedral during the next two decades. When completed, it will be the fifth largest of the world's cathedrals.

Although the cathedral is the seat of the presiding bishop of the Protestant Episcopal Church and the bishop of the diocese of Washington, Christians of many denominations worship here. During one period Russian, Syrian, and Polish Orthodox congregations were holding services at the same hour in different chapels. A Jewish congregation also worshiped here for a year until its synagogue was completed.

Following the Westminster Abbey precedent, the cathedral is intended as a tomb for the nation's illustrious dead. Woodrow Wilson, Admiral Dewey, and Cordell Hull are buried here, as is Ann Sullivan, Helen Keller's lifetime companion.

On the cathedral grounds are five educational institutions: Beauvoir elementary school; National Cathedral School for Girls and St. Albans School for Boys, both preparatory schools; College of Preachers for training of clergy; and College of Church Musicians for training organists and choirmasters.

West of the cathedral lie the newer residential districts of Wesley Heights, along Foxhall Road, and Spring Valley, where President Lyndon B. Johnson lived until he moved into the White House. Nestled in this affluent setting is the eighty-acre campus of the American University at Ward Circle, the intersection of Massachusetts and Nebraska avenues. The youngest of the city's four large universities, American was established by the bishops of the Methodist Episcopal Church and incorporated by Congress in 1893. While the uptown campus was being developed, graduate instruction began at a temporary downtown center in 1914 with an inaugural address by President Wilson. During World War I the uptown campus became a training base for the Army's gas and flame division; and here chemists discovered the deadly lewisite gas. After the war the graduate school downtown expanded into buildings east of the George Washington campus, purchased with funds allocated by the government as reimbursement for its wartime services. The liberal arts college finally opened uptown in 1925, and the campus has been expanding ever since. Today American, with over ten thousand students, is second only to G.W. in enrollment. It is coeducational and nonsectarian in its teaching but maintains its Methodist affiliation.

Changing Sixteenth

Like Massachusetts Avenue, Sixteenth Street beyond the business district has for decades been lined with fine mansions turned embassies. Notable are the Soviet Union's Embassy in the Pullman residence above L Street, Bulgaria's in the Charles Evans Hughes house at V Street, and Spain's in a house at Fuller, whose builder tried in vain to sell it to the government as a home for vice-presidents. New apartments are going up, one of them where Senator Robert M. La Follette lived at Park Road. The street's impressive religious institutions remain, such as the Jewish Community Center, All Souls Unitarian, the Mormon Temple, and National Baptist Memorial Church at the intersection of Columbia Road. Meridian Hill Park, a walled Italian-style garden with tumbling cascades, fountains, statues of Dante and Joan of Arc amid twelve acres of greenery, is still the city's most formal park, if a bit on the seedy side. Rock Creek Park, one of America's largest urban parks, bordering upper Sixteenth Street on the west for many blocks, is the city's principal family playground. From dawn to dusk through much of the year, its bridle paths, hiking trails, golf course, picnic spots, and winding parkways invite retreat from the clanging city. Its zoo, with Smokey the Bear and the white tiger and the fords through Rock Creek at either end, delights more youngsters than anything else in town. The park's outdoor Carter Barron Amphitheater, on a starlit summer's night, is incomparable for ballet and popular entertainment.

The most significant change in upper Sixteenth is in the residential section around the amphitheater. Washington's most successful Negro business and professional men have built or purchased expensive houses in several residential pockets between Sixteenth and the park, where not long ago only whites could live. The largest of these is in the northern apex of the District just before Sixteenth Street enters Silver Spring, Maryland—as far as one can get in the District from the areas of wretchedness occupied by poor Negroes downtown. The great green divide, Rock Creek Park, separates black and white Washington. Few Negroes penetrate the city's most desirable neighborhoods west of the park except as domestic servants. East of the park, however, there are vast areas of the upper District—Brightwood, Petworth, Brookland, and Kenilworth—in which middle-class Negroes live in neat, pleasant neighborhoods, tending lawns and gardens, painting shutters just as did the whites who preceded them before departing for the racially exclusive developments that sprang up in suburban Maryland and Virginia after the war. Segregation in public places in Washington vanished in the mid-fifties, but residential integration is still rare in the mid-sixties. One exception is in the upper Georgia Avenue area above Walter Reed Hospital, where citizens of both races, organized as Neighbors, Inc., have demonstrated the practicability of the mixed neighborhood.

Northeast

The Brookland section of the Northeast quadrant draws a million pilgrims every year. They are bound for a spiritual-academic island visually dominated by the magnificent Byzantine dome of America's largest Catholic church, the National Shrine of the Immaculate Conception. The shrine stands on the edge of the campus of Catholic University facing Michigan Avenue. Like the Washington Cathedral, the shrine is a work of delicate art and craftsmanship. Its cornerstone was laid in 1920 and the crypt church completed in 1926. The upper church, with its bell tower and great dome of vivid blue, yellow, and red tiles, was dedicated in 1959. Work on the interior will continue for years. As funds become available, the buff brick interior walls are faced with marble, the plastered interior domes furnished with mosaics depicting scenes of holy splendor. Over twenty-one million dollars has been spent of the estimated thirty-five million the completed shrine is expected to cost.

Catholic University's 140-acre campus, largest in Washington, was founded on the sixty-acre Middleton estate and the cornerstone laid in 1888 before an assembly of clerical and secular dignitaries, including President Cleveland. It was founded, and is controlled by, the Roman Catholic bishops of the United States to serve as the national pontifical university in America. By the turn of the century it had begun to fulfill one primary purpose as a fountainhead of higher learning for the various religious orders of the Church. Today there are eighty-seven houses of study and religious communities grouped around the campus, such as the Franciscans, whose monastery sits a few blocks north on South Dakota Avenue, and the Paulists, who established the Apostolic Mission College on campus.

Catholic U. emphasizes graduate work to educate not only leaders but leaders of leaders, particularly professors and priests to serve other Catholic colleges. Sometimes referred to as the West Point for United States Catholic clergy, it uses Latin as the classroom language in its schools of canon law and sacred theology. It has more graduate than undergraduate students in its student body of six thousand-plus. Originally only priests taught priests, but today lay faculty members outnumber priests three to one and two thirds of the students are lay men and women, most of them pursuing nonclerical studies in the arts and sciences. The diversity of secular studies is exemplified by the fame that Catholic U.'s drama department has gained.

Also northeast of the Capitol, between Florida and New York avenues, is unique Gallaudet College, the world's only school of higher learning for deaf mutes. Incorporated by Congress in 1857, the school was organized on land donated by Amos Kendall, a local philanthropist who had been President Jackson's Postmaster General. It was named for Dr. Thomas Hopkins Gallaudet, world-famous teacher of the deaf, whose son was its first superintendent. Initially it taught only children, but in 1864 President Lincoln signed an act authorizing it to confer degrees in liberal arts and sciences. Gallaudet today can take a child from kindergarten through graduate school if the student wishes to prepare for a teaching career, as many have. Its nearly eight hundred students include many from foreign countries. Congress appropriates funds annually to cover about 70 per cent of Gallaudet's operating budget, and in recent years has provided some fourteen million dollars for new facilities on its ninety-two-acre campus.

The Northeast quadrant is bisected by the meandering Anacostia River and pierced by the tracks of the Pennsylvania and the Baltimore and Ohio Railroads fanning north from Union Station. Much of the city's industrial property borders the tracks or the arterial roadways linking the capital with Baltimore.

Anacostia

Swinging south on the Kenilworth Freeway, the first link to be built in a complex of inner city expressways, one enters Anacostia, the Latinized name for the Nascotine Indians, who lived along the Anacostia River. The Anacostia flats are most famous as the camp ground of the bonus marchers. Longtime residents vividly recall the campfires and rude shacks of these desperate men whose descent on the capital brought home the harsh reality of the Depression to a city whose steady government payroll makes it all but impervious to the country's economic fluctuations. Similarly, Coxey's "army of the unemployed," a ragtag throng of several hundred who demanded relief from Congress, awakened Wash-

ington to the recession of the 1890s when they clashed with police on the Capitol grounds. After mounted officers and billy-club-swinging Capitol guards drove them off and arrested Coxey for walking on the grass, most of his army deserted the cause. The bonus marchers were more persistent. Of the some twenty thousand who arrived in the spring of 1932, about two thousand camped here through July after the Senate had killed a bonus bill passed by the House. When the veterans refused the government's offer of free transportation home, officials used the stick. General Douglas MacArthur was sent from Fort Myer on horseback leading a troop of cavalry with drawn sabers, infantry with fixed bayonets, and six whippet tanks. The commander of the tanks that blockaded the Anacostia bridge while troops cleared the flats and burned the camp would one day become President of the United States, Dwight D. Eisenhower.

The most famous home in Anacostia is a twenty-room Colonial at 1411 W Street, S.E., once owned by a wealthy slaveholder but later acquired by a Negro abolitionist, Frederick Douglass. After his escape from a Maryland plantation and rise to fame as writer and lecturer, Douglass became Recorder of Deeds for Washington, a post that ever since has traditionally gone to a Negro. The Park Service administers the house as a public museum.

The most promising development for Anacostia is a planned conversion of the 585-acre Bolling Air Base along the Potomac and Anacostia. Changing it into a model community with waterfront parkland would enhance the beauty and recreational value of this neglected section of town.

New Southwest

In a 560-acre triangle south of the Mall to the waterfront, the capital's worst slums have been supplanted by the city's most modern community. The redevelopment of Southwest Washington is uniquely different from restoration in Georgetown and Capitol Hill. Instead of trying to preserve and refurbish,

The interiors of expensively remodeled Capitol Hill houses are generally much more elaborate than those of the originals, built mostly as working-class homes after the Civil War. The exteriors follow the Georgetown style.

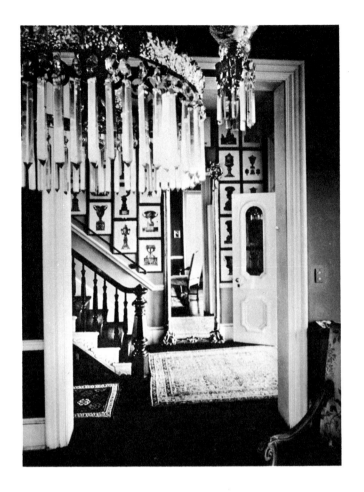

Woodrow Wilson House (left), at 2340 S Street, is the only one of five homes of former presidents in the Kalorama section that is open to the public. The Wilsons moved here from the White House. The President's widow lived on here after his death in 1924 and, before she died in 1961, arranged for it to be preserved with his mementos as a museum.

Decatur House (opposite), home of naval hero Stephen Decatur until his death in a duel, was later occupied by Henry Clay. Preserved for the public by the National Trust for Historic Preservation, its nineteenth-century furnishings include the pistols (above the mantel) used in the fatal exchange at the dueling ground in Bladensburg, Maryland, and the decanters pictured below.

Southwest has annihilated the past. Bulldozers not only obliterated the area's fifty-seven hundred dilapidated houses, reeking privies, and junk-strewn alleys; but city planners abolished the time-honored building lot system. In place of narrow lots marked off from city blocks, the Southwest plan allocated spacious parcels of land to developers to permit freedom of design. Some parcels were awarded on the basis of the best competitive designs. Chloethiel Woodard Smith, the architect for Capitol Park development, had some thirty acres on which to arrange four elevator apartment towers, clusters of two-story town houses, and open spaces. When completed, new Southwest will comprise about five thousand apartments and nine hundred town houses for middle- and upper-income residents and nearly a thousand public housing units for low-income families; churches, office buildings, schools, shops, a delightful waterfront of seafood houses and small-boat piers along the tranquil Washington channel, and a Florentine bridge of shops and restaurants across the channel to East Potomac Park and the new national aquarium.

Southwest has kept its few historic homes and integrated them neatly into the modern group design. The oldest are known as Wheat Row, at 1313–21 Fourth Street, the city's first row houses, built by speculators in 1793. At 456 N Street is a home built for Colonel Washington Lewis, a cousin of George Washington. On Sixth between N and M is the Law House, built in 1795 for Thomas Law, who married a granddaughter of Martha Washington. The Laws made it an early center of social life, entertaining such visiting dignitaries as Louis Philippe before he took the French throne. Law had a profound influence on the early character of this section of the city. After losing heavily in real-estate speculation in the 1790s, he and associates got a charter from Congress to build a canal through Southwest from the Anacostia River north to the foot of Capitol Hill, then west along what is now Constitution Avenue to the

Historic Georgetown's narrow streets are lined with interesting variations on an architectural theme protected against modernization by the Commission of Fine Arts. The Federal and Georgian houses include the city's oldest, finest, and most expensive residences. Jacqueline Kennedy moved from the White House into this house (opposite) owned by Averell Harriman, and later purchased a house nearby before moving with her children to New York.

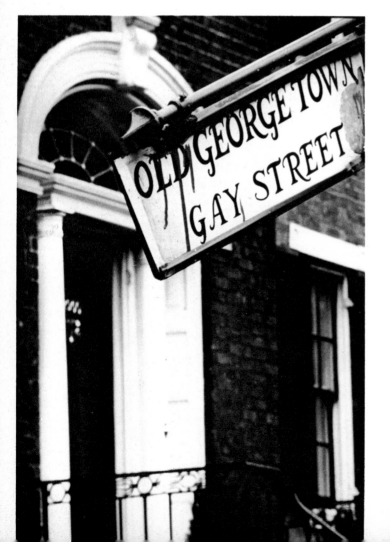

Potomac. Finished in 1815 but never a great success, the canal was filled during Shepherd's improvement program in 1873. Canal Street marks sections of its route. The canal and the railroad that later sliced across the top of Southwest from Virginia tended to wall off the area from the main body of the growing city. Instead of better residences, builders put up tiny brick row dwellings for workers. Until 1869 the city jail was at Greenleaf Point, where now stands Fort McNair at the confluence of the Anacostia with the Potomac. Seven conspirators in Lincoln's assassination were held, tried, and four of them hanged in this jail. John Wilkes Booth was buried there until removed to Baltimore.

Before the Southwest slums were razed in the early 1950s, the area was largely populated by poor Negroes. Over 70 per cent of their houses had no central heat and nearly half had no bathrooms. Appropriately, new Southwest offered the first new high-quality housing in the inner city to residents of both races. Negroes account for about 10 per cent of the occupants of private housing here and virtually all of the public housing. Most of the dispossessed residents moved to other slum areas that were spreading in a widening arc north of Union Station.

Hell's Bottom

The remaining slums cover Washington's most densely populated sections between Massachusetts Avenue and Howard University, west to 16th Street and east to the Anacostia River. To the prisoners of this rotting core the visible new city appears as a cold white glacier bearing down on them with relentless unconcern. They can find no high ground in these wretched lowlands of poverty, discontent, ignorance, crime, and hopelessness.

For generations Washington has had such estranged regions into which genteel folk feared to tread. A century ago the toughest section was called Murder Bay, a cluster of tar-paper shacks and junk heaps along the old Washington Canal behind the White House on the Ellipse and the Washington Monument grounds. The commercial heart of Murder Bay was a row of houses occupied by camp followers who catered to General Hooker's Union Division encamped nearby during the Civil War. "The Division," as this notorious red-light district came to be called, flourished and spread nearly to the foot of

Dumbarton Oaks, in Georgetown, once the estate of John C. Calhoun, gained international recognition as the site of the 1944 conference that drafted the proposed United Nations charter.

Capitol Hill until suffragettes in 1914 persuaded Congress to pass the red-light bill, ending open countenance of prostitution in Washington. The government later demolished "The Division" facing lower Fifteenth Street, to make way for its own Department of Commerce.

Besides Murder Bay, other notorious sections included Bloodfield in Southeast, and Rum Row, a collection of saloons and gambling dens near Fourteenth and Pennsylvania around the Willard Hotel. When they were cleaned up, vice traffic shifted north to Hell's Bottom, a section south of Soldiers' Home. To shield the less athletic old soldiers from the temptations of Hell's Bottom, Congress in 1891 prohibited sale of intoxicants within a mile of the home. Today the city's relatively tame vice remains near old Hell's Bottom, principally on Fourteenth and Seventh and T and U streets, N.W., the commercial heart of the inner city slums.

None of Washington's vice is controlled by organized crime syndicates. The most popular form of gambling is the numbers racket, a clandestine lottery based on three digits determined each day by the outcome of certain horse races. The lure of a 600 to 1 payoff for a winner, despite the 1,000 to 1 odds against the bettor, draws thousands of participants daily, most of them betting less than a dollar, some only nickels and dimes. The headquarters of a numbers writing operation is often moved each week to evade the police, whose suspicions about a given place must be backed up by five days' observation in order to establish a probable cause for a raid. The largest numbers operator ever apprehended by Washington police had a ten-thousand-dollar-a-day business. There are probably fewer than a dozen big gamblers doing five thousand dollars a day, realizing a net profit of about 20 to 25 per cent of their gross. Most of them in turn lose large sums gambling at nearby racetracks, in dice games at private social clubs, or on pilgrimages to Reno and Las Vegas.

Heroin is the most widely used narcotic in Washington. Most of it comes through the port of New York, some through Baltimore. Several of the city's twelve hundred or so addicts can usually be observed standing at Fourteenth and U streets, waiting with the requisite sum for a palmed delivery of capsulized escape. Though the police, like society, feel compelled to imprison homosexual and heterosexual prostitutes, they send dope addicts to D.C. General Hospital as required by law.

Most Washingtonians accept the city's vices but have become alarmed over its rising crime rate, particularly among juveniles. Serious felonies increased 83 per cent from 1957 to 1964. Every day in the District of Columbia sees an average of seven robberies, seven assaults, thirteen auto thefts, and twenty-three housebreakings. There are a dozen homicides every month and a woman is raped every other day. More than 90 per cent of these crimes are committed east of Rock Creek Park in black Washington, mostly in the rotten core of the inner city. Negroes are not only the perpetrators but the victims of most of the city's crimes. Unable to escape this vast urban concentration camp, many are first- or second-generation immigrants from the rural South, unskilled, uneducated, and unemployed, the bitter fruit of the old plantation system.

Forge of Freedom

Ever since the capital, sanctuary of the national conscience, was located south of the Mason-Dixon line, it has suffered the moral agony of its racial conditions. Of the town's 3,210 inhabitants in 1800, 623 were slaves and 123 were free Negroes, one of whom, Benjamin Bannecker, was appointed by George Washington to help organize the new capital. By 1830 there were more than six thousand free Negroes here but just as many slaves. Conditions of servitude outraged sensitive souls. Slave ships plied the Potomac, unloading their black cargoes into "Georgia pens" along the waterfront, there to await auction time at local markets. This was the Washington that impelled Thomas Moore to write:

Even here beside the proud Potomac's streams...
The medley mass of pride and misery
Of whips and charters, manacles and rights
Of slaving blacks and democratic whites...

The abolition movement took hold in the capital about 1815 when a Negro woman, about to be sold apart from her husband, leaped from an attic window of a tavern at Thirteenth and F. Her cries

The National Gallery's permanent collection of twenty-seven thousand paintings, sculptures, prints, and decorative art, representing the work of some two thousand artists, fascinates visitors.

Intersections of the city's diagonal avenues named for the states are marked by many circular or rectangular parks. Dupont Circle, where Connecticut, Massachusetts, and New Hampshire avenues come together, is a popular meeting place.

awakened the mayor's wife – and the city's humanitarian instincts. Abolition gained such adherents in Washington as Senators William H. Seward and Salmon P. Chase and Congressman Abraham, Lincoln. Washington churches and houses in Georgetown became "underground railroad" stations. Harriet Tubman, the courageous Negro leader on this escape route, slept in a Washington park beneath a sign advertising a reward for her capture.

Congress at length prohibited the slave traffic in Washington as one provision of the historic Compromise of 1850. Slave ownership was not abolished until 1862, however, when the Civil War had removed slavery's influential defenders from Congress.

After Lincoln signed the Emancipation Proclamation on January 1, 1863, Negroes flocked to Washington, an exodus that continues to this day. A Freedmen's Village accommodating fifteen hundred ex-slaves was established on Robert E. Lee's old estate, now Arlington Cemetery.

Negro leaders hoped to make Washington the center of Negro civilization in its highest form. The government created the Freedmen's Bureau in 1865 to foster new opportunities and better social conditions for ex-slaves. Two years later, Howard University, named for the Civil War general Oliver Otis Howard, who headed the bureau, was founded here. Congress enacted legislation allowing Negroes to vote in Washington's local elections; city ordinances were adopted prohibiting racial discrimination in places of public accommodation; a few government jobs began to open to Negroes; and the city directory in 1869 discontinued using a *c* to denote colored residents.

The high promise of this beginning was compromised after the Reconstruction era, however. In 1874 Congress repealed the city's home-rule statute, and asserted authority to manage the city's affairs, partly because of congressional objections to Governor Shepherd's big spending on public works and partly because of the return to Congress of white supremacists from the South. Lacking a vote, local residents formed neighborhood citizens associations in the 1870s to gain a voice in the management of local affairs. Negroes, unwelcome to these groups, formed their own civic associations. White property owners and real-estate interests skillfully used the citizens associations to resist the free movement of Negroes outside the traditional colored blocks. Builders sub-divided the long building lots, which L'Enfant had provided to give each house its garden, and erected cheap row housing facing the alleys. By the turn of the century, about a fifth of Washington's ninety thousand Negroes lived in three hundred alleys such as Pig Alley, Louse Alley, and Slop Bucket Row. Field hands, finding no work in white-collar Washington, turned to ragpicking and to crime and became the progenitors of today's lost generation of despairing multitudes who swell the rosters of the welfare office, the police court, the charity wards, who try their luck on the numbers, take solace in the bottle or the needle, and blame their troubles on "The Man." Washington, in a word, became a Jim Crow town. Negroes were turned away from restaurants and ice-cream parlors and, later, from taverns and other public places catering to whites. Government hiring practices, reflecting white-supremacy attitudes, disheartened Negro leaders who had expected more from the Teddy Roosevelt, Taft, and Wilson administrations.

Although Negroes fought in France to help save the world for democracy, race relations only worsened in Washington after their return. On a hot night in July 1919, rumors had spread among servicemen that the wife of a sailor had been attacked by a Negro. About a hundred sailors, soldiers, and marines on leave invaded the old Southwest and beat up several colored men and women. Negroes retaliated by importing guns from Baltimore and distributing them at Seventh and T during the next several days. Then the Washington *Post*, not yet the liberal institution it was to become, published an inflammatory article on its front page in effect inviting all available servicemen to join in a "cleanup" of the colored sections. The city's seven hundred police, aided by four hundred cavalrymen from Fort Myer and four hundred marines from Quantico, were unable to control the mobs that surged through the streets. When it was over, two policemen, one marine, and two Negroes lay dead, hundreds were injured, and racial antagonism became a fixture of a period marked elsewhere by the night riders of the Ku Klux Klan.

Washington Negroes reacted to segregation by creating their own caste system based on pigmentation. They, too, favored those of lightest color. At the turn of the century Negro society in Washington was dominated by seven hundred octoroons and eleven hundred quadroons who augmented the advantage

The baseball Senators have a loyal following, even though Washington, as the saying goes, is first in war, first in peace, and last in the American League.

Fans of the professional football Redskins pack Washington's new stadium on the banks of the Anacostia, and cheerleaders urge the players on.

of light skins with other advantages such as old family ties to free Negroes, money, education, and positions in business, real estate, banking, and politics. Washington's aristocratic Negro "Four Hundred" comprised sixty to seventy families. Many might easily have passed for white. They were the descendants of white planters and favorite slaves who were freed before emancipation. By carefully marrying off their children within the group, they maintained a closed society. One Negro church painted its entrance hall a creamy beige and turned away worshipers whose color was any darker.

The Negroes for decades kept all dark-skinned Negroes out of Dunbar High School, which was considered the college preparatory school for children "of quality." Washington's other high schools for Negroes in the long period of segregated schools were Armstrong and Phelps, which emphasized the vocational philosophy of Booker T. Washington, and Cardoza, which specialized in preparation for clerical jobs. These schools educated the second-tier mulattoes. At the start of this century there were about eighteen thousand mulattoes of "doe-nut or ginger-cake color [who] said those blacker than themselves should be ignored," notes one historian. The bottom tier was composed largely of full-bloods who worked as laborers or domestics or were unemployed. Until recent times, most of the children in the bottom tier seldom received more than an elementary education.

As the bridge designed to cross these chasms of caste, culture, and color, Howard University just north of Florida Avenue commands a brooding view of black Washington. In its first half century Howard concentrated on bringing its students up to the college level. In 1898, for instance, only forty-two of its 367 students were taking college courses. Since then Howard has become the stellar institution of higher learning for Negroes in the United States, the gateway to a better life. One determined charwoman at the Library of Congress whose husband was a dining-car waiter before getting a government job as a printer, told her three children, "Either think with your head or work with your hands like I do." One son, a Howard graduate, holds a responsible government position in architecture.

Howard has graduated more Negroes in medicine, dentistry, pharmacy, engineering, music, law, and social work than have all the colleges of the Old South combined. It has graduated more teachers than anything, most of whom went South because segregated schools offered more teaching jobs to Negroes than did integrated schools in the North. Because of Howard, Washington has attained some measure of that high civilization envisioned after emancipation: the last census showed that nearly forty thousand Negroes in Washington had been to college and one in ten Negro families earned at least ten thousand dollars a year.

Education, alone, could not unlock every door. It took more direct action to smash segregation, and sometimes it came unexpectedly. In 1939 the Daughters of the American Revolution aroused national sympathy for Miss Marian Anderson and her race by denying her the use of their Constitution Hall. Interior Secretary Ickes offered the steps of the Lincoln Memorial, and seventy-five thousand persons came for her Easter Sunday recital. This incident may have been the turning point in the long struggle against discrimination; at any rate, the white conscience had been visibly pricked.

Simultaneously, legal scholars at Howard, directing a new quest for civil rights, entered the courts. After their first victory in 1938, one triumph followed another until the high court in 1954 struck down segregation in the public schools. Washington immediately integrated its schools with scant local dissent. And the old laws prohibiting discrimination in Washington's public places were held to be still valid, thus opening theaters, hotels, restaurants, and the like for the first time in three quarters of a century.

What the courts did to Jim Crow in Washington, the arrival of the black diplomats from the new Africa did to the colored caste system. "Status used to be determined by how close to white you were," explained a graduate of Dunbar and Howard. "Now it's how close you are to full blood. Tradition used to be the determining factor. Now it's heritage." Howard contributed to this new sense of identity by admitting more foreign students than any other American college (one out of seven students in recent years). Today its campus is a community of blending

Among Washington's six major universities, Howard is unique—a federally supported institution launched after the Civil War to educate Negroes. Students of varied national and racial origins, such as these cheerleaders, can be found on its campus on a knoll overlooking downtown Washington.

The National Shrine of the Immaculate Conception, America's largest Roman Catholic cathedral (opposite), on the edge of the Catholic University campus in northeast Washington, attracts a million pilgrims each year. The Roman Catholic bishops of the United States, who founded and operate Catholic University, periodically meet in northeast Washington. The Knights of Columbus (right), in full regalia, gather to honor them.

Sea food fresh from Chesapeake Bay is sold on the Maine Avenue waterfront.

shades and features, suggesting the world in microcosm. The intellectual growth transplanted from Howard to schoolrooms and parliaments the world around will perhaps prove to be the most lasting contribution of black Washington to this age.

Washington's prolific Negro community has given the capital the reputation of being the first major American city with more colored than white residents. This is a half-truth. Negroes constitute 55 per cent of the population within the District; but in greater Washington, whites predominate by a three-to-one ratio as they have done for the last half century.

Negro predominance in the inner city does, of course, possess political significance. Ostensibly, the city is governed by three commissioners appointed by the President. In fact, the commissioners are timid servants of the sovereigns of Capitol Hill, who determine, along with great issues of war and peace, the salaries of District teachers and policemen, the tax on liquor, the strings on welfare payments, and the size of rockfish sold in local markets. Ever since Congress took away home-rule power from District residents nearly a century ago, prosegregation congressmen have blocked all legislation to return it. They claim credit back home for preventing the possible election of a Negro mayor. Worse, some of the city's overseers on the House District Committee, attempting to demonstrate that racial mixing won't work, frustrate the city's most progressive attempts to meet its social problems by curbing necessary urban re-

newal and slashing school and welfare budgets.

During the past decade influential citizens have tried to offset this lopsided congressional power through such organizations as the Federal City Council. Its progressive businessmen backers, favoring reforms and redevelopment, contrast with the conservative business interests behind the Board of Trade, chief defender of the status quo, and certain special interests such as parking lot operators speculating in real estate. The system itself by which District affairs are managed guards the status quo. The system is replete with commissions, boards, and committees that simply plan and suggest, but it is stultified by the absence of any ultimate single possessor of the power to act.

The very survival of the District as a viable community under this form of nongovernment is remarkable in itself. Yet survival is not enough. Blight is spreading through the old city faster than renewal in all its private and public forms. The 1950 census showed that one in every eight houses was substandard; by 1960, after all the slums of Southwest had been razed, and additional poor housing had been reconstructed in Georgetown, Foggy Bottom, and Capitol Hill, the census showed that one of every six houses was substandard. The National Capital Planning Commission is seeking measures to check this cancerous growth. Whether this proud capital, or any contemporary metropolis, can cure its urban cancer is one of the most imperative public questions of this affluent age.

Southwest, once Washington's worst slum, is being transformed into the city's most modern residential section. The largest urban renewal project in America, it is composed of apartments and town houses that extend from the Maine Avenue waterfront to South Capitol Street.

*Lincoln Memorial Bridge, one of the gateways to the outer city,
is jammed with rush-hour traffic. Many other bridges also
connect the capital with its burgeoning suburbs.*

CHAPTER THIRTEEN

The Outer City

A recent visitor of Alice Roosevelt Longworth's, taking tea in her comfortable old town house near Dupont Circle, was asked where he lives. When he said Chevy Chase, Washington's favorite dowager hooted, "Oh, you live in the country." This "old Washington" point of view illuminates Washington's most swiftly changing dimension. Chevy Chase does have its country club, in fact two of them – but they are miles from the country now.

Since World War II, Chevy Chase, Falls Church, Bethesda, Alexandria, Silver Spring, Clarendon, Takoma Park, and other satellite towns have spread across pastoral Virginia and Maryland, dividing and subdividing like giant amoebas until they are hardly distinguishable from one another. They maintain their identity chiefly as political units of the outer city.

More attractive than most city suburbs, Washington's environs are universally clean because of the city's lack of heavy industry. Though dominated by low-down-payment ramblers and miniature manors, the outer city has nevertheless succumbed to the pressures of population and profit. Builders sell row dwellings as "town houses" twenty miles from downtown. And apartment houses have risen at such a rate that population density is fast becoming as great as in the District. As one suburbanite from Iowa put it, "My family just can't believe there are more people in this development than in all of Mediapolis."

The resultant traffic congestion intensifies the warfare between city beautifiers and commercial interests. When faced with the cost of beauty in public works, Congress tends to side with the late Senator Bob Kerr's derision of "ass-thetics." It will strap a six-lane concrete belt around Washington's expanding waist, throw a half dozen utilitarian spans across the river, dissect parks and residential neighborhoods with high speed expressways, but balk (because of

the cost) at putting parked cars out of sight underground. Washington's commitment to the principle of one man, one vote, takes second place to its insistence on one man, one auto, and the God-given right to park it on public property each day. As Will Rogers once put it, "Politics ain't worrying this country one tenth as much as parking space." Washington's worst eyesores are no longer its temporary government buildings but its temporary parking lots, jammed with the chariots of the invaders from the outer city.

The Science Ring

A less noticeable, but more broadly significant, postwar phenomenon of the outer city is its prominence in the world of modern science. Washington today rivals Boston, New York, and Los Angeles for the greatest concentration of scientists and engineers in the country. The formation of a ring of more than thirty government laboratories and more than three hundred private research and development plants around the capital has been stimulated largely by government explorations in the fields of medicine, outer space, agriculture, and weapons. Today about 70 per cent of all scientific research in the United States is nourished by the federal government, currently at the rate of ten billion dollars a year, and a generous share feeds Washington's growing science complex.

The largest organization is the National Institutes of Health at Bethesda, Maryland, headquarters for the nation's war on cancer, heart disease, mental illness, arthritis, and other ills that plague mankind. Here more than two thousand scientists and doctors on a staff of some ten thousand are engaged in four-

The Virginia side of the outer city is George Washington country. He roamed its woods and hills as a young surveyor, helped to lay out the city of Alexandria, and frequented its famous Gadsby's Tavern. While serving as the nation's first President when the capital was at New York, he returned to the Potomac Valley to select the site of the permanent capital. Washington's rifle, powder horn, and knapsack, shown here in the woods where he might have used them, are from the collection in the museum at Mount Vernon overlooking the Potomac, ten miles south of Alexandria. Great Falls is pictured opposite.

George Washington's home, Mount Vernon (following pages), is glimpsed through the trees across the Potomac.

196

The old-fashioned carrousel, with its brass ring, draws
multitudes of children to Great Falls Park, Virginia.

Race tracks in nearby Maryland whet the sporting instincts of residents of the relatively puritanical nation's capital. The International, run on the grass at Laurel on Veterans Day, features thoroughbreds from many foreign countries and Washington society (following page).

teen hundred research projects designed to find the secrets of better health and longer life. N.I.H. also funnels millions of dollars annually into medical schools, universities, hospitals and other non-federal institutions and it awards thousands of annual grants to individual scientists to support their research.

Federal medical research here dates from the late nineteenth century when the government's Hygienic Laboratory was shifted from Staten Island, New York, to Washington. Renamed the National Institutes of Health in 1930, this child of the storied U. S. Public Health Service was moved to its present Wisconsin Avenue site in 1938 after Mr. and Mrs. Luke I. Wilson of Bethesda donated the land for this purpose. Congress, meanwhile, responding to public demand for an intensified attack on a single dread disease, created the National Cancer Institute in 1937, to be followed after the war by other separate institutes, most recently one devoted to child health and human development from pre-conception genetic resources to old age. Today N.I.H. occupies a compound of some thirty buildings, including an attractive modern creation housing the National Library of Medicine.

Over the years N.I.H. scientists have discovered that pellagra results from dietary deficiency, developed a vaccine for Rocky Mountain spotted fever, found that one type of cancer can be suppressed by chemotherapy, developed an effective and simple emergency treatment for burn shock, and partially cracked the so-called genetic code, which lies at the heart of the systematic reproduction of all living matter. They are still working on the common cold.

Across Wisconsin Avenue the world-famous Bethesda Naval Medical Center, like Walter Reed Army Medical Center at Sixteenth and Alaska, N.W., performs research, treats ailing VIPs and military and civilian personnel flown in from all over the world for specialized treatment.

The heart of space research here is Goddard Space Flight Center on a five-hundred-fifty-acre campus near Greenbelt, Maryland. Established in 1959 as the first major American lab devoted to peaceful research in space and named after Dr. Robert H. Goddard, the American rocket pioneer, it has a staff of thirty-seven hundred and an annual budget of nearly a half billion dollars. Goddard conducts the satellite program designed to map conditions between the earth and moon, administers space tracking stations located around the globe, and operates a mammoth bank of computers serving Cape Kennedy, Florida.

Nearby the Department of Agriculture operates its famous eleven-thousand-acre Beltsville experimental farm, complete with laboratories, greenhouses, orchards, pastures, and fields for fundamental and applied research covering the wide range of poultry, livestock, foodstuffs and their production to benefit farmer and consumer. The small Beltsville turkey, which has become popular in this country, is one appetizing result of this research.

Most military research and development in Washington's science ring is performed at the Naval Ordnance Laboratory near Silver Spring, Maryland; the Naval Research Laboratory across the Potomac from Alexandria; the Naval Oceanographic Office at Suitland, Maryland; Fort Belvoir, Virginia, home of the U. S. Army Corps of Engineers south of Mount Vernon; David W. Taylor Model Basin near Cabin John, Maryland, which tests new designs for civilian as well as military vessels; and in scores of private industrial plants specializing in electronics, missile propellants, computers, communications, plastics, optics, acoustics, and other industrial frontiers of this age.

The location of these laboratories and industrial parks, along with the shift of the Bureau of Standards to Gaithersburg, Maryland, the Atomic Energy Commission to Germantown, Maryland, and the Central Intelligence Agency to McLean, Virginia, helped stimulate the rapid residential growth of the outer city. In addition, two completely new towns, Reston, Virginia, and Columbia, Maryland, are rising on the fringe of greater Washington, both uniquely planned to integrate the most desirable features of city and suburb for their residents.

Alexandria

Anchored by deep historic roots, Alexandria, Virginia, secures its individual identity against the tides of contemporary suburban sprawl. Older than the national capital by half a century, it glories in having been the home town of George Washington, George Mason, and Robert E. Lee. Washington helped found the town by surveying its streets in 1749.

Located on the Potomac and on the King's Highway that ran between Williamsburg and New England, Alexandria flourished as a port and popular social center whose taverns attracted the stagecoach trade and the nearby planters, the Lees, Washingtons, Custises, Masons, and Fairfaxes. Its harbor was crowded with ships bringing from Europe the best that Virginia tobacco could buy for the plantations.

Alexandria's prosperity, like Georgetown's, lasted little more than a century. During the Civil War it remained within the Union, hence was spared much of the destruction suffered by other Southern towns. After the war it slowly declined but was sustained by a few industries until the growth of Washington and the federal payroll brought Alexandria a new era of prosperity.

Today Alexandria basks in the sunshine of spiraling real-estate values. Fashionable Washingtonians have discovered its charming restored Colonial, Georgian, and Federal period houses. Like Georgetown in this respect, it has attracted VIP residents, only more slowly because it is farther from the city's heart.

The best preserved of the historically interesting private homes include those that once belonged to Dr. James Craik (210 Duke Street), George Washington's physician throughout the Revolution; Dr. William Brown (212 South Fairfax Street), surgeon general of the Continental Army, who wrote the first *American Pharmacopaeia* in 1778; George William Fairfax (207 Prince Street), one of Washington's instructors in engineering, later owned by Robert Adam, founder of the Masonic Lodge, and still later by Alexandria's Civil War congressman, Lewis MacKenzie, who installed the town's first bathroom with a tub whose overflow spilled into Prince Street; the Lawrason house (301 South Saint Asaph Street), where Lafayette stayed; Robert E. Lee's boyhood home (607 Oronoco Street); and Captain's Row, a picturesque cluster of unpretentious eighteenth-century houses facing Prince Street's cobblestones laid by Hessian prisoners after the Revolutionary War.

The most significant historic building in Alexandria is Carlyle House at 123 North Fairfax Street. Built in 1752 by John Carlyle, a Scottish merchant who was one of the town's founders, the stately Georgian mansion is a public museum furnished with period pieces. General Braddock met here with five royal governors to plan the campaign against the French and Indians in 1755 and to recommend a tax on the Colonies to help pay for the war. After the Revolutionary War, a Carlyle House meeting on

tariffs helped stimulate the calling of the Constitutional Convention.

Gadsby's Tavern at Royal and Cameron streets, comprising the City Tavern built in 1752 and City Hotel built in 1792, is of comparable historic interest. George Washington not only slept here but used it as his military headquarters several times, celebrated his last birthday here, and from its steps reviewed his troops for the last time and reputedly declared, "Fall out, men, and go home. The wars are over." A convention meeting here approved George Mason's liberal declaration of rights, which influenced Jefferson's draft of the Declaration of Independence a year later. Lafayette was feted here on his last visit to America in 1824.

Alexandria has two Colonial churches: the austere Old Presbyterian Meeting House, 321 South Fairfax Street, where many patriots were buried; and Christ Church, at Cameron and Columbus streets, typical of Georgian church architecture, where Washington, Lee, and many presidents have worshiped. Roosevelt and Churchill observed a national day of prayer here together a month after Pearl Harbor. Other old public places are the Apothecary Shop on Fairfax Street, the Friendship Veterans Fire Engine Co. at 107 South Alfred Street, which has a fire engine presented by Washington in 1775, and the museum and tower overlooking the city at George Washington Masonic National Memorial.

Plantation Mansions

Most romantic of all the landmarks of the outer city are the great old houses of the planters, splendidly restored and furnished and serenely sited on the rolling countryside of Virginia. Mount Vernon, Woodlawn, Gunston Hall evoke awe and envy for the tranquillity of plantation life. The Custis-Lee mansion, surrounded by the graves of war dead in Arlington, reminds one of the cost of the plantation system to those who fought over the issues it raised.

The Lee house was built in 1802 by Martha Washington's grandson, George Washington Parke Custis, on an estate of eleven hundred acres. He named it Arlington after the ancestral homestead of the Custis family on Virginia's eastern shore. The estate at that time lay within the borders of the District of Columbia, as did Alexandria. But after Virginia protested the location of the government buildings on the Maryland side of the river, Congress in 1846 retroceded Virginia's share, most of which was named Arlington County.

The only Custis daughter was married to Lieutenant-Colonel Robert E. Lee in the mansion in 1831. Six of their seven children were born here, and Lee took leave from the Army to manage the estate after his father-in-law's death in 1857, only four years before making the agonizing decision that caused the Lees to depart from Arlington forever.

During the Civil War, Arlington became an armed camp, and the mansion served as headquarters for the Union general commanding nearby forts that guarded the capital. The government subsequently confiscated the estate for nonpayment of taxes and set aside two hundred acres for a national cemetery; but the Supreme Court later returned title to Lee's son, who sold it to the government for a hundred and fifty thousand dollars. It stood empty until after 1925, when Congress approved its restoration and its designation as a memorial to the Confederate Commander. Its portico affords a magnificent view of Washington and is a stirring view itself; at night, its lighted columns beacon the traveler from the bluff above the Virginia end of Memorial Bridge.

Mount Vernon lies south of Alexandria at the end of the most refreshing ten-mile drive in the outer city. The scenic parkway following the Potomac is shielded by trees from the housing developments that crowd the old plantation lands to the west.

The parkway passes Wellington farm, once part of Mount Vernon's five-thousand-acre estate, which Washington gave for life tenure to Tobias Lear, his faithful secretary; and Collingwood, another part of the original estate, which became notorious as a Colonial dueling ground; and Fort Hunt, one of the Civil War-era outposts used as a prison camp during the Spanish-American War.

The Mount Vernon property, patented in 1674 by George Washington's great-grandfather, was inherited by George in 1754, five years before he married a wealthy widow, Martha Custis. His half-brother Lawrence had built a house here in the 1740s, naming it after his British commander, Admiral Edward Vernon. George renovated and enlarged it in 1773 and drew plans for the later addition of the banquet room and library at either end. After returning from the Revolutionary War, Washington developed his farms and gardens until recalled six years later in 1789 to accept the presidency under the new constitutional government. In 1799, two years after he returned to private life, Washington died and was entombed at Mount Vernon. His widow was buried beside him in 1802. The estate passed first to a nephew, Bushrod Washington, a justice of the Supreme Court, and then to subsequent heirs until it was acquired for two hundred thousand dollars in 1858 by the Mount Vernon Ladies' Association, a society organized by Ann Pamela Cunningham of South Carolina to restore and preserve it as a national shrine.

Congress tried to move Washington's remains to a crypt in the Capitol, the Virginia legislature wanted to enshrine his body at Richmond, and a drunken workman at Mount Vernon, after being fired, broke into the old tomb and tried to steal the President's skull. None succeeded, but the grave-robber was caught with the skull of a Washington nephew buried in the same tomb. Consequently, a new tomb was built on a slope overlooking the Potomac. In its outer vault were placed the sarcophagi of George and Martha, in its inner vault a number of their heirs, and in 1855 the doors were locked and the key thrown into the river.

Today Mount Vernon, unsurpassed among America's historic homes, is visited by well over a million visitors annually. Many of them continue three miles farther to Woodlawn, the handsome plantation given as a wedding present by Washington to his adopted daughter, Nelly Parke Custis, when she married his favorite nephew, Lawrence Lewis. Woodlawn's handsome Georgian mansion, designed by the first architect of the Capitol, William Thornton, passed out of the family in the mid-nineteenth century, was owned in the 1920s by Senator Oscar Underwood of Alabama and later by Roosevelt's Secretary of War, Harry Woodring. It was acquired in 1948 by the National Trust for Historic Preservation and restored and furnished as a public museum.

Gunston Hall, George Mason's mansion a few miles farther south, was built in 1758. It is a relatively plain brick house with extraordinarily fine interior finishings, notably the carved woodwork of the drawing room, and superb gardens divided by magnificent boxwood hedges. Mason wrote Virginia's Declaration of Rights here. He also built a schoolhouse, now restored, in which his nine children were educated by a tutor who lived in the loft.

Washington today rivals Boston, New York, and Los Angeles as a center for scientists and engineers. They work in government laboratories and in more than three hundred private research and development firms that ring the capital. One of the most unusual laboratories is the Navy's David W. Taylor Model Basin on the Potomac near Cabin John, Maryland, where new designs for war and commercial vessels and planes are tested in huge tanks and wind tunnels.

Pohick Church, built in 1769–74 to serve these plantation families, still stands. Its rector, "Parson" Weems, is said to have started the apocryphal cherry-tree yarn about his most famous parishioner. During the Civil War, Union cavalry stabled their horses in the church, using the font as a trough, and practicing marksmanship against the east wall. Bullet scars are still visible.

Other Virginia Landmarks

The Civil War battlefield at Manassas is a favorite souvenir-hunting ground. Fashionable Washingtonians, anticipating an easy Union victory in the battle of Bull Run, drove in their carriages to Manassas to watch but retreated in terror when the Confederates routed the North's defenders there.

The Fairfax Courthouse, built in 1800, has pre-served the wills of George and Martha Washington and court records showing arrests "for failing to attend church services" and for "profane swearing." Mrs. Calvin Coolidge, on visiting the courthouse, remarked that she had thought all swearing was profane. In this seat of Fairfax County General John S. Mosby conducted one of his most spectacular raids, capturing Union General Edwin H. Stoughton, his staff, and horses at Payne's Church a block west of the courthouse. Lincoln, on receiving this news, said he didn't mind losing a general, because another could be created with a stroke of his pen, but he didn't know how to replace the horses.

John Randolph and Henry Clay dueled with pistols near the Virginia end of Chain Bridge. Randolph's perforated coat was the only casualty. The bridge itself takes its name from an early structure supported by chains. Great Falls Park, a popular picnic spot on the Virginia side, preserves the remains of two un-

successful commercial ventures: the Potomac Canal and Matildaville, a town site named for the mother of Robert E. Lee. Both were inspired by George Washington's vision of the Potomac Valley as the best route to the west; as a youth, he explored and surveyed the region for Lord Fairfax. The Potomac Canal Company built five skirting canals around unpassable sections of the river between Washington and Harpers Ferry, one of them at Great Falls, where the Potomac drops 76.5 feet through a mile-long rocky gorge. Ruins of the old locks are explained for visitors by park rangers. The Potomac Canal was abandoned when the Chesapeake and Ohio Canal, on the opposite side of the river, running 186 miles out to Cumberland, Maryland, was opened in 1828. Matildaville failed to survive the death of the canal. It had an ironworks and a gristmill, whose ruins are visible, but apparently only its tavern and jail flourished.

Rosslyn and McLean

The downstream community of Rosslyn, opposite Georgetown, was given great expectations when Congress approved an aqueduct bridge across the river to carry barges from the C & O Canal to another canal going to Alexandria. The bridge backers went bankrupt, and Rosslyn degenerated into a vice center and commercial slum. The piers of the bridge, just above Key Bridge, are the only visible remains of the original dream. Now, however, Rosslyn has claimed a new destiny as an extension of Washington's booming business district. Towering office buildings have recently sprouted along the Potomac's shore and eclipsed the view of Washington for many a Rosslyn hilltop resident.

The residents of the McLean area upstream blocked this sort of progress when builders wanted to erect apartment houses along the Potomac above Chain Bridge on the Merrywood estate, where Jacqueline Kennedy lived as a girl. For years McLean has been highly regarded for its country estate atmosphere so convenient to town. Its name honors John R. McLean, a publisher of the Washington *Post,* who built a spur of the Great Falls and Old Dominion Electric Railway to McLean along what is now Old Dominion Drive. President and Dolley Madison fled to this area the night of the British invasion, and the next

morning watched Washington burn from a nearby hill. The President stayed at Salona and the First Lady at Rokeby. Both of these mansions, along with Hickory Hill, housed Union generals during the Civil War. Hickory Hill subsequently was owned by Justice Robert H. Jackson, Senator John F. Kennedy, and now his brother Robert, the New York senator.

Many exceptionally fine privately owned homes scattered across the Virginia countryside are opened to the public in the spring during historic garden week, sponsored by the Garden Club of Virginia. Among them is Oak Hill, built in 1823 by President Monroe ten miles south of Leesburg. The plans were drawn by Jefferson and construction supervised by James Hoban, builder of the White House. While vacationing here, Monroe drafted his message to Congress enunciating the Monroe Doctrine. Oak Hill, considered the outstanding example of Palladian residential design, has a lovely Italian-style garden.

Spring brings not only house tours but horse events. The social center for Washington's horsy set is fashionable Warrenton, where the Gold Cup Steeplechase in early May has been a famous event for over forty years. Paul Mellon and other wealthy Washingtonians have handsome estates here and patronize the hunt clubs. Potomac, Maryland, is a closer center of horsy activity. The outstanding race of the year, the International, attracts thoroughbreds from all over the world and much of fashionable Washington to the Laurel track on Armistice Day.

Bladensburg

On the Maryland side of the outer city, historic roots go down deepest at Bladensburg, on the Anacostia River. Another tobacco port, it also prospered on the coach traffic between the northern and southern colonies. Of its dozen coaching taverns, the most noteworthy was the George Washington Tavern, built as "The Indian Maid" in 1732, the year of Washington's birth. Washington stayed overnight here in 1774 while en route to the First Continental Congress at Philadelphia, and again in 1790 as President when selecting the site for a national capital. This tavern was also favored as overnight quarters by gentlemen who met at dawn on the nearby Bladensburg dueling ground. Of the more than thirty duels fought here, the most unorthodox involved cousins, Brigadier General Armistead Mason and Colonel John McCarty. As the challenged party, McCarty could select the weapons. He proposed they both leap from the Capitol dome. The challenger refused. Next he suggested they both sit on a keg of gunpowder and be blown up. Again he was refused. Hand to hand with dirks was also turned down. When Mason agreed to shotguns at ten paces, later modified to rifles at twelve paces "to the death," McCarty killed him.

The American militia moved to Bladensburg to meet the British invaders in 1814, and Madison rode out to take personal command. This was the only time a President has taken to the field as commander-in-chief. The rout of the Americans made it an inauspicious precedent.

When the Anacostia began to silt up and the railroads chuffed past the old coach stops, Bladensburg lapsed into obscurity, never to catch on as a fashionable community in the manner of Georgetown and Alexandria.

Beyond Bladensburg, in the midst of the Prince Georges County suburban complex, lies the three-hundred-acre campus of the Washington area's largest educational institution, the University of Maryland at College Park. Established in 1856 by a group of farmers as Maryland Agricultural College, it became the state's land-grant college in 1864 and in 1920 was merged with the University of Maryland at Baltimore. With some twenty-five thousand students at College Park, it is the thirteenth largest university in the nation.

Chevy Chase

Washington's oldest suburb as such is charming Chevy Chase, a village of comfortably spacious homes set back from shaded lanes, on the northwest edge of the District. Senator Francis G. Newlands of Nevada promoted the Chevy Chase Land Company in 1890 and built one of the first homes, the stone château on Chevy Chase Circle. The name comes from fourteenth-century border raids, called *chevauchiées*, between the Scots and English. A ballad of the period tells of the battle of Chevy Chase in 1388 in which the English Lord Percy raided the Cheviot Hill chase of the Scottish Earl Douglas, who was killed defending his lands. The name first ap-

peared here on a 1725 land grant, perhaps as a tribute to Scottish settlers. Today it is applied to the residential section surrounding the Circle as far east as Rock Creek Park and west to Wisconsin Avenue, an area inhabited by many foreign diplomats. Residents of the Village, however, regard their community as the only true Chevy Chase.

Chevy Chase Village is a 225-acre tract in Montgomery County with a New England town meeting-type government. "Noise, whooping, profanity or vulgar language" are forbidden by village ordinance at the annual town meeting and, for that matter, are frowned upon throughout this genteel community. The village is so quiet that during the war a whistling mailman could be heard summoning housewives with the mating call of the cardinal whenever he brought a letter from a husband in the service. The laughter of children at play has been heard more in recent years as the houses of old settlers are passing to a new generation.

Beyond this village of twenty-four hundred residents, nearly a half million more upper- and middle-class settlers have converted Montgomery County into the most affluent quarter of greater Washington. Median income per family exceeds ten thousand dollars, highest for any county in the nation. Arlington and Fairfax counties, Virginia, are not far behind. The greatest concentration of high-income families is in Bethesda, whose sixty thousand residents enjoy a median family income of over twelve thousand dollars. New shopping centers abound throughout the outer city, soaking up these liquid assets like giant sponges.

Washington's well-publicized abundance of unattached women (fifty thousand more than men) stops at the city line. The outer city, in the main, is the habitat of the young married. In Montgomery County about 70 per cent of the residents are under forty, and 96 per cent are white. The fertility rate of these suburban whites is comparable to that of the urban blacks, contrary to popular myth. Indeed, the women of suburban Wheaton and Rockville have been more prolific than those of either race anywhere else in greater Washington.

Closer to the cradle than to the grave, the outer city is like a gangling youth, constantly outgrowing last season's trousers, satiated with the things of the market place, and rushing exuberantly into the uncertain future of the American megalopolis.

CHAPTER FOURTEEN

Treasure Troves

In Washington, America's Treasure Island, congressmen and foreign diplomats, seeking to enrich their constituencies, prospect in the Departments of Defense, State, Agriculture, and Interior, and the World Bank. Tourists and students, mining the wealth of heritage, dig in and about the city's museums, galleries, and shrines.

Though Washington yields generously to both kinds of prospectors, the latter depart with the more lasting gain. For who will ever lose the memory of approaching the saintly Lincoln, that brooding figure of strength and forbearance seated in his Parthenon by the Potomac? Who will not cherish the sense of reverence inspired by scanning Jefferson's words on the old parchment that set the world atremble, "all men are created equal"? Who will forget his admiration upon inspecting the space capsules of Shepard and Glenn or Lindy's *Spirit of St. Louis?* Or the reverie of a quiet afternoon with a Rembrandt or Monet painting? All these gems of the mind and spirit, Washington shares with millions of visitors every year.

Among its treasure troves, none is more absorbing to young and old than the red castle on the Mall, the Smithsonian Institution. It owes its founding to an English scientist, James Smithson, who died in 1829, leaving five hundred and fifty thousand dollars to the United States Government "to found at Washington,

The Folger Shakespeare Library on Capitol Hill contains the world's foremost collection of Shakespeareana, including an excellent small-scale replica of the Globe Theater and a full-scale reproduction of another typical Shakespearean playhouse. The exhibition hall shown here is a reproduction of the great hall of an Elizabethan palace.

under the name of the Smithsonian Institution, an establishment for the increase and diffusion of knowledge among men." It was not established until 1846. Congress, unaccustomed to receiving aid to this underdeveloped country, was not only perplexed by such benefaction from a kingdom America had so recently fought in two wars, but embarrassed by Smithson's origins. Born out of wedlock to aristocratic parents, Smithson thus expressed the frustration of his untitled circumstances: "The best blood of England flows in my veins . . . but this avails me not. My name shall live in the memory of man, when the titles of the Northumberlands and the Percys are extinct and forgotten."

And so it has. Persuaded by Congressman John Quincy Adams that Smithson's gold sovereigns would prove a national asset, Congress, after years of debate, finally established what has become the world's most impressive museum. The Smithsonian contains more than fifty-five million items of priceless historical, artistic, scientific, or industrial importance. It is fondly called "the nation's attic" because each year ten million visitors rummage through its mementoes. In addition to its fine public exhibits, the Smithsonian makes available other articles and specimens to research scholars, undertakes scientific research and exploration, and, through its International Exchange Service, circulates scientific tracts throughout the world. Obedient to Smithson's directive, it diffuses knowledge without regard to national borders or hostile regimes. Moreover, the Institution administers four scientific bureaus, four art galleries, two museums, the National Cultural Center, and the Washington Zoo. Congress has multiplied Smithson's gift many times over to pay for all these facilities; it annually appropriates some fifteen million dollars just to operate them.

Seven of its buildings are on the Mall. Dominating all is the red Norman castle, the original Smithsonian, built in 1855. It was supplemented by the Arts and Industries Building in 1881, and further in 1964 by the Museum of History and Technology (across the Mall). The old hangarlike Aircraft Building, built in World War I as a testing laboratory, is to be replaced with a modern National Air Museum. The Natural History Museum, recently expanded, was built of granite in 1911. The galleries came later, Freer in 1923, the National in 1941. A new portrait gallery will be installed in the old Patent Office at Eighth and F streets, N.W.

On display in these museums is everything from a nugget found in Sutter's mill race that set off the California gold rush of 1848 to the stuffed hide of the largest elephant on record and a ninety-two-foot model of a magnificent blue whale. There is also Whitney's cotton gin, the Morse telegraph key, and a classic collection of autos, locomotives, and aircraft. America's cultural origins are traced through marvelous life-size models of Indians. Specimens of the vanishing wildlife of the continent are also realistically preserved.

The Smithsonian is complemented by a host of collections exhibited by other public and private museums all over town. The Folger Shakespeare Library on Capitol Hill, run by Amherst College, contains the world's best collection of Shakespeareana and materials in English dealing with the seventeenth and eighteenth centuries. Its exhibition hall is a reproduction of the great hall of an Elizabethan palace. The Folger contains an excellent small-scale model of the Globe Playhouse and a full-scale reproduction of another Shakespearean theater, unfortunately too small to stage the tragedies or comedies depicted in bas-relief panels on the front of the building.

The Library of Congress, originally intended only for the use of the national legislature, was moved in 1897 from the Capitol to its massive Italian Renaissance building on First Street, S.E. It has probably the world's most extensive collection of books, periodicals, newspapers, and photographs, more than forty million items all told. Although not a lending library, it compiles a master reference list of its works for other libraries and permits them to borrow books

At dawn, before the invasion by sight-seeing hordes, the deserted Smithsonian Institution broods like an ancient castle on the Mall.

A recent addition to the Smithsonian complex is the Museum of History and Technology (above) on Constitution Avenue between Twelfth and Fourteenth streets, which opened in 1964. The Smithsonian collection is so vast, some sixty million items, that there is space to exhibit only about one per cent of it at any time. Among the History Museum's exhibitions are models of clipper ships (left) and this statue of George Washington in a Roman toga. The latter drew much congressional ridicule after its unveiling at the Capitol in 1841 and was subsequently moved to the Smithsonian, "the nation's attic."

Neptune and his sea nymphs (above) greet visitors in front of the Library of Congress on Capitol Hill. The library stores and catalogues some forty million books, periodicals, newspapers, photographs, and music manuscripts. This Stradivarius violin (left) is in the music collection. The ornate Renaissance architecture of the library befits this early Latin lectionary (opposite) and the three-volume Gutenberg Bible that is also exhibited there.

The first light of dawn strikes the marble columns of America's Parthenon, the Lincoln Memorial, as the moon sets behind it. The peerless figure of the country's sixteenth President, lighted throughout the night, can evoke an unforgettable sense of reverence in the visitor who stands at its feet.

not available locally for scholarly purposes. Students come from all over the country to mine its lode of specialized materials. An annex was built on Second, S.E., in 1938, expanding the library's space to forty-three acres. Another annex is needed to relieve the congestion of this bibliomania.

The million visitors yearly who pass the fountain of old Neptune and his sea nymphs to inspect the library's interior find a multitude of Old World adornments, from thirty-three heads sculpted over the windows to illustrate the races of man, to painted wall panels pointedly suggesting the joys of temperance and the pain of bad government. On permanent exhibition are the three-volume Gutenberg Bible, one of three perfect vellum copies in existence. It was the first large book printed by movable type, the invention that made modern libraries possible. The library also displays Jefferson's rough draft of the Declaration of Independence, with penned changes by Franklin and Adams, and Lincoln's two drafts of his Gettysburg Address.

The originals of the Declaration of Independence, the Bill of Rights, and the Constitution repose in the National Archives on Pennsylvania Avenue midway between the Capitol and White House. After being displayed each day in the exhibition hall, the great charters are lowered into a fireproof, bombproof vault which has fifteen-inch-thick steel and reinforced concrete walls. The display cases, in which the public sees them, are filled with helium and fitted with laminated glass filters that give the documents a yellow cast but shield them from damaging ultraviolet rays.

When the British advanced on Washington in 1814, these treasured documents were stuffed into coarse linen sacks and carried by horse cart to Leesburg, where they remained until the British fleet had left Chesapeake Bay. During World War II they were stored with the bullion at Fort Knox. For many years in the last century the Declaration of Independence hung in the old Patent Office Building opposite a tall window, exposed to the erosion of varying temperatures, dust, and direct light. President Grant lent it

One of the most moving symbols of death is this statue by Augustus Saint-Gaudens in Rock Creek Cemetery. Commissioned by historian Henry Adams in memory of his wife, the shrouded figure was called "Beyond Pain and Beyond Joy" by the sculptor but is popularly known as "Grief."

to the city of Philadelphia for its Centennial Exposition in 1876, and the State Department exhibited it in a cabinet until 1894, when it was removed from public viewing, wrapped and placed flat in a steel case at State. The Library of Congress took possession of both it and the Constitution in 1921. The Bill of Rights remained at State until transferred to the Archives in 1938. The three charters were brought together in 1952 when the Declaration and the Constitution were ceremoniously moved in an armored car from the Library to the Archives.

Archives also houses the Emancipation Proclamation, the Japanese and German surrender documents that ended World War II, the Treaty of Paris, which concluded the Revolutionary War, the Articles of Confederation, and a profusion of lesser documents collected from nearly every government agency for safe deposit in this national strongbox. Of the tons of records created by the government's activities, about 20 per cent are retained permanently.

The expense of sorting, cataloguing, and storing this stockpile is justified by the five hundred thousand queries (half from ordinary citizens) taken care of each year at Archives. Little old ladies who, for a consideration, will trace your family tree can always be found in its search rooms, poring over old military and census records. Carl Sandburg went through the Mathew Brady collection of Civil War photographs for his book, *Storm Over the Land*, and Margaret Landon spent over a month here reading Siamese consular records to provide authentic background for *Anna and the King of Siam*. Oil companies check the validity of land titles before setting up their drilling rigs. And every year some ten thousand citizens come seeking proof of age or citizenship, often to establish eligibility for Social Security.

Archives has provided invaluable data for many public ventures. When the Ohio Turnpike was built, engineers wanted to bypass the state's many abandoned mine shafts but didn't know where they were until Archives produced records of the WPA project that had sealed their openings. Before General Eisenhower picked the date for the Normandy invasion, his weather experts sifted thousands of Weather Bureau records here to determine probable weather conditions. When General MacArthur was planning his invasion of the Philippines, Archives supplied the Pentagon with a hundred and fifty Spanish-made maps taken from Spain in 1898, some so detailed they showed jungle trails. It is little wonder that the most widely remembered public inscription in Washington is the Shakespearean quote near the entrance to Archives: "What is past is prologue."

The Federal Bureau of Investigation, in the Justice Department building a block to the west of Archives, draws more than a half million visitors a year to its museum of criminology. Guided by FBI fledglings who sing the praises of the agents who almost always get their man, the visitors see exhibits from the gangster era of the thirties, when the G-men gunned down Dillinger and "Baby Face" Nelson and "Pretty Boy" Floyd, the espionage cases of the forties, and the almost perfect 2.7-million-dollar Brink's robbery case of the fifties.

Most fascinating is the FBI laboratory, in which experts annually examine some two hundred thousand specimens of evidence sent in by state and local police. Tiny flecks of paint found on a hit-and-run victim's clothing could identify the offending vehicle. Handwriting or typewriting on a ransom note, compared with samples on file or obtained from suspects, can help identify a kidnaper. Fingerprints found at the scene are checked in a few minutes against a file of a hundred and sixty-nine million sets of prints, fifteen million from persons with police records. Markings on bullets, bloodstains, hairs, fibers, toolmarks, footprints, tire treads are all grist for the technicians whose testimony in court is often sufficient to bring a guilty verdict. The FBI tour ends in a blaze of gunfire in the basement firing range, where an agent perforates the head and belly of a man-shaped paper target with his .38 service revolver and a Thompson submachine gun.

Ford's Theatre, a few blocks north of the FBI at 511 Tenth, contains a Lincoln museum on the first floor. The National Park Service is rebuilding the second floor so that visitors may visualize the actual scene of Lincoln's assassination. Across the street the Petersen House where Lincoln died has been restored with copies of the original furnishings. A few things actually were there at the time, such as the pillow on which Lincoln lay.

The National Gallery of Art, the sparkling pendant in the necklace of museums ringing the Mall, is an esthetic masterpiece. It was designed by John Russell Pope and constructed of pinkish Tennessee marble, which doesn't glare in the summer sun and turns a mystic mauve in the rain. The central rotunda opening out to the galleries is set off by twenty-four columns of green Italian marble circling a fountain topped by the fleet figure of Mercury.

Washington's leading galleries symbolize America's unique route to the arts. What royalty did for the galleries of Europe, American capitalists did for the National, the Corcoran, the Freer, and the Phillips, and just in the nick of time. They collected paintings all over the world and brought them to America before export restrictions and skyrocketing art prices curtailed trade in the masters.

The National, opened in 1941, was inspired by a gift of fifteen million dollars and a hundred and twenty-five paintings from Andrew Mellon, the Pittsburgh financier who served as Secretary of the Treasury for Harding, Coolidge, and Hoover. Mellon's selfless insistence that it be a truly national gallery, rather than one named for him, encouraged other wealthy art collectors to contribute their masterpieces, thus bringing to the National the Widener, Kress, Rosenwald, and Dale collections.

The enterprise of these collectors – and the persuasiveness of David Finley, the National's first director, who talked the capitalists out of their art treasures – consummated the dream of an American gallery to compare with those of the Old World. Today the National contains more than twenty-seven thousand works of art in its permanent collection of paintings, sculpture, prints, drawings, furniture, tapestries, ceramics, and other examples of the decorative arts. They represent the work of nearly two thousand artists.

The Freer Gallery was a gift to the government by Charles Lang Freer of Detroit, who made a fortune building freight cars, and retired at forty-six to travel and collect art works, mostly American and Asiatic. When he offered his collection to the government, President Theodore Roosevelt accepted. The Freer Gallery, financed and endowed by the philanthropist, was built on the Mall west of the Smithsonian, which has administered the gallery since its opening in 1923.

The Corcoran Gallery of Art, emphasizing the work of American artists, was chartered in 1870 by William Wilson Corcoran, a Georgetown banker who made a killing in bonds sold to finance the Mexican War. Originally the Corcoran was in the building at Seventeenth and Pennsylvania, later used by the U. S. Court of Claims. It moved to its present building at Seventeenth and New York around the turn of the century. After the death of former Senator William Andrews Clark of Montana, the Corcoran secured his elaborate collection and the Clark family built a new wing to house it. Clark, whose fortune was made in mines, railroads, utilities, and foodstuffs, offered his collection to the Metropolitan in New York but it was declined because of a condition that it be exhibited as a unit.

The Phillips Gallery was opened in 1918 by Duncan Phillips in his family's four-story brick home at 1612 Twenty-first, built in 1897. The gallery added a new wing in 1960 but maintains the intimate mood of a private home. This was the earliest museum of modern art in the country. The Phillips collection includes works from many periods and artists whose paintings are intermingled "the better to show the universality of art and the continuities of such ancient seeing habits as realism, expressionism and abstraction"; but twentieth-century art dominates. A favorite is Renoir's "The Luncheon of the Boating Party."

The Washington Gallery of Modern Art opened in 1962 in another old private home a block south at 1503 Twenty-first. Its chief benefactors were the Eugene Meyer and Edgar Stern foundations. Like the Corcoran, it has a list of members whose dues help sustain it and to whom it rents paintings for modest fees. Unlike the other major galleries, the Modern charges a small admission fee and is devoted largely to touring exhibitions.

The very creation of this major new gallery and its popular support speaks for Washington's heightened interest in the arts. When Franz Bader opened the first commercial gallery at the old Whyte Book Shop on Seventeenth Street in 1938, he recalls, "If we sold one picture a month it was sensational." Today his art business is flourishing in a little gallery at 2124 Pennsylvania Avenue, N.W. He has dropped all books except art books; and paintings, most by Washington artists, dominate his trade. Washington now has a galaxy of small galleries throughout the city. Several coffee houses have exhibitions, notably the Potter's House on Columbia Road, where Lyndon B. Johnson, as Vice-President, attended a show by Jimilu Mason, Washington sculptor who has done his bust. The Corcoran's membership, now over four thousand, nearly doubled from 1960 to 1964. Enrollment in the Corcoran art school has also dou-

bled since the nationwide art boom hit the capital.

In other museums there are several outstanding permanent collections. Dumbarton Oaks features the superb Robert Woods Bliss collection of pre-Columbian art as well as jewelry, metalwork, and textiles of the early Christian and Byzantine periods. The Pan American Union exhibits contemporary Latin American artists. The Museum of African Art, 315 A Street, N.E., one of the city's newest, reflects the rising interest in the heritage of Africa. The National Geographic Society's Explorers Hall, in its handsome new quarters at Seventeenth and M, exhibits photographs and artifacts from some of the Society's most memorable expeditions. Hillwood, the sumptuous home of Mrs. Marjorie Merriweather Post filled with objets d'art from imperial Russia, will some day be turned over in its entirety to the Smithsonian.

Outside the Smithsonian there is astonishingly small attention paid to military affairs in Washington museums. The Air Museum includes war planes, from World War I dogfighters with machine guns mounted on the cowl, to Navy fighters from World War II. The Truston-Decatur Naval Museum at 1610 H Street, N.W., and the Navy Yard Museum depict famous naval engagements and heroes; Fort Washington has a postage-stamp-size museum on the War of 1812; and the Medical Museum of the Armed Forces Institute of Pathology displays military medical material, along with such other exhibits as various stages in the prenatal growth of a baby.

Any lack of status for the military within the city's museums is more than overcome, however, by the numerosity of military statuary in the parks. The Grant Memorial at the Capitol end of the Mall, comprising twelve horses, eleven soldiers, four lions, eight lampposts, an artillery battery, and the general, is the largest equestrian statue in America (Victor Emmanuel's in Rome is the only one larger).

A curious fact about the thirty-eight military memorials in Washington is that twenty-nine honor heroes of eighteenth- and nineteenth-century battles, ranging from George Washington to Simón Bolívar, but those memorializing the terrible wars of the twentieth century honor the group and not the man. Not even Colonel Teddy Roosevelt or General Black Jack Pershing rates a statue. The Iwo Jima Memorial, for example, commemorates the Marine Corps's many campaigns without mention of a single individual.

Twentieth-century Washington is more inclined to

honor its statesmen. The name of the city and its towering memorial, the Washington Monument, honor a soldier-statesman; but the other great memorials, planned or completed, suggest a contemporary recognition that the pen is indeed mightier than the sword in the long course of national and world affairs.

Thus Teddy Roosevelt's memorial, an island in the Potomac, recalls not his military exploits on the island of Cuba but the progressive measures of his presidency to conserve the country's natural resources. Theodore Roosevelt Island lies offshore from Georgetown's waterfront. A tiny ferry carries visitors across the channel. Once owned by George Mason of Gunston Hall, whose son built a fine brick mansion there in the 1790s and farmed the island until about 1832, it later became a resort for family outings. It was bought in 1931 by the Theodore Roosevelt Memorial Association and turned over to the government to be maintained in its natural state in honor of the vigorous conservationist.

The John F. Kennedy Center for the Performing Arts and the Robert A. Taft statue and carillon on Capitol Hill were both designated memorials to political leaders who died in office under tragic circumstances. Imposing memorials for Franklin Roosevelt and Wilson and Madison are planned.

The most impressive memorials built in this century are those for Jefferson and Lincoln. The Jefferson Memorial, honoring our greatest political philosopher, was dedicated in 1943. This marble edifice amid the Japanese cherry trees on the tranquil Tidal Basin was designed by John Russell Pope to reflect Thomas Jefferson's admiration for the circular-domed Pantheon in Rome. (His preference for the Roman style is further shown in Jefferson's own design of Monticello, his home at Charlottesville, Virginia, 110 miles south of Washington.) Rudulph Evans'

heroic statue of the nation's third President and the author of its Declaration of Independence, standing, scroll in hand, conveys the strength of his commitment to freedom, as though he were saying, "Here I take my stand." On interior panels the visitor reads Jefferson's noble expressions on inalienable rights, on freedom of the mind, the evil of slavery, and the necessity of change in institutions.

This memorial forms a north-south axis with the Washington Monument and the White House. Some years ago a few trees were removed to give the President a clear view of the Jefferson shrine from his office, and more recently lights were added to illuminate the exterior after twilight.

The Lincoln Memorial forms the east-west axis along the Mall with the Capitol. The city already had two outdoor statues of the sixteenth President, one in Judiciary Square on Indiana Avenue, the other in Lincoln Park on East Capitol Street, when Congress authorized the Lincoln Memorial in 1911. Henry Bacon designed the building in classic Greek style, similar to the Parthenon, the temple on the Acropolis to the goddess Athena. Lincoln belongs in a temple; for, more than any other American leader, Lincoln posthumously became a godly figure to his countrymen. Daniel Chester French's peerless marble figure, portraying power in repose, evokes a spirit of reverence in the visitor.

Lincoln's treasured words at Gettysburg and at his second inaugural, inscribed on stone tablets in the temple, seize the visitor's heart and mind with the power of Holy Writ: "With malice toward none, with charity for all, with firmness in the right as God gives us to see the right, let us strive on to finish the work we are in..."

Lincoln still speaks for his country. And the banks of the River Potomac tremble beneath the burden and the glory of his goodness.

The privately endowed Museum of African Art on Capitol Hill (upper left) was established in 1964 as the first American Museum dedicated solely to the cultural heritage of Negroes, who now comprise over half the population of the District of Columbia. Many of the wooden objects, such as the Luba mask (lower right) from the Congo, are believed to be more than a century old. A superb collection of Chinese art at the Freer Gallery includes the female Buddha figure from the sixth century.

CHAPTER FIFTEEN

Rites and Pageants

In the citadel of the common man, pageantry is devoted largely to the ceremonials of birth and death, of arrival and departure – the birth of new administrations, the arrival of potentates, the advent of spring, the death of soldiers and presidents. Washington enjoys a minimum of pomp. The President, representing every common man, sets the style of plainness. He permits virtually no ostentation to embellish his person or office. He never mounts a stallion to review his troops. No gold carriages, only severe black autos, transport him through the crowded streets. He wears a conservative business suit, whether he is attending church services that mark the opening of a new Congress, or tossing out the first ball at D. C. Stadium to open the baseball season, or laying a wreath at the Tomb of the Unknowns on Memorial Day, or welcoming the most splendidly garbed ruler from a faraway land.

This avoidance of showy display characterizes the political community's desire to appear as one with the electorate. Only the military carry on the tradition that rank merits special costuming. Yet, when entering the Cabinet or an ambassadorship or the presidency itself, the most decorated general changes to mufti. This obsession with ceremonial austerity reaches even to the sentries at the White House gates. The changing of the President's guards, disregarding all palace-guard tradition, is rather more like streetcar conductors changing shifts at the terminal.

A splendid exception to the political rule of plainness is the inauguration of the President. Cutaways and high silk hats are traditional, but each President may set his own style. President Eisenhower broke with tradition to wear a homburg. President Johnson overturned tradition entirely by wearing a business suit and a fedora.

The inaugural is a wonder of continuity, a reminder that as a continuing unbroken republic we are an old nation. This change of command does not wait upon a ruler's death, or wars and uprisings. Through even the most terrible of civil wars the change has occurred, always at its appointed time, always by the process agreed upon, and never once by fraud or violence. In the light of the history of modern nations, this is a remarkable demonstration of a people's ultimate devotion to principle above party and to laws above men. The world today thinks of American influence in terms of power: in a sense, our real influence derives from political steadiness.

Take the first inauguration at Washington. The election between Thomas Jefferson and Aaron Burr had been thrown into the House of Representatives by a tie in the Electoral College. The House met in a charged atmosphere. One roll call followed another as each man's supporters struggled for supremacy. Jefferson did not win until the thirty-sixth ballot. Yet once this decision was reached, the House members, friend and foe of the new Chief Executive, gathered about him for the oath-taking in the Senate's first temporary chamber. The oath was administered by Chief Justice John Marshall, who was hostile to Jefferson's democratic philosophy and later used his judicial authority to check presidential power.

Whatever the antagonisms of its participants, the inaugural reaffirms the unity of purpose of the three branches of the federal government. And in this final rite of the national election, the President is consecrated to the high calling of serving all of his countrymen.

The presidential oath has not varied since Washington took it: "I do solemnly swear that I will faithfully execute the office of President of the United States, and will to the best of my ability preserve, protect and defend the Constitution of the United

Cherry blossoms, flowering around the Tidal Basin usually in early April, have become symbolic of Washington. The trees were a gift from the city of Tokyo, during the Taft Administration. The annual Cherry Blossom Festival, timed to meet the expected arrival of the pink blooms, goes forward with or without blossoms, regardless of weather.

The city-beautiful movement in America began at the turn of the century when the McMillan Commission projected new parks, fountains, and gardens for the nation's capital. The movement gained new impetus from President and Mrs. Johnson. Lady Bird personally planted some of the many flowers that adorn Washington. The Rose (opposite), official flower of the District of Columbia, graces the Treasury Department grounds near the White House end of historic Pennsylvania Avenue.

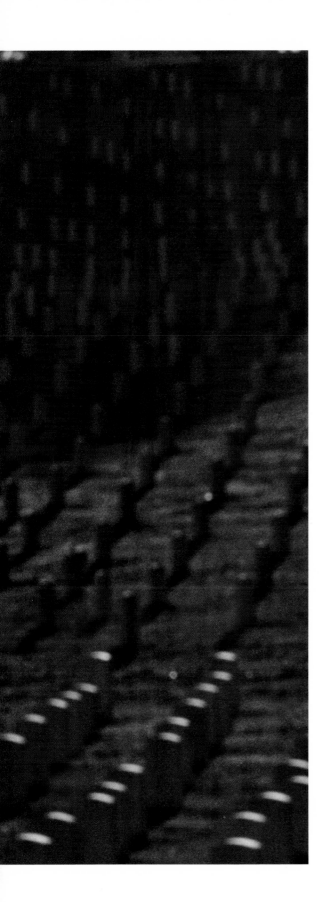

The autumn of life evokes thoughts of death for everyone; but the ranks of the dead in Arlington Cemetery are filled with youths who gave their lives to help preserve liberty.
Since Robert E. Lee left these Virginia hills to lead the Confederate army, the Lee estate overlooking the capital has become the nation's largest national cemetery. More than a hundred and fifty thousand persons, including some wives and children of servicemen, have been interred here.

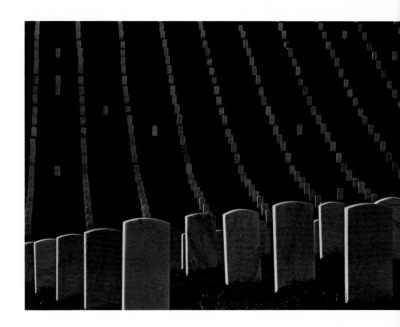

States." In other respects the inaugural has undergone a telling transition. Attendance at Jefferson's inaugural was limited to those of the political elite who could crowd into the tiny Senate chamber, and some of them could not hear his inaugural address because Jefferson's many talents did not include oratorical power. Lincoln, too, lacked a strong speaking voice but by the time of his inaugural the ceremony had been moved outdoors to the Capitol's east portico, where several thousand citizens gathered to hear the Emancipator as best they could. Radio extended the range of the pageant to a national audience in time for most Americans to hear Franklin Roosevelt saying, "All we have to fear is fear itself." Today television makes the inaugural visible to the entire nation.

Andrew Jackson would be pleased. For it was Jackson who made the inaugural a ceremony for the people rather than for Washington's political aristocracy. Jackson changed the locale to the Capitol steps so that his admirers, the commoners, could watch. The event was nearly a disaster. The crowd was quiet enough for Jackson's address; but when he concluded by ceremoniously kissing the Bible and bowing to the people, these joyous sovereigns surged forward to embrace Old Hickory. Although he had walked to the Capitol from his hotel, Jackson now had difficulty reaching the foot of Capitol Hill where a horse awaited, to carry the new President to the White House.

Celebrants had taken command there, too, milling boisterously through the old mansion like the Paris mobs at the Tuileries, upsetting the punch, muddying the carpets, and toasting their hero and his rescue of their government from the aristocrats.

Since then, the inaugural pageant has been captured by the middle class. Except by the pickpockets who work the crowds along the Pennsylvania Avenue parade route, propriety is faithfully observed today. The parade itself is the Americana one expects of parades anywhere in the nation: brass bands, high-stepping majorettes, decorated floats, a ceremonial display of military prowess, flag-bearers by the hundreds, and cowboys and Indians to delight people of all ages. Entertained until dusk in the raw January air, the crowds are diverted from whooping it up on the White House grounds. The President sets the example by spending the afternoon in a drafty reviewing stand in front of the Executive mansion.

The climax of this festival is the inaugural ball. It, too, has outgrown the White House. Garfield's inaugural ball was held in the Smithsonian's then new Arts and Industries Building on the Mall, and Cleveland's was held in the more spacious Pension Building at Fourth and G streets. But in recent years it has divided into many balls held in various downtown hotels and the Armory, a vast concrete shed next to the stadium on the Anacostia River. The number of invited dancers and minglers has so increased with each election that the question in every guest's mind is whether he will catch a glimpse of the host and hostess. To accommodate their guests, the President and First Lady dash through the night from ball to ball with scarcely time for taking a turn around any ballroom. Television cameras follow their breathless journey because the public still likes Jackson's idea of a public inaugural.

A less public ceremony but no less minutely planned is the arrival of a visiting foreign ruler. The jet age and America's power have made these visitations more frequent than ever before. As recently as the Truman era only three heads of state were invited each year; now they come with fortnightly regularity. Before the ruler's arrival, the State Department compiles a complete dossier on his tastes, habits, hobbies, idiosyncrasies. One Latin American disliked seasoned foods, would not tolerate smoking in his presence, was fearful of drafts, liked his bedroom warmed to an uncommonly high temperature, and had a passion for ballet. State planned a visit that gratified his every whim.

The President gives a formal dinner for his guest in the White House, the Secretary of State is host at another meal, and the guest reciprocates with two separate dinners before his departure. Such repetitious bread-breaking strikes pragmatic Washington as too much of a good thing. However, there is no tampering with it. It is rigidly prescribed by the Treaty of Vienna of 1815 in which the great powers, besides carving up Napoleon's former empire, set down rules of courtesies due every head of state. For a century no wars were fought over diplomatic rudeness until the shooting of Archduke Ferdinand, clearly a violation of protocol.

The public pageantry of a ceremonial visit centers on the guest's arrival. By dawn the city's sanitation crews have rinsed the streets and mounted flags of both nations on the lampposts along his way. The fire department has raised two aerial ladders, usually near Fourteenth and Pennsylvania, to form a great arch, hung with a mammoth flag of the visitor's country, under which the convoy of notables will pass. Protocol dictates that the President meet his guest when he alights from his train or plane in Washington, after which the convoy usually passes along a prescribed route from Union Station or Andrews Air Base to the White House.

President Kennedy altered this traditional entry by encouraging visitors to arrive by helicopter on the White House lawn. Kennedy saw it as a time-saver but some foreign dignitaries feared it might demean them. The Emperor of Ethiopia, for one, noted that by his country's standard, the farther a host travels to receive a guest the greater homage he pays. So when Haile Selassie came by rail, Kennedy went to Union Station to meet him. Others less wedded to tradition, starting with Ben Bella of Algeria, have dropped from the skies onto the President's lawn and been accorded all appropriate pomp: military bands trumpeting the arrival, cannons booming salute, honor guards presenting the colors, and parading ranks of polished troops.

The arrival of the Japanese cherry blossoms, coincident with a week-long festival, though fraught with no international peril, is even more difficult to manage because of Washington's unruly spring weather. Weeks before the festival, government horticulturists make their annual forecast of when the trees will bloom. Whether or not the blossoms enter on time, and whether they are crowned with sunshine or snow, the pageant of maidens, in décolleté gowns, goes bravely on as it has for three decades.

The princesses of this festival represent their home states, for each has been selected by a state society, the organization of that state's residents "temporarily" working in Washington. In selecting a Cherry Blossom Queen from among the princesses, Washington takes no chances with judges playing favorites. She is chosen by the turn of the wheel.

The Easter Egg Roll on the White House lawn is one of those traditions, on the Monday following Easter, that have survived for nearly a century after a chance beginning. Egg rolling apparently began on the grassy slopes of Capitol Hill. In the spring of 1878, however, the Capitol grounds were unceremoniously closed to the children who came, baskets in hand, for the frolic. In protest, a small band of children marched to the White House, where President Hayes obligingly let them use the grounds. They've been coming ever since. President Roosevelt stopped the custom in 1941 during the war and President Eisenhower resumed it in 1953. Adults are admitted only if accompanied by children; so some enterprising youngsters peddle their services to any childless adults found peering through the iron fence at the festivities within.

The event has an old-fashioned Sunday-in-the-park flavor. Children bring their own hard-boiled eggs but quickly tire of trying to roll them through the thick grass of the flat lawn. A military band entertains near the fountain, which is protectively screened for the occasion. If the President is in town, he often greets the crowd, sometimes from the balcony of the mansion, occasionally by mingling. The crowd runs to about ten thousand, apparently because it is the only chance for the public to frolic in the President's back yard.

Washington welcomes these rites of spring as festivals of rebirth, for it is ever conscious of the nearness of death. The city's flags seem to fly at half-mast most of the time. Virtually every foreign dignitary lays a wreath at the Tomb of the Unknowns. And the white stones on the hills of Arlington become more numerous each passing day.

Since the old Lee estate was converted to a burial ground for Civil War dead a century ago, it has become the country's largest national cemetery. It is said that the general who selected the site did so to avenge what he regarded as Lee's treason in leading the Confederates. Nearly a hundred and fifty thousand persons, including some wives and children, have since been interred there.

Arlington offers continuous military pageantry at the Tomb of the Unknowns. Throughout the day and night, the heat and the cold, vigil is conducted by a solitary Army private, rifle shouldered, bayonet fixed, pacing crisply before the monument with the precision of a metronome. Every hour on the hour the changing of the guard is executed. No drums. No bugles. No banners waving. All of it conveys a soundless sense of reverence.

Washington expresses its hope for universal peace at Christmas time when the President lights a giant tree on the Ellipse, opening the annual Pageant of Peace.

Peace Monument (left), at the foot of Capitol Hill, suggests the sorrow that Americans feel over war's terrible waste. Sculpted in Rome to memorialize Navy Civil War dead, its marble figures depict America weeping on the shoulder of History.

It is an honor reserved for fallen statesmen to lie in state in the Rotunda of the Capitol. On Sunday, November 24, 1963, the flag-draped coffin (opposite) of a young President was borne on a caisson from the White House to the Capitol and placed upon the catafalque that had cradled Abraham Lincoln in this same Rotunda. Throughout the day and cold night, a never-ending line of mourners waited their turn to pass the bier of John Fitzgerald Kennedy.

Since 1921, when an unidentified soldier killed in World War I was laid in a sarcophagus and placed within the hollow of a massive block of Colorado marble, kings, queens, presidents, and multitudes of many lands have stood solemnly before this tomb in recognition of the sacrifice of America's finest young men. In 1958 the remains of unknown servicemen killed in World War II and in Korea were interred beneath two white marble caps set flush in the gray granite of the plaza of the tomb, a memorial to all Americans who die unknown to all but God.

Arlington is also the resting place of men known to all – Pershing, Wainwright, Marshall, Dulles, Kennedy. A funeral for such as these is marked by unexampled solemnity: the flag-draped casket on a caisson drawn through the streets by six matching gray horses, across the Memorial Bridge, up the winding lanes; the riderless black stallion, empty boots reversed in the stirrups; the mournful cadence of muffled drums, the measured footfalls of marching men. And then the terrible hush after the last words have been spoken and the piercing notes of taps have echoed through the oaks, that moment that finally divides the quick from the dead.

This generation will never forget the four days that began with a burst of rifle fire in Dallas and ended with a solemnly beautiful widow lighting the Eternal Flame in Arlington. In the year after the death of John Fitzgerald Kennedy, nearly eight million persons came to stand before his grave, there on the velvet green slope overlooking the great city on the River Potomac.

No matter how aggrieved, Washington is never paralyzed by the death of a President. The ceremonials of vice-presidential succession, so swift and sure, have given the country three strong leaders already in this century – Theodore Roosevelt, Harry S. Truman, and Lyndon B. Johnson — who might otherwise have been lost in the footnotes of history. So, even in moments of death, Washington remains a capital of hope.

Washington expresses its basic political aspirations on July Fourth, when several thousand citizens gather at the foot of the Washington Monument to recall the Declaration that set America free and to thrill to the fireworks that cast their brilliance on the noble thrusting shaft. In this and all its rites, the capital of hope reflects America's pervading spirit. Americans hope and work for something better for their youngsters, for themselves, for men everywhere. Let anything go wrong, a child lost in a suburban woods or an earthquake in Asia, and America rushes out to help. Point to an injustice, and America tries to right the wrong. America did not seek its global involvement but neither could it avoid it without denying its nature. If America conquers any country it will only prove the wisdom of the ancient Greek Xenophon, who said the only real way to conquer is by generosity.

Thus, America's capital finds its fullest meaning in sharing – sharing the wisdom of Jefferson, and the heart of Lincoln, and the experience of nearly two centuries of democratic order. Washington, in sum, lives to liberate the human spirit, wherever it may be.

From the Rotunda, the coffin of President Kennedy was taken to St. Matthew's Cathedral on Rhode Island Avenue for low requiem mass. Kneeling at the altar rail is the President's widow Jacqueline and his brother Robert. In pews behind them sit monarchs and prime ministers among the two hundred and twenty world leaders, representing ninety-two nations, who came to Washington to pay their respects. From the pulpit the Most Reverend Philip M. Hannan began his eulogy with one of John F. Kennedy's favorite biblical passages: "There is an appointed time for everything . . . a time to be born and a time to die . . ."

The Inaugural is a wonder of continuity. The change of national command waits not upon a ruler's death or wars and uprisings. Ever since the adoption of the Constitution it has occurred at the appointed time, always by the process agreed upon, and never once by violence or fraud. Since Andrew Jackson's inaugural, the ceremony has been held on the east front of the Capitol, so that it might be witnessed not only by the nation's most influential persons, shown clustered behind President Lyndon B. Johnson (above), but by the common people who gather on the Capitol Plaza.

The inaugural parade descends Capitol Hill on Constitution Avenue, veers into Pennsylvania Avenue near the National Gallery of Art (left), and proceeds toward the White House. The south side of Pennsylvania Avenue forms the hypotenuse of the Federal Triangle, a concentration of government office buildings. The north side, faced mostly with old private buildings, is scheduled for major improvement. The Americana of an inaugural parade must include pretty drum majorettes. The President spends his first afternoon in office in a drafty reviewing stand in front of the White House along Pennsylvania Avenue. The President and Vice-President and their wives, flanked by Secret Service men, watch the inaugural parade from behind a shield of bullet-proof glass.

Washington, profoundly grieved but never paralyzed by the death of a President, adheres to the constitutional provision of vice-presidential succession. It carries on as the capital of hope, a shining star beckoning and leading in man's quest for freedom around the world.

INDEX

NOTE: Italicized page numbers refer to picture captions.

Adams, Henry, *221*
Adams, John, 31, 55, 143, 221; rated, 48
Adams, John Quincy, 22, 32, 157; election of, 48; and George Washington University, 156; rated, 48; signature of, *153;* and Smithsonian, 211; tomb of, 160
Adam, Robert, 204
AFL-CIO, 127
Africa, 9; dancers from, *140, 147;* diplomats from, *140;* Museum of African Art, 223, *225*
Agriculture, Department of, 203
Air Force, 107, 108, 109, *110*
Air Museum, 223
Alcohol, use of. *See* Drinking
Alexandria, 143, *196,* 203-4
Algerian Embassy, 94
Algonquin Indians, *22*
Allen, Robert S., 124
Ambassadors, 46, 87 ff. *See also* specific embassies
American Broadcasting Company, 123
American Institute of Architects, 156
American Medical Association, 129
American Petroleum Institute, 127
American University, 168
Amherst College, 212
Anacostia, 170
Anacostia River, 19, 24, 170
Anderson, Marian, 187
Anderson House, 161
Andrews Air Force Base, 32, 107
Anna and the King of Siam, 221
Apothecary Shop (Alexandria), 204
"Apotheosis of Washington," *56*
Arena Stage, *139,* 141, 155
Arlington (Lee estate), 20, 204-5, *231*
Arlington Cemetery, 182, 204, 205, *231,* 234-39; L'Enfant's tomb, 20
Arlington County, 20, 209
Armed Forces Institute of Pathology, 223
Armory, the, 160, 233
Armstrong, Louis, *140*
Armstrong High School, 187
Army, 107, 108; Band, 143
Art. *See* Galleries; Museums; specific works; etc.
Arthur, Chester A., 48, 160
Associated Press, 120, 123
Atomic Energy Commission, 203
Attorneys, 81, 127-28; solicitor general, *80,* 81
Automobiles, 195
Azaleas, *164*
Bacon, Henry, *225*
Baltimore and Ohio Railroad, 20
Baltimore *Sun,* 124
Bannecker, Benjamin, 178
Barlow, Joel, 161
Bates, Edward, 67
Belgian Embassy, *100*
Bell, Alexander Graham, 160
Bell, Jack, *119*
Bella, Ahmed Ben, 234
Belmont, Alva, 157
Belmont House, 157
Bennett, James Gordon, 120
Bethesda, Maryland, 209
Bethesda Naval Medical Center, 203
"Big man" view of presidency, 46-48
Bill of Rights, 221
Bischoff, J. W., 143
Bladensburg, Maryland, *172,* 208-9
Blaine, James G., 161
Blair, Francis Preston, *162*
Blair, Montgomery, 156
Blair House, 156, *162*

Bliss, Robert Woods, 223
Boggs, Mrs. Hale, 136
Bolling Air Base, 170
Bonus marchers, 170
Booth, John Wilkes, 143, 177
Borglum, Gutzon, *56*
Braddock, Edward, 204
Brady, Mathew, 221
Brandeis, Louis, 161
Brazilian Embassy, 87
Bretton Woods Conference, 102
Brightwood, 169
Brookings Institution, 160
Brookland, 169
Brown, William, 204
Brumidi, Constantino, 55, *56, 119*
Bryan, William Jennings, 99
Buchanan, James, 22, 84, 160, 168; rated, 48
Budapest String Quartet, 143
Budget Bureau, 34, 116
Bulgarian Embassy, 168
Bull Run, 206
Bunau-Varilla, Philippe, 129
Bureaucracy, 115-17
Burr, Aaron, 227
Byrd, Charlie, *140*
Cabinet, 34, 46. *See also* specific posts
Cafritz, Gwendolyn, 134
Calhoun, John C., *119,* 145, 156, 160, *177*
Calhoun, Mrs. John C., 134
Cameron, Simon, 120
Cameroon, 94
Capitol, the, *16, 21,* 22, 27, 55-59 ff, *63,* 67, *70,* 79; Kennedy coffin in, *236;* rotunda, *56, 239*
Capitol Hill, 157-60, *170. See also* specific buildings
Captain's Row, 204
Card-calling days, 134-36
Cardoza High School, 187
Carlyle, John, 204
Carlyle House, 204
Carnegie Library, 160
Carpenter, Frank G., 70
Carroll, Daniel, 157
Carter, Robert, 20
Carter Barron Amphitheater, *140,* 145, 169
Case, Francis, 129
Catholic University, *139,* 143, 169-70, *189*
Central Intelligence Agency, 99, 203
Chain Bridge, 19, 206
Chamber of Commerce, United States, 127
Charismatic leaders, 49-52
Chase, Salmon P., 182
Chase, Samuel, 79
Cherry blossoms, 27, *164, 228,* 234
Chesapeake and Ohio Canal, 20, 160, 208
Chevy Chase, 195, 209
Chicago *Daily News,* 123
Chicago *Tribune,* 123
Christ Church, 157, 160
Christ Church (Alexandria, Virginia), 204
Christian Science Monitor, 123
Christmas, *34, 36,* 234
Chrysanthemums, *164*
Churchill, Sir Winston, 204
Circuit Court, 22
City Hall, 160
Civil rights. *See* Negroes
Civil service, 115-17
Civil War, 16, 55, 177-78, 182, 206, *231;* Alexandria and, 204; Arlington and, 205; Brady photos, 221; combat commissions, 67; forts, 107; and hiring of women, 115; and news, 120; and offer of Union command to Lee, 156; and Supreme Court, 79
Clark, William Andrews, 223

Clay, Henry, 48, *119,* 156; and Decatur House, 156, *172;* duel, 70, 206; signature, *153*
Cleveland, Grover, 31, 168, 169, 233; rated, 48
Cleveland Park, 168
Clipper-ship models, *214*
Coffee houses, 223
Coffelt, Leslie, plaque for, *162*
Collingwood, 205
Colt, Samuel, 128
Columbia, Maryland, 203
Columbia Broadcasting System, 124
"Columbus Doors," *56*
Commerce, Department of, 178
Commission of Fine Arts, *174*
Computers, 105, 109
Congress, 34-46, 55-74, *63, 67,* 107, 116. *See also* Lobbyists; etc.; specific houses, legislators
Congressional Cemetery, 160
Congressional *Record,* 74
Connecticut Avenue, 168
Constitution, 46, 48, 60, 221
Constitution Hall, *143,* 187
Coolidge, Calvin, 60, 161, 222; and news conferences, 122; *Post* backs, 119; rated, 48; and wife's portrait, *32*
Coolidge, Mrs. Calvin, *32,* 206
Corcoran, William Wilson, 222
Corcoran Gallery of Art, 222-23
Correspondents, 119-26, *119, 121, 126*
Corruption, 67, 117
Cosmos Club, 156, 161
Couriers, diplomatic, *103*
Court of Claims, 222
Court packing, 79-81
Courts, 52, 81. *See also* Supreme Court
Court of Appeals, 81
Coxey's army, 170
Craik, James, 204
Crime, 178
Crocuses, *164*
Cromwell, William N., 129
Culture, 141-43
Cunningham, Ann Pamela, 205
Custis, George Washington Parke, 204
Custis, Nelly Parke, 205
Custis-Lee mansion. *See* Lee estate
Custom House, 160
D.C. Stadium, 157-60, *184*
Danish Embassy, 90
Daughters of the American Revolution, 187
Davis, Jefferson, 160
Dawes, Charles G., 99
Deaf mutes, 170
Decatur, Stephen, 156, *172*
Decatur House, 156, *172*
Declaration of Independence, 221
Defense, 105-12
Defense, Secretary of, 108
Defense Department, 116
Dewey, Admiral George, 160, 168
Dickens, Charles, 19
Diplomats, 87-103 (*see also* specific ambassadors, countries); ambassadors and State of the Union address, 46
Dirksen, Everett McKinley, *70*
Districts Courts, 81
Dogwood, *164*
Dooley, Mr., 81
Douglas, William O., 157
Douglass, Frederick, 170
Dred Scott Case, 84
Drinking, 67-70, 84, 136
Duels, 70, 208-9
Dulles, John Foster, 9
Dulles International Airport, *9,* 24
Dumbarton House, 154
Dumbarton Oaks, 154, *177,* 223
Dunbar High School, 187
Dupont, Henry A., 160

Dupont Circle, 161, *180*
Early, Jubal, 107
Easter Egg Roll, 234
Eaton, Peggy O'Neale, 134
Education, Negro, 187
Eisenhower, Dwight D., 33, 134, 168, 234; and bonus marchers, 170; golf at White House, 31-32; inauguration, 227; and natural-gas bill, 129; and news conferences, 122; and Normandy invasion, 221; use of helicopter, 32
Elections, 48-52, 128
Embassies, 87-100, *90, 94, 100. See also* specific countries
Entertainment, *139-48, 140, 143, 148. See also* Music; Theater; etc.
Evans, Rudulph, 225
Executive Office Building, *15. See also* State, War, and Navy Department Building
Ex Parte Milligan decision, 79
Export-Import Bank, 102
Fairbanks, Charles W., 160
Fairfax, George William, 204
Fairfax County, 209
Fairfax Courthouse, 206
Farm Bureau, 129
Farragut Square, 160
Federal Bureau of Investigation, 157, 222
Federal courts, 81
Federal employees, 115-17
Federal Triangle, 157, *243*
Fichandler, Zelda, 141
Filibusters, 61, 66
Fillmore, Millard, 48
Finance, international, 102
Fine Arts Commission, 27, 154, 160
Finley, David, 222
First Ladies, 46, 136, 141 *(see also by name)*; portraits of, 32
Fish, Hamilton, 160
Flemming, Arthur, *126*
Foggy Bottom, 155-56
Folger Shakespeare Library, *211*, 212
Ford's Theatre, 141-43, 222
Foreign correspondents, 122
Foreign dignitaries, visiting, *46*, 233-34
Foreign diplomats, *46*, 87-100. *See also* specific diplomats, embassies
Foreign governments, lobbying for, 129
Foreign Service Institute, 102
Forsythia, *164*
Fort Belvoir, 107, 203
Fort Hunt, 205
Fort McNair, 19, 107, 109, 177
Fort Myer, 107
Fort Stevens, *76*, 107
Fort Washington, 107, 223
Franciscans, 169
Francis Scott Key Bridge, 24
Franklin, Benjamin, 221
Freedmen's Bureau, 182
Freer, Charles Lang, 222
Freer Gallery, 222, *225*
French, Daniel Chester, 225
French Embassy, 94, 161
Friday Evening Parade, 112
Friendship House, 157
Friendship International Airport, 24
Friendship Veterans Fire Engine Company, 204
Fulbright, William, *59*
Fund-raising dinners, 128
Funerals, *236, 239, 239*
Furniture, bureaucracy and, 116
Gadsby's Tavern, 143, *196*, 204
Gallatin, Albert, 157
Gallaudet, Thomas Hopkins, 170
Gallaudet College, 170
Galleries, 222-23, *225*
Gambling, 178

Garden Club of Virginia, 208
Garner, John, 74, *119*
Garfield, James A., 33, 48, 117, 160; inaugural ball, 233
Gaslight Club, *147*
Georgetown, *24*, 149-55, *174*
Georgetown University, *24*, 27, 155
Georgetown Visitation Convent, 155
George Washington University, 155-56
Georgia Avenue, 169
German Embassy, 90
Gettysburg Address, 221, 225
Ghent, Treaty of, *153*
Gilman's Drug Store, 160
Gizycka, Count Joseph, 134
Goddard, Robert H., 203
Goddard Space Flight Center, 203
Goldberg, Arthur, *83*
Gold Cup Steeplechase, 208
Gore, Albert, *73*
Government Printing Office, *74*, 84
Grant, Ulysses S., 22, 79, 117, 221; Memorial, *76*, 223; rated, 48
Great Britain. *See* Britain
Great Falls, *196, 200*, 206-8
Gridiron Club, 123
Gunston Hall, 205
Gutenberg Bible, 221
Haile Selassie, 234
Haiti, 94
Hamilton, Alexander, 19, 48, 70
Hammond, John Hays, 161
Hanna, Mark, 129, 156
Hannan, Philip M., *239*
Harding, Warren G., 119, 122, 161, 222; rated, 48
Harlan, John M., 81
Harlech, Lord and Lady, *88*
Harriman, Averell, *174*
Harrison, Benjamin, 24, 48
Harrison, William Henry, 31, 48, 49, 156
Harvey's restaurant, 157
Hayes, Rutherford B., 48, 160, 234
Hays, Mrs. Rutherford B., 136
Healy, Patrick F., 155
Healy Tower, 155
Hearst papers, 123
Helicopters, 32
Hell's Bottom, 177-78
Herblock, cartoons of, *124*
Heroin, 178
Hickory Hill, 208
High schools, 187
Hillwood, 223
Historic landmarks, 160-61. *See also* specific landmarks, places
Hoban, James, 31, 208
Hoey, Clyde, 60
Holmes, Oliver Wendell, 81, *83*, 136, 160
Hooker, Joseph, 177
Hoover, Herbert, 34, 60, 134, 161, 222; and news conferences, 122: rated, 48
Horses and horse racing, *201*, 208
House of Representatives, 22, 46, 55 ff, *63*; and Jefferson's election, 227; and lobbies, 129; new office building, 157; and television, 123
Houston, Sam, 70
Howard, Oliver Otis, 182
Howard University, 182, 187, *187*
Hughes, Charles Evans, 81, 161, 168
Hull, Cordell, 97, 168
Humphrey, Hubert, *73, 133, 243*
Humphrey, Mrs. Hubert, *133, 243*
Huntington, Collis P., 128
Ickes, Harold, 187
Inaugurations, *121*, 227-33, *241-43*
Indian artifacts, 22
Indonesian Embassy, 87, 94
Industrial College of the Armed Forces, 112
Inter-American Defense Board, 103
Inter-American Development Bank, 102

Inter-American Social Progress Trust Fund, 103
Internal Revenue Bureau, 156
International (horse race), *201*, 208
International Ball, *92*
International Bank for Reconstruction and Development, 102
International Development Association, 103
International Finance Corporation, 102-3
International Monetary Fund, 102, 103
Iranian Embassy, 90
Islamic Center, 161-68
Israel, 52
Italian Embassy, 90, *98*
Iwo Jima Memorial, 223
Izvestia, 122
Jackson, Andrew, 33, 46, 70, 134, 170; and civil service, 117; election of, 48-49; inauguration of, 226; rated, 48
Jackson, Robert H., 208
Japanese Embassy, 90, *94*
Jefferson, Thomas, 33, 97, 161, 208, 221; and Christ Church, 157; financial distress of, 20; improves Pennsylvania Avenue, 22; inauguration, 223, 227; Justice Chase assails, 79; Memorial, *12*, 225; and the press, 119, 124; rated, 48; and site of capital, 19; and State of Union address, 46; and White House design, 31
Johnson, Andrew, 48, 79, 156
Johnson, Lyndon B., 32, *49, 53, 121*, 168, 228, 239; and the arts, 143, 223; and churches, 157, 159; inauguration, 227, *241, 243*; and news conferences, 122-23; and Pennsylvania Avenue, 157; and Perle Mesta, 134
Johnson, Mrs. Lyndon B., *228, 243*
Johnston, Eric, 136
July 4th, 239
Justices. *See* Courts
Kalorama, 161-68, *172*
Keller, Helen, 168
Kendall, Amos, 170
Kenilworth, 169
Kennedy, Caroline, 32, *42*
Kennedy, John F., 32, *38, 42*, 134; assassination, funeral, 32, 33, *236, 239, 239;* and Dulles airport, *9;* and foreign rulers, 234; former homes, 154, 208; and Lafayette Square, 156; and Negroes, 102; and news conferences, 122; office, *45;* and Pennsylvania Avenue, 157; on presidency, 33, 97
Kennedy, Mrs. John F. (Jacqueline), *36, 42, 45*, 208, *239;* house of, *174;* and Lafayette Square, 156; parties, 136
Kennedy, John F., Jr., 32, *42*
Kennedy, Robert, 208, *239*
Kennedy Center for the Performing Arts, 143, 155, 225
Key, Francis Scott, 157
Key, Philip B., 70
Kindler, Hans, 143
Knights of Columbus, *189*
Know-Nothings, 24
Korean War, 239
Krock, Arthur, 124
Kuwait Embassy, 90
Labor, and lobbies, 127
Lafayette Marquis de, 55, 154, 156, 204
Lafayette Square, 32, 156
La Follette, Robert M., *119*, 168
Landon, Margaret, 221
Latrobe, Benjamin, 55
Laurel track, *201*, 208
Law, Thomas, 174
Law House, 174
Lawrason house, 204
Lawrence, David, 124
Lawyers. *See* Attorneys
Lear, Tobias, 205
Lectionary, early Latin, *216*

Lee, Robert E., 154, 182, 203 ff, 208, 231, 234; and Blair House, 156
Lee estate, 20, 204-5, 231
Lee house, 162
L'Enfant, Pierre Charles, 16, 20, 22, 24, 157
Lewis, John L., 63
Lewis, Lawrence, 205
Lewis, Washington, 174
Library of Congress, 10, 21, 22, 55, 157, 212-21, 216; concerts at, 143
Libya, 94
Limousines, 70, 74, 115
Lincoln, Abraham, 32, 70, 182, 218, 266; assassination, 33, 141, 143, 222; and "big man" view of presidency, 46; Borglum head of, 56; and cabinet, 34; and Capitol dome, 16, 55; and combat commissions, 67; drafts of Gettysburg Address, 221; and Fort Stevens attack, 107; and Gallaudet College, 170; inauguration 233; and Lee 156; Memorial (see Lincoln Memorial); and office-seekers, 117; on presidency, 33; and the press, 120; rated, 48; summer home, 22, 160
Lincoln, Mrs. Abraham, 143
Lincoln, Robert, 160
Lincoln, Willy, 31
Lincoln Memorial, 21, 24, 28, 155, 218, 225; Marian Andereson and, 187
Lincoln Memorial Bridge, 24, 194
Lind, Jenny, 141
Lindens, The, 161
Lippmann, Walter, 124
Little Falls, 19
Little Theatre of Alexandria, 143
Lobbyists, 127-29
Lodge, Henry Cabot, Sr., 160
Longworth, Nicholas, 74, 134, 161
Longworth, Mrs. Nicholas (Alice R.), 134, 136, 137, 161, 195
Los Angeles Times, 123
Louis Philippe, 174
McAdoo, William Gibbs, 160
MacArthur, Douglas A., 67, 170, 221
McCarty, John, 209
McCormick, Robert R., 87, 120
McGrory, Mary, 126
MacKenzie, Lewis, 204
McKinley, William, 32, 33, 48
McLean, Evelyn Walsh, 87, 134
McLean, John R., 119, 208
McLean, Virginia area, 208
McMillan, James, 24
McMillan Commission, 24, 228
Madison, Dolley, 31, 156, 160, 208
Madison, James, 20, 48, 119, 153, 208; and churches, 156, 157; and George Washington University, 156; and Octagon House, 153, 156; rated, 48; takes command against British, 209
Magazines, 123
Magnum, Ed, 141
Malawi Embassy, 94
Mali, 96
Mall, the, 24
Manassas, Virginia, 206
Maret School, 168
Marine Corps, 107, 112, 223; Band, 42, 136, 143; Commandant's House, 160
Markets, 160
Marshall, John, 79, 81, 84, 227
Marshall, Peter, 70
Martin, Joseph P., 70, 74
Maryland, 38, 208-9. See also specific places
Maryland, University of, 209
Mason, Armistead, 209
Mason, George, 20, 203, 204, 205, 225
Mason, Jimilu, 223
Matildaville, 208
Mellon, Andrew, 221
Mellon, Paul, 208

Memorials, 223-25. See also specific memorials
Mencken, H. L., 124
Menemencioglu, Ambassador and Mme., 100
Meridian Hill Park, 168-69
Merrywood, 208
Mesta, Perle, 134
Mexican Embassy, 98
Meyer, Eugene, 119, 223
Miller, William M. ("Fishbait"), 46
Mithcell, Howard, 208
Monroe, James, 20, 55, 119, 208; rated, 48
Montgomery County, 209
Monticello, 225
Moore, Thomas, 178
Moroccan Embassy, 96
Morris, George Maurice, 161
Morris, Robert, 22
Morton, Levi, 161
Mosby, John S., 206
Mosque, the, 161-68
Mount St. Alban, 150
Mount Vernon, 196, 205
Museums, 211-14, 211, 212, 213, 214. See also specific museums
Music, 143
Narcotics, 178
Nascotine Indians, 170
National Archives, 156, 221-22
National Capital Planning Commission, 160, 192
National City Christian Church, 159
National Civil Service Reform League, 117
National Gallery of Art, 21, 24, 148, 178, 222, 243
National Geographic Society, 159, 223
National Institutes of Health, 195-203
National Press Club, 123
National Shrine of the Immaculate Conception, 169, 189
National Society of Colonial Dames of America, 154
National Symphony, 143, 143; Ball, 133
National Theater, 141, 143
National Trust for Historic Preservation, 156, 172, 205
National War College, 112
National Woman's Party, 157
Naval Observatory, 107
Naval Oceanographic Office, 203
Naval Ordnance Laboratory, 203
Navy, 107, 108; Band, 143
Navy Yard, 160; Museum, 223
Negroes, 169, 177, 178-92; civil rights bills, 66; as diplomats, 101; Supreme Court and, 81
Neighbors, Inc., 169
New Deal, 60, 70, 81, 117; and press, 122
New Republic, 124
New Year's, 134, 143
New York City, 60
New York Courier, 120
New York Evening Post, 124
New York Herald, 120
New York Herald Tribune, 123, 124
New York Times, 122, 123, 124
New York World, 124
Newhouse papers, 123
Newlands, Francis G., 209
Newspaper correspondents, 119-26, 119, 121, 126
Niagara Falls, 38
Nicaragua, 128
Northeast section, 169-70
Northwest section, 149, 168
Noyes, Crosby S., 119
Numbers racket, 178
Oak Hill, 208
Occidental, The (dining room), 157
Octagon House, 22, 153, 156
Ohio Turnpike, 221
Old Presbyterian Meeting House, 204
Old Soldiers' Home, 22, 160

Old Stone House, 154
Olney, 143
Organization of American States, 102
Opachankano, Chief, 19
Oratory, congressional, 61-66
Owen, Ruth Bryan, 99
Page boys, 81
Pan American Health Organization, 103, 155
Pan American Union, 223
Panama Canal, 128
Parks, 24 (see also specific parks); statuary in, 76, 223
Parties, 131-34th ff, 140. See also specific hosts, occasions
Patent Office, 55
Patterson, Eleanor (Cissy), 134, 161
Paulists, 169
Peace Monument, 236
Pearson, Drew, 124
Pennsylvania Avenue, 22, 148, 156-57, 162, 228, 243
Pennsylvania Railroad, 24
Pension Building, 233
Pentagon, 99, 105-12, 105, 106, 110, 117
Perkins, Frances, 115
Peter family, 154
Petersen House, 143, 222
Petworth, 169
Phelps High School, 187
Phillips, Duncan, 223
Phillips Gallery, 223
Pierce, Franklin, 22, 48, 119
Pinchot, Gifford, 160
Piscataway Indians, 19
Pius, Pope, 155
Plantation mansions, 204-6. See also specific houses
Pohick Church, 206
Political community, 27-28, 31
Polk, James J., 48
Port Saïd, 147
Pope, John Russell, 161, 222, 225
Post, Marjorie Merriweather, 134, 223
Post Office Department, 22
Postal Service, 116
"Potomac," 19
Potomac, Maryland, 208
Potomac Canal, 208
Potomac River, 19-20, 19, 22, 28
Potter's House, 223
Powhatan, Chief, 19
Pravda, 122
President, the, 31-52, 52, 74, 136, 141 (see also specific presidents); and baseball season, 160; "Church of Presidents," 156; death of, 239; as diplomat, 94, 97; and Easter Egg Roll, 234; and foreign rulers, 233-34; inaugurations, 121, 227-33, 241-42; news conferences, 122-24; office of, 33, 45, 49; seal of, 38
Press, the, 119-26, 119, 121, 126
Pride, 70
Prince Georges County, 209
Prostitution, 70, 177-78
Protocol, 94-97, 233-34. See also specific occasions
Public opinion, 49, 128
Puerto Ricans, 70, 156
Pullman, George, 87, 98
Radio, 123
Randolph, John, 206
Rathbone, Henry R., 143
Rayburn, Sam, 74
Reed, Stanley, 81
Reedy, George, 121
Residential community, 27, 28, 149 ff. See also specific areas
Reston, James, 124
Reston, Virginia, 203
Revolutionary War, 106-7, 204. See also Washington, George

Ribicoff, Abraham, *119*
Rites and pageants, *226*, 227-43, *228-42*, *234*, *236*
Rivers, Larry, 143
Rock Creek Cemetery, *221*
Rock Creek Park, 22, 24, 32, *164*, *167*, 169. *See also* Carter Barron Amphitheater; Zoo
Rockville, Maryland, 209
Rogers, Randolph, 56
Rogers, Will, 49-52, 59, 60, *76*, 195
Rokeby, 208
Roosevelt, Franklin D., 32, *38*, 60, 226, 234; and Adams' prayer, 31; and "big man" view of presidency, 46; and Christ Church (Alexandria), 204; and the press, 121, 122; rated, 48; staff, 34; and Supreme Court, 79-81; and women, 99, 115
Roosevelt, Theodore, 31, 32, 160, *167*, 239; and "big man" view of presidency, 46, 48; and Freer Gallery, 222; Kalorama home, 161; Memorial, 225; on presidency, 33; and the press, 122; rated, 48; staff, 34; and Washington Cathedral, 168
Roosevelt Island, 225
Roosevelt Island Bridge, 154
Root, Elihu, 160
Rose, the, *228*
Rosslyn, 208
Russian Embassy, 87, 90, 94, *98*, 168
Russian newspapers, 122
Saarinen, Eero, *9*
Saint-Gaudens, Augustus, *221*
St. John's Episcopal Church, 156
St. Louis *Post-Dispatch*, 123
St. Mark's Episcopal Church, 157
St. Matthew's Cathedral, *239*
Salona, 208
Sandburg, Carl, 221
Saudi Arabian Embassy, 90
Scheyven, Baron and Baroness, *100*
Schlesinger, Arthur M., 48
School of Foreign Service, 155
Science, 195-203
Scott, Winfield, 119
Scripps-Howard, 120, 123
Sea food, *190*
Seal, presidential, *38*
Secret Service, 32, 33, 46, *243*
Secretaries, 34, 94. *See also* specific cabinet posts
Senate, 22, 55 ff, *59*, *63*, *67*, *70*, *119*, 157; and State of the Union address, 46; and television, 123
Seward, William H., 32, 182
Shadows, The (night club), *147*
Shady Grove, 143
Shakespeareana, *211*, 212
Shaw, Carolyn Hagner, 131, 136
Shepherd, Alexander, 22, 160, *164*, 177, 182
Shouse, Mrs. Jouett, *133*
Showboat (night club), *140*
Sickles, Daniel, 70
Sixteenth Street, 168-69
Skyline, *21*, 27
Slums, 170-78
Smith, Chloethiel Woodward, 174
Smith, Howard W., *63*
Smith, John, 19
Smithson, James, 211
Smithsonian Institution, 22, 32, *167*, 211-12, *212*, *214*, 233
Snowfall, *79*
Social List of Washington, 131
Society, 131-36, *140* (*see also* specific members); Negro, 182-87

Society of the Cincinnati, 161
Solicitor General, *80*, 81
Sousa, John Philip, 143, 160
Southwest section, *139*, 170-77, *193*
Spanish Embassy, 168
Speaking fees, 128
Spoils system, 117
Spring Valley, 168
Standards, Bureau of, 203
Stanford, Leland, 160
State, Secretary of, 94-97, *100*, 233
State courts, 81
State Department, 94-99, *100*, 103, 116, 155
State of the Union addresses, 34-46
State, War, and Navy Department Building, *15*, 22, 34, 97
Statuary, *76*, 223-25. *See also* specific memorials
Stern, Edgar, 223
Stone, Edward Durell, 155
Stone, Harlan Fiske, 79
Storm Over the Land, 221
Storr, Paul, *41*
Stoughton, Edwin H., 206
Stuart, Gilbert, 31
Sudan, 94
Sullivan, Ann, 168
Sumner, Charles, 70
Supreme Court, *10*, 22, 46, 55, 79-84, *79*, *80*, *83*, *84*, 129, 157; and television, 123
Taft, Robert A., *119*, 225
Taft, William Howard, 27, 48, 161
Taft, Mrs. William Howard, 27
Tass, 122
Tayloe house, 156
Taylor, Zachary, 31, 48, 160
Taylor Model Basin, 107, 203, *206*
Teamsters' Union, 127
Television, *121*, 123
Theater, *139*, 141-43
Thomas Circle, *159*
Thornton, William, 55, 205
Timmons, Bascom, 123
Tomb of the Unknowns, 234, 239
Treasury Department, 22, 115, *228*
Truman, Harry S, 31, 32, 134, *162*, 239; assassination attempt, 156; and foreign rulers, 233; and MacArthur, 67; and news conferences, 122
Truman, Margaret, 31
Truston-Decatur Naval Museum, 223
Tubman, Harriet, 182
Tudor Place, 22, 154
"Tuesday-through-Thursday Club," 60
Turkish Embassy, *100*
Twain, Mark, 60, 115
Tyler, John, 48, 156, 168
Underwood, Oscar, 205
Union Station, *16*, 24, 160
United Auto Workers, 127
United Nations charter, *177*
United Press International, 123
U. S. Information Agency, 97
U. S. News & World Report, 124
Van Buren, Martin, 22, 48, 156, 168
Vernon, Edward, 205
Veterans' Administration, 116
Vice, 70, 178
Vice-President, the, *73*
Vietnam, 94
Villard, Henry, 120
Vinson, Carl, *63*
Violence in Congress, 70
Violin, Stradivarius, *216*
Virginia, *196*, 203-8, *231*. *See also* specific places

Wall Street Journal, 123
Walsh, Thomas F., 87
War Department, 106-7
War of 1812, 107, *153*, 209, 221; burning of Washington, 31, 55, 159, 208; museum, 223
Warnecke, John Carl, 156
Warrenton, 208
Washington, Booker T., 187
Washington, Bushrod, 205
Washington, George, 178, 196, 203, 204, 205, 208; belongings in museum collection, *196*; and "big man" view of presidency, 46; in Bladensburg, 208; creates Foreign Affairs Department, 97; and federal employees, 116; financial distress of, 20; lays Capitol cornerstone, 55; Monument (*see* Washington Monument); Mount Vernon shown, *196*; and neutrality proclamation, 48; one secretary, 34; portrait, 31; and presidential oath, 227; rated, 48; and site of capital, 19, 20; statue in toga, *214*; and University, 155; and War Board, 106, 107; will, 206
Washington, Mrs. George (Martha), 205, 206
Washington, Lawrence, 205
Washington Cathedral, 27, *150*, 168
Washington Club, 161
Washington *Daily News*, 120
Washington *Evening Star*, 119, 121, *126*, 131
Washington Gallery of Modern Art, 223
Washington Masonic National Memorial, 204
Washington Monument, *21*, 24, 27, *28*, 239
Washington National Airport, 24
Washington *National Intelligencer*, 119
Washington *Post*, 31, 119-29, 182, 208; Herblock cartoons, *124*
Washington Redskins, 160, *184*
Washington Senators, 160, *183*
Washington *Times-Herald*, 120
Webster, Daniel, *119*, 157
Weems, "Parson," 206
Wellington farm, 205
Wells, Sumner, 161
Wesley Heights, 168
Westinghouse, George, 161
Wheat Row, *174*
Wheaton, Maryland, 209
Whigs, 49
Whisky a Gogo, *147*
White, Josh, *147*
White House, *15*, 22, *26*, 31-32, *36*, *38*, *42*, *162* (*see also* specific occupants, occasions); at Christmas, 34, *36*; correspondents, *121*; dinners at, 31, *41*, *42*, 136-41; East Room, 22, 31, 32, *36*, 136; Easter Egg Roll, 234; Marine Band at, 136, 143; renovation, *162*; staff, 34
Whitman, Walt, 127, 156
Wilson, Mr. and Mrs. Luke, 203
Wilson, Woodrow, 31, 32, 46, 99, *124*; and American University, 168; Kalorama home, 161, *172*; and news conferences, 122; on presidency, 33, 46; rating of, 48; tomb of, 168
Wilson, Mrs. Woodrow (the first), 31
Women, 209; in civil service, 115-16; as diplomats, 99; of the press, 123, *126*; in society, 131th ff
Woodlawn, 205
Woodley mansion, 168
Woodring, Harry, 205
Woodrow Wilson House, *172*
World War I, 117, 168, 182, 239
World War II, 122, 123, 221-22, 239
Wriston, Henry M., 99
Zoo, *167*, 169